Ways Women Orgasm
By Jane Thomas

Ways Women Orgasm
9780956894700

Published by *Nosper Books* 2011
www.nosper.com

Copyright © Jane Thomas 2011

Printed in the United States of America

With thanks to all
those who have contributed
along the way
and
with special thanks to
my husband Peter
for his practical and moral support.

# Contents

| | |
|---|---|
| Introduction to Ways Women Orgasm | 2 |
| Female sexuality | 4 |
|     Sexual desire | 6 |
|     Female masturbation | 8 |
|     Sexual arousal | 10 |
| Orgasm during sex | 12 |
|     Clitoral stimulation | 14 |
|     Sexual fantasies | 16 |
|     Orgasm techniques | 18 |
| Investing in your sex life | 20 |
|     Enjoying sex play | 22 |
|     Emotional intimacy | 24 |
|     Physical intimacy | 26 |
| Stories: Sexual desire | 29 |
|     A sexual relationship | 30 |
|     Understanding female sexual desire | 32 |
|     Young and sexy | 34 |
|     Women who fake orgasm | 36 |
|     The sexual politics of female sexual desire | 38 |
|     Sexual promiscuity | 40 |
|     How female sexuality differs to male sexuality | 42 |
|     Women's sexual desire | 44 |
|     Female orgasm is not required for reproduction | 46 |
|     Women have a lower sex drive | 48 |
| Stories: Female masturbation | 51 |
|     Female masturbation is relatively uncommon | 52 |
|     Women's sex drive to orgasm during sex | 54 |
|     Women's sexual arousal and orgasm are not automatic | 56 |
|     Women have to learn how their sexual arousal works | 58 |
|     Women have to learn how to orgasm | 60 |
|     Techniques women use to reach orgasm | 62 |
|     How a woman can learn how to masturbate | 64 |
|     How to use a vibrator to discover orgasm | 66 |

| | |
|---|---|
| Comparing orgasm from female masturbation and with a partner | 68 |
| How we enjoy our best orgasms | 70 |

## Stories: Sexual arousal — 73

| | |
|---|---|
| Women's sexual arousal | 74 |
| Sexual arousal during intercourse | 76 |
| The mystery of female sexual arousal | 78 |
| Confusion over female orgasm | 80 |
| Some women never tune into eroticism | 82 |
| Women often assume sexual arousal during sex | 84 |
| Sexual arousal from romantic emotions | 86 |
| Male nudity does not cause female sexual arousal | 88 |
| Why sexual arousal is more elusive for women | 90 |
| Understanding women's sexual arousal | 92 |

## Stories: Clitoral stimulation — 95

| | |
|---|---|
| Enjoying sexual pleasure | 96 |
| The 'non-genital' orgasm | 98 |
| Real female orgasms | 100 |
| Understanding the G-spot | 102 |
| Most women are not aiming for orgasm though genital stimulation | 104 |
| The facts of female sexuality | 106 |
| How to orgasm | 108 |
| Women's sexual dysfunction | 110 |
| Lack of arousal during sex | 112 |
| What if female sexuality truly equalled male sexuality? | 114 |

## Stories: Sexual fantasies — 117

| | |
|---|---|
| Clitoral stimulation is not everything | 118 |
| How to give a woman an orgasm during sex | 120 |
| Arousal comes from appreciating eroticism | 122 |
| Not every woman enjoys eroticism | 124 |
| Women's sexual arousal relies on sexual fantasies | 126 |
| Sharing sexual fantasies | 128 |
| Women who use fantasy for sexual arousal | 130 |
| How women enjoy eroticism through sex stories | 132 |
| Reaching orgasm | 134 |
| How to enjoy your sexual fantasies | 136 |

## Stories: Orgasm techniques — 139

| | |
|---|---|
| Why foreplay techniques don't always work as we think they should | 140 |

| | |
|---|---:|
| Transferring masturbation techniques to sex | 142 |
| Positions and techniques for sexual intercourse | 144 |
| Difficulties in applying orgasm techniques to sex | 146 |
| Women's psychological sexual arousal | 148 |
| True female sexual arousal and orgasm | 150 |
| The ideal male lover | 152 |
| Women's sexual arousal tends to be assumed or overlooked | 154 |
| Lack of orgasm is not a sexual dysfunction | 156 |
| The 10 facts of female sexuality | 158 |
| **Stories: Enjoying sex play** | **161** |
| Eroticism | 162 |
| How do women achieve sexual arousal during sex? | 164 |
| Lust is good | 166 |
| Why sex is fun | 168 |
| Difficulty reaching orgasm during sex | 170 |
| Women who enjoy their own sexual arousal | 172 |
| Sexual relationships favour male orgasm | 174 |
| Making the most of sex play | 176 |
| Pleasuring a woman | 178 |
| How a woman can enjoy sex play | 180 |
| **Stories: Emotional Intimacy** | **183** |
| Female sexuality in perspective | 184 |
| Sex and love | 186 |
| A man's sexual arousal can be very flattering | 188 |
| Why do women not always appreciate displays of male sexuality? | 190 |
| Why do so many women dislike eroticism? | 192 |
| Sheltering young women from eroticism | 194 |
| How to get laid | 196 |
| Women settle for emotional intimacy over sexual arousal | 198 |
| Intercourse does not facilitate female orgasm | 200 |
| Why sex is called 'making love' | 202 |
| **Stories: Physical intimacy** | **205** |
| Emotional intimacy may lead to physical intimacy | 206 |
| Women who enjoy sexual pleasure | 208 |
| Why is sexual pleasure still taboo? | 210 |
| Very few women talk about orgasm | 212 |
| Sexual pleasure | 214 |
| Women who want to enjoy sexual pleasure | 216 |

| | |
|---|---|
| Sharing physical intimacy with a partner | 218 |
| Some women do explore sexual pleasure | 220 |
| How to pleasure a man | 222 |
| Spice up your sex life | 224 |

## Stories: Misconceptions — 227

| | |
|---|---|
| Interpreting experiences of female orgasm | 228 |
| Talking to women about female orgasm | 230 |
| Women who appear to want sexual pleasure | 232 |
| Bluffers, fakers and sex surveys | 234 |
| Is sexual arousal with a partner really so easy? | 236 |
| Sexual fact versus sexual fantasy | 238 |
| Why it can be difficult to discuss our sexual experiences | 240 |
| Why do so few women comment on sexual pleasure? | 242 |
| Taking the ego out of sex advice | 244 |
| The sexual revolution set false hopes for female sexuality | 246 |

## Stories: Understanding men — 249

| | |
|---|---|
| Men are fascinated by sex | 250 |
| Men's sexual fantasies | 252 |
| The marvel of male sexuality | 254 |
| Men's sexual arousal is usually easy | 256 |
| Male sexuality involves a high sex drive | 258 |
| Holding men responsible for women's sexual arousal | 260 |
| How men appreciate sex and love | 262 |
| Long-term sexual relationships | 264 |
| Men hope a lover will enhance their sexual arousal | 266 |
| Sex for life | 268 |

## Stories: Sex advice today — 271

| | |
|---|---|
| Sex advice for women is often misleading | 272 |
| Explanations for women's sexual arousal | 274 |
| The truth about female sexuality | 276 |
| Sex experts deal with sexual dysfunction | 278 |
| How do women reach orgasm with a partner? | 280 |
| Defending the modern image of female sexuality | 282 |
| The problem with sex advice today | 284 |
| What sex experts have told me | 286 |
| Advice on female orgasm | 288 |
| Bringing more realism to sex advice | 290 |

Appendix — 293

| | |
|---|---:|
| About the author | 294 |
| My story | 296 |
| Contact | 298 |
| Member Forum | 300 |
| Bibliography | 302 |

This book accompanies the website www.WayWomenOrgasm.org, known as 'Ways Women Orgasm'. The book replicates the text on the site (as at 2011) including 18 pages of core content and 120 stories.

The main difference between the two is that the website provides an opportunity for interactive comment on each of the 120 stories as well as dialogue on the Member Forum page. The stories were originally published as articles and so each one stands alone to some degree.

The forum is constantly evolving to reflect feedback. Any suggestions for improving or correcting the text will be gratefully received.

# Introduction to Ways Women Orgasm

For many women, orgasm is never an issue. Sex fulfils all their expectations for a romantic and passionate 'love-making' act.

Women, who approach sex purely through their relationship, hope for little more than the sensual and emotional aspects of sex.

Others appreciate that orgasm involves sexual arousal and genital stimulation.

Women who are familiar with orgasm from female masturbation find that orgasm during sex doesn't 'just happen' but they struggle to find answers given the vague and conflicting advice currently available.

A man would never try to become aroused by focusing on loving emotions. Neither would he attempt orgasm without stimulating his penis. Yet female sexuality is still defined as if sexual arousal and orgasm arise in completely different ways for men and women.

Many women dislike the eroticism that leads to sexual arousal and so they are offended by the suggestion that a woman might need to use fantasy and stimulate her genitals if she is ever to achieve orgasm.

**Ways Women Orgasm** is for couples who appreciate that women need to use orgasm techniques during sex as much as men do.

A truly 'sexual woman' enjoys eroticism through her fantasies and hopes for a sexual relationship where female sexual arousal is discussed.

### The female sexuality forum

**Ways Women Orgasm** provides sex education for adults so that couples can compare notes on how women enjoy true sexual arousal and orgasm.

Anyone who registers can join the Member Forum and comment on 120 stories that use real women's experiences to explore the facts as well as the myths that surround our understanding of female sexuality today.

The main aims of **Ways Women Orgasm** are:

- **FEMALE SEXUALITY:** To *highlight the known facts* to help couples differentiate between fact and fiction and to RE-

DEFINE women's sexuality in terms that the AVERAGE woman might reasonably hope to experience.

- **ORGASM DURING SEX:** To *present women's real life experiences* openly and honestly including explaining the sexually explicit orgasm techniques that SOME women learn OVER TIME to enable them to orgasm during sex.

- **INVESTING IN YOUR SEX LIFE:** To *suggest how couples can explore sex play* over the longer-term by understanding how men and women's sexual responses DIFFER and by investing PROACTIVELY in their intimate time together.

**Ways Women Orgasm** aims to inform and reassure women of all ages: all the pictures are clean.

The site aspires to be open-minded but there is nothing that should offend.

The discussion is based on honesty not sexual ego and covers: sex drive, the role of sexual fantasies and why orgasm from female masturbation may always be different to orgasm from penetration.

Jane Thomas, author of **Ways Women Orgasm**, is unique as a modern sex writer because she talks openly about her own personal experiences, both of masturbation and of sex with a partner.

Her conclusions are supported by other expert opinions.

**Ways Women Orgasm** is the most comprehensive and explicit source of information about female orgasm available today.

Even well-informed and sexually experienced women can make more of their sexual relationships with men by appreciating the facts.

Certainly any couple interested in exploring sex together over many years needs to know 'The 10 facts of female sexuality' – p158.

# Female sexuality

Sex is associated with pleasure (through sexual arousal and orgasm) as well as with reproduction (through family and relationships).

However male and female sexuality are, often implicitly, defined differently in terms of the importance of the relationship aspects of sex.

For example, men are motivated to enjoy their own sexual arousal and orgasm regardless of a relationship. So they enjoy masturbation and are willing to pay for both pornography and sex.

Female sexuality is often defined more in terms of a woman's attractiveness to men than her ability to orgasm so many people are confused when a woman asks about orgasm during sex.

It was Kinsey's revelation ('Sexual behavior in the human female' published 1953) that SOME women do experience orgasm (commonly from masturbation alone) that lead to the popular belief that EVERY woman should be able to orgasm during sex 'naturally and easily'.

So even today it is suggested that women with 'the right attitude' (i.e. attractive and sexually willing) can hope to experience sex differently to other women simply by willing it to be so.

Others believe that a woman needs 'the right man' to 'enjoy' sex fully. There is nothing wrong with finding sex wonderful, for romantic or emotional reasons, but this is not true sexual arousal.

Since female orgasm is not needed for reproduction sex does not facilitate female arousal.

A woman's challenge during sex is how to achieve the MENTAL arousal required for clitoral stimulation to lead to orgasm.

So although manual or oral stimulation of the clitoris are both more likely to lead to orgasm, women often prefer 'love-making'.

Intercourse allows a woman to assist with the much easier task of facilitating male orgasm rather than aiming for her own.

This is Nature's design, which explains why, although female masturbation is very NORMAL, it is also quite UNUSUAL.

Relatively few women explore their own sexual arousal either alone or through genitally focused sex play with a partner.

## Female orgasm during sex

Traditionally female sexuality has been defined almost entirely in reproductive terms (through vaginal intercourse within marriage).

**Ways Women Orgasm** provides women with the factual background to their sexuality in terms of a genital focus (through their own sexual arousal and orgasm) to help modern women make sense of their sexual experiences.

The discussion of **female sexuality** covers the following:

- **SEXUAL DESIRE**: women's own sexual desire is often confused with how sexually desirable they are to men.

- **FEMALE MASTURBATION**: women's sexual arousal is not automatic and so most women never discover masturbation.

- **SEXUAL AROUSAL**: sexual arousal may be evidenced by the physical but it is fundamentally PSYCHOLOGICAL in nature.

Whereas men's need for PHYSICAL stimulation during sex is clearly focused on the penis, it is often mistakenly assumed that female orgasm arises from the stimulation of the vagina.

Unfortunately the vagina (as part of the birth canal) has very few nerve endings. Only the clitoris, the female sex organ and source of female orgasm, has a sensitivity comparable with the penis.

Similarly, whereas men rely on explicit eroticism (pornography) for their PSYCHOLOGIAL sexual arousal, it is often mistakenly assumed that female sexual arousal depends on emotional criteria.

But women need explicit eroticism to achieve sexual arousal just as men do. It's simply that women's fantasies (effective when alone) do not always help with orgasm during sex.

*"As Ann Koedt put it, in 'The Myth of the Vaginal Orgasm': 'Perhaps one of the most infuriating and damaging results of the whole charade has been that women who were perfectly healthy sexually were taught that they were not.'" (Shere Hite; The Hite Reports; 1993)*

# Sexual desire

Kinsey shocked the world in the 1950s with his revelation that SOME women experience orgasm. The popular message became: all women 'naturally' orgasm during sex. But this was never true.

*"In the later teens, when... the average male was at the peak of his sexual capacity and activity -, there was still nearly a half (47 per cent) of the females who had not had their first orgasm.*

*With this relatively limited background of experience and limited understanding of the nature and significance and desirability of orgasm, it is not surprising to find that a goodly number of the married females never or rarely reach orgasm in their marital coitus." (Alfred Kinsey; Sexual behavior in the human female; 1953)*

Women, who know how to achieve true sexual arousal, commonly orgasm through masturbation or oral sex because both of these include the clitoral stimulation needed for female orgasm.

BUT first a woman must know how her sexual arousal works. How can all women orgasm during sex without the orgasm techniques or familiarity with orgasm from masturbation that men have?

Equally how can women's sexual desire and ease of arousal equal men's when they need mechanical assistance (vibrators) to orgasm? Why do only women need G-spot stimulation for orgasm?

John Gray states his view (my emphasis): *"Biologically and hormonally, men are MUCH MORE driven to be sexual than women are." (John Gray; Mars & Venus in the Bedroom; 1995)*

Frankly, regardless of their orgasmic ability, you have to be pretty naïve to believe that women get as much out of sex as men do.

Not only is female sexual arousal much more obscure than male but also women are not motivated by sex in the way that men are.

So even young women's magazines discuss relationship issues rather than provide women with sexual turn-ons.

**Women do not have the same drive to orgasm during sex**

Of course, women can enjoy sex. But any woman who suggests that women's sexual desire is as strong as men's throughout their lives is not only exposing her inexperience but also her ignorance of the facts.

Women do not achieve sexual arousal or orgasm nearly as easily as men do. Many women are not even interested in these aspects of their sexuality.

As Sheila Kitzinger points out, for many women, orgasm is simply not a priority:

*"For most women orgasm does not have this central role in life. And if it does, it tends to be for a small part of their lives, and often to melt into the background against other significant experiences and other expressions of their sexuality."* *(Sheila Kitzinger; Woman's Experience of Sex; 1983)*

This is simply about balancing EFFORT versus REWARD.

Firstly a woman has to make much more conscious effort to engage on her sexual arousal and secondly the rewards of orgasm are fundamentally just not as critical to women as they are to men.

The film '40 days and 40 nights' (2002) suggests that men cannot cope without orgasm even for 24 hours.

The other facts that indicate that men have a stronger sexual desire or sex drive than women include:

- men's greater willingness to initiate sex with a partner;
- men's much more evident interest in eroticism and almost any aspect of sex;
- the fact that men masturbate much more frequently than women; and
- men's willingness to pay for sex.

Nevertheless a woman can enjoy sexual pleasure especially if she is willing to explore sex beyond intercourse.

**Ways Women Orgasm** discusses how women's sexual arousal works and explores techniques that might make female orgasm more likely.

# Female masturbation

As our bodies develop through puberty, young men and women become aware of themselves as very different sexual beings.

Boys have erections as early as 8 or 9. During puberty the penis increases substantially in size and becomes much more responsive to stimulation, both mental and physical. By the age of 12 or 13, most boys have learnt how to reach orgasm through masturbation.

There is no similar natural trigger for a girl to explore her own sexual arousal and discover how her genitals respond to physical stimulation.

When girls reach puberty they get breasts and periods: body changes linked to women's child-bearing role. So even today women often approach sex from the perspective of family and relationships.

*"While women read romantic novels, men read pornography. While romance packages sex with love, fidelity and marriage, pornography packages sex with violence, possession and promiscuity*

*This means that women and men often have very different views of sex and what it is all about." (Sheila Kitzinger; Woman's Experience of Sex; 1983)*

Through masturbation boys learn how to use genital stimulation to bring a psychological state of sexual arousal to orgasm.

Yet, against all logic, it is often implied that women can hope to orgasm during sex without the benefit of the same learning process.

Sometimes it is even suggested that there is some mysterious disadvantage to female masturbation.

It's not that women who do not masturbate have more success with sex but that, with no comparison, they have no reason to question their sexual experiences.

Most women are not aiming for orgasm through genital stimulation so they interpret sexual relationships as 'love-making'.

**Female masturbation is relatively uncommon**

The publicity given to women's use of vibrators today leads many people to assume that every young woman masturbates.

After ten years of talking to women in the UK, I now realise that female masturbation is relatively unusual.

If female masturbation were common more women would empathise with men's use of pornography because they would understand that anyone who masturbates needs to use a source of eroticism to achieve the kind of sexual arousal that leads to orgasm.

By the way, it's never too late to learn. See 'How a woman can learn to masturbate' – p64.

A woman needs the opportunity and privacy to explore her own body's responses, usually during a period of being single.

If they do discover masturbation to orgasm, women are typically in their twenties or thirties and often they have already had the experience of a sexual relationship.

Some women say that they find masturbation uninteresting or lacking in emotional context. I remember as a teenager occasionally experimenting by touching my body, in the bath for instance, just to see if anything sexual might happen.

Of course it never did because women's sexual arousal and orgasm are not automatic as a man's tend to be.

Any ineffectual touching of a person's genitals could be described as masturbation and little girls often touch themselves in this casual way.

A better definition would be to describe masturbation as an activity where a person has at least the intention of enjoying sexual arousal and orgasm. Girls learn to masturbate later than boys because their fantasies are more complex.

On the positive side, female masturbation is an innocent pleasure that has no harmful side effects either for the individual or for the couple's sexual relationship.

Women can learn how to orgasm by combining a conscious mental focus on their sexual fantasies together with genital stimulation if they are provided with knowledge about their bodies and their sexual psychology.

## Sexual arousal

Sexual arousal is a mental state that arises when the mind responds to PSYCHOLOGICAL stimuli (of an erotic or sexual nature).

Sexual arousal is evidenced by PHYSICAL phenomena such as increased blood flow to the erectile organ (penis/clitoris).

Both sexes can express their sexuality through sexual arousal and orgasm but since men's arousal happens spontaneously (beyond their conscious control), the progression from sexual arousal to genital stimulation and orgasm is much easier for boys to discover.

*"Men and women are mismatched in this respect because a man is much more easily and quickly aroused, and reaches orgasm in a very short time in almost any situation." (Miriam Stoppard; Healthy Sex; 1998)*

Men's physical arousal is very evident because a man's erection is difficult to miss. Likewise a man's orgasm is easy to identify because it usually coincides with ejaculation.

Women's sexual anatomy and physiology do not allow for the same kind of irrefutable evidence.

This makes it easier for women to fake but also for everyone to be less sure about how women's arousal is achieved.

Another reason that men are confident about male orgasm is because they are familiar with orgasm from masturbation.

Since relatively few women ever learn how to masturbate to orgasm, there is much less clarity and certainty over how women reach orgasm.

Andrew Stanway lists male turn-on's, which include most parts of a woman's body.

He notes that women can be attracted to assertive or competent men but no one is suggesting that these attributes assist with female sexual arousal.

He concludes: *"It is less easy to assess psycho-sexual triggers for women than for men." (Andrew Stanway; Loving Touch; 1993)*

## How do women become sexually aroused enough to reach orgasm?

Anyone who is familiar with orgasm will know that, despite all the fuss made about physical stimulation, this aspect of sex can be a complete red herring. In other words, knowing which body part to stimulate is useful but not the whole story.

Clitoral stimulation is not everything. After all, our ability to reach orgasm ultimately depends on what happens in the brain. Yet we rarely acknowledge the PSYCHOLOGICAL aspects of sex.

If she is ever to reach orgasm, a woman first needs to know how to become sexually aroused enough (both mentally and physically) for clitoral stimulation to lead to orgasm.

We often talk about sexual arousal as if an erection or orgasm, for that matter, is caused purely by physical stimulation. This is partly because men's psychological sexual arousal is usually a given.

Women who masturbate know that they have to take a vastly different approach in order to CONSCIOUSLY generate sexual arousal and orgasm.

Men think about sex much more than women but they only use fantasy to enhance arousal when they are engaged in activities such as masturbation alone, unimaginative sex or sex with an uninspiring partner.

Under more ideal circumstances (e.g. adventurous sex with a stunning partner) men don't need to use fantasy. Fantasy is more critical to female sexual arousal.

*"Women fantasize more than men, and their fantasies are extremely explicit" (Rachel Swift; Satisfaction Guaranteed; 1996)*

True sexual arousal follows as a response to our senses (sight, smell and touch) as well as our imagination (fantasy).

A lover's body does not cause female sexual arousal any more than images of naked men (porn) during masturbation.

So if sight is less effective in arousing women it makes sense that they need to use other means, such as imagination, to substitute.

# Orgasm during sex

Unfortunately, modern day sexology is not a science based on facts and logic but more a collection of beliefs and opinions.

One expert will claim that all women orgasm by the age of 19; another asserts 30.

Some say that clitoral stimulation is needed for orgasm and others that clitoral stimulation is irrelevant to female orgasm.

If female orgasm is so easy, then why do so many people ask about how women orgasm? No one EVER asks about male orgasm.

Orgasm involves a release of sexual tension that is built up as a person becomes aroused. Even for a woman, a true orgasm is followed by a period of resolution before another orgasm is possible.

In fact the link between clitoral stimulation and female orgasm comes NOT from women's experience of sex BUT from female masturbation.

The discussion of **orgasm during sex** covers the following:

- **CLITORAL STIMULATION**: clitoral stimulation does lead to female orgasm during female masturbation BUT ....

- **SEXUAL FANTASIES**: FIRST a woman needs to focus on sexual fantasies to become aroused enough for orgasm.

- **ORGASM TECHNIQUES**: so women are likely to find orgasm during sex more elusive than during female masturbation.

## Women's orgasm techniques

**Ways Women Orgasm** presents the orgasm techniques (often suppressed by other sources) that women use to orgasm during sex in terms that women who are familiar with orgasm from masturbation can relate to.

(1) Clitoral stimulation is needed for female orgasm...

*"... certainly, it is easier for most women to be orgasmic during masturbation than during intercourse. ... For most women, masturbation involves some form of stimulation of the clitoris,*

*whereas with intercourse, the clitoris is only stimulated indirectly, ..."* (Masters & Johnson; Human Sexuality; 1995)

If the answer to achieving female orgasm were as simple as providing PHYSICAL stimulation, there wouldn't be a problem in the first place.

After all this isn't rocket science. When a man is sexually aroused, he knows which body part to stimulate.

*"Many women indicated that they could not even suggest that their male partner was not satisfying them because if they did he would just fall apart. I felt a little insulted by that. I'm a big boy. If I'm not stimulating your clitoris correctly or whatever, tell me. I can handle that. I think most men can."* (Shere Hite; The Hite Reports; 1993)

(2) BUT clitoral stimulation by itself (whether by the woman or her partner) does not guarantee female orgasm. Why not?

Unlike men, most women do not approach sex just short of an orgasm. So even a woman who masturbates does not necessarily consider stimulating her clitoris during sex with a partner simply because she is not MENTALLY aroused enough for genital stimulation to make sense.

Genital stimulation only leads to orgasm once a person is mentally aroused.

*"Few of us reach orgasm without fantasy ..."* (Tracey Cox; Hot Sex; 1998)

Since the naked body of a sexual partner does not cause a woman to become aroused enough to orgasm, she is likely to need to use her sexual fantasies during sex.

The truth is that a woman is lucky if she finds even ONE way to orgasm.

# Clitoral stimulation

William Masters and Virginia Johnson's research in the 1960s focused on intercourse but even they acknowledged that the clitoris is the source of female orgasm (NOT the vagina as is often assumed).

To explain female orgasm during intercourse, they suggested that the hood of the clitoris is pulled each time the penis thrusts into the vagina, thus providing enough clitoral stimulation for orgasm.

But in 1976 Shere Hite concluded that this indirect clitoral stimulation was INSUFFICIENT to allow MOST women to orgasm during sex through intercourse alone.

These conclusions were not generally popular and, having failed to gain general acceptance, have been marginalised in modern day explanations for women's sexual experiences.

Possible reasons for their rejection include:

- Although heterosexuals can engage in other sexual activities, vaginal intercourse is seen to be core to how a man and a woman enjoy their sexual relationship;
- Given the difficulty in identifying female sexual arousal and orgasm, it was natural to assume that women's response to intercourse must be similar to men's;
- The belief that women orgasm during sex as easily as men enhanced women's attractiveness, not only in men's eyes, but also in terms of how women saw themselves;
- Female masturbation is relatively rare and so most women approach sex through intercourse as a loving and sensual experience rather than aiming for orgasm through genital stimulation; and
- Hite's conclusions reassure women who masturbate but they don't help women understand how to orgasm during sex.

## Clitoral stimulation is needed for orgasm

Clitoral stimulation is inevitable during female masturbation but there is a misconception that the clitoris is irrelevant to orgasm during sex.

Not so: the clitoris is a woman's sex organ and the source of female orgasm however she achieves it.

Amazingly, not all experts today agree that clitoral stimulation is required for female orgasm. The issue remains contentious because relatively few women understand that genital stimulation is required for a person to experience orgasm.

So although few men would attempt to reach orgasm without stimulating their penis, many women claim to orgasm without clitoral stimulation simply because they assume (as most men do) that female orgasm arises when the penis stimulates the vagina.

Women can enjoy many aspects of touching, penetration or non-genitally focused stimulation just as men do. But if a woman wants to orgasm during sex (or alone for that matter) then she needs to stimulate her clitoris.

Men orgasm by stimulating their penis directly, through masturbation, oral sex or intercourse but even they have difficulty with orgasm when genital stimulation is reduced e.g. by a condom. It is ludicrous to suggest that women can orgasm with less genital stimulation than men need.

*"The source of an orgasm, then, is clitoral. But a woman can feel orgasm mainly in her clitoris or the area beneath it, or in her vagina, or both, or in the whole pelvic area including her uterus, or – indeed – flooding her whole body." (Sheila Kitzinger; Woman's Experience of Sex; 1983)*

The clitoris is highly sensitive to touch much as the glans of the penis is. So when we talk about direct stimulation of the clitoris, my personal experience is that this involves stimulating the clitoris through the skin around (the labia) and over (the hood of) the clitoris. I tend to rub downwards from my vulva above the clitoris and press one or two fingers from each hand over the clitoris.

The sensitive clitoris is pressured through the protective layer of skin immediately around it. During masturbation, my stimulation of the clitoris is not particularly vigorous or even direct.

However, stimulation can be focused at crucial moments of arousal and is far more direct than the total lack of sensation that I experience during vaginal intercourse.

# Sexual fantasies

On approaching masturbation, my first task is to identify a fantasy that will arouse me enough to reach orgasm.

If I cannot achieve the necessary sexual arousal from fantasy then it makes not a jot of difference how vigorously or for how long I stimulate my clitoris. I know that orgasm is impossible.

*"However we feel about fantasies, it is clear that sex is not, for most of us, just a rubbing together of bodies, but involves our minds ... We take our minds with us into each sexual encounter." (Sheila Kitzinger; Woman's Experience of Sex; 1983)*

It came as a revelation to me that women might also use fantasies to help them orgasm during sex.

After all men don't take their pornographic magazines into sex with a partner, so why would women take their sexual fantasies?

Surely the 'real thing' should be better than the substitute used during masturbation?

The hitch is that men use erotic images, which transfer fairly naturally from masturbation to sex (in the form of a lover's naked body).

Understandably many people feel insulted by the idea that their lover may fantasise during sex.

A drawing (reproduced from Playboy November 1977) of a couple in bed, shows the man looking forlorn and the woman saying,

*"I think you're being silly. Would you like it better if I was thinking of you and sleeping with Robert Redford?" (Masters & Johnson; Human Sexuality; 1995)*

Perhaps because of this taboo, women's use of fantasies during sex is rarely acknowledged. Since women are not aroused visually as men are, they are likely to need to use sexual fantasies for orgasm.

## Some women find fantasies are ineffective during sex

It would seem that some women's sexual fantasies may not be compatible with sexual activity with a partner.

More involved mind-based sexual fantasies may only be suitable for use alone.

*"Among the most common varieties of sexual fantasies are those that can best be described as old familiar stories. The origin of such a fantasy, if it can be traced at all, might have been a book, a movie scene, or an actual experience. ...*

*Sometimes the primary fascination with this sort of fantasy lies in its sexual arousal, while at other times the pleasure may be more related to the 'director's role'- being able to control the scene, plot, and actors.*

*In many instances, the complexity of this fantasy makes it more suitable for use in solitary situations than during sexual activity with a partner." (Masters & Johnson; Human Sexuality; 1995)*

Let's be quite clear though.

Women may fantasise about many different things: an exotic holiday, winning the lottery or even Brad Pitt making love to them (romantic fantasy).

Sexual fantasies, in the context of women's sexual arousal, are quite different. Specifically women's sexual fantasies are focused on SURREAL but EXPLICITLY sexual scenarios with a complex psychological context.

Typically they involve taboo acts that are highly embarrassing to admit to and the people are no one you've ever met (or likely to meet). This kind of fantasy does not easily transfer to sex (no matter how kinky your sex life!).

*"There is a startling gulf between fantasy and what a woman is really seeking in a sexual relationship and she may find this very disturbing." (Sheila Kitzinger; Woman's Experience of Sex; 1983)*

An alternative is for a woman to incorporate her sexual fantasies into her sexual relationship either by reading erotica as a precursor to sex or by including ideas from her fantasies into physical sex play with her partner.

# Orgasm techniques

The web shows just what an extraordinary level of interest there is (both from men and women) in suggestions for how a woman can orgasm during sex.

Just to give a flavour, here are a few tips from the experts:

- Don't worry because orgasm is not that important;
- Relax a bit more and stop concentrating on orgasm;
- Try incorporating a fair amount of leg, abdominal, and buttock tension;
- Rhythmically squeeze your pelvic floor muscles;
- Breathe deeply or pant to get oxygen to those tensing muscles;
- Arch your back or try a different position to maximise clitoral stimulation;
- Stimulate the lubricated clitoris for long enough to guarantee an orgasm; and
- Escape into fantasy to block out any negative thoughts or distractions!!!

I am not saying that these approaches do not work. Presumably they work for the people who suggest them. I am just saying that they do not work for me. Anyway isn't female orgasm during sex supposed to happen 'spontaneously' as it does for men?

Shere Hite explained in 'The Hite Report' (1976): some women obtain the DIRECT clitoral stimulation they need for orgasm by stimulating their clitoris by hand during sex with a partner while other women find a position for intercourse that maximises the INDIRECT clitoral stimulation from male thrusting.

Although this second approach is ideologically appealing, orgasm is likely to be more difficult to achieve with indirect genital stimulation – imagine men settling for a partner thumping against their groin!

The huge omission from The Hite Report (and other sex books) is that there is no acknowledgement of the psychological aspects of sex. No one explains how women become sexually aroused enough for clitoral stimulation to lead to orgasm.

## Women use orgasm techniques (just as men do)

Many women (even those advising others) are uncomfortable with eroticism and explicit sexual behaviours. So although men know that their PSYCHOLOGICAL sexual arousal depends on an appreciation of eroticism (images of the body of a real or imagined sexual partner), women are often advised that female sexual arousal arises simply from love and romance.

Women are not even told that clitoral stimulation is needed for female orgasm. Women would need to be MORE SEXUAL than men if they could orgasm during sex without making use of (physical and psychological) orgasm techniques as men do.

Experts sometimes suggest that women should use their orgasm techniques (learnt from masturbation) during sex with a partner. With all the fuss that is made about clitoral stimulation it is easy to overlook other vital aspects of masturbation.

*"Fantasy and masturbation go together like bacon and eggs and lots of people have one favourite that always guarantees an orgasm. Studies show more than 50 per cent of us fantasise every time we make love with our partner." (Tracey Cox; Hot Sex; 1998)*

Despite suggestions to the contrary, men and women are not only from the same planet but also from the same species. Why should men and women experience the physical and psychological aspects of sexual arousal and orgasm totally differently?

It is quite possible that there are differences between male and female sexuality relating to levels of sex drive, ease of arousal and the importance of orgasm. Nevertheless enjoying our sexuality through sexual arousal and orgasm involves:

- achieving PSYCHOLOGICAL sexual arousal through an appreciation of eroticism (images for men; stories for women); and
- (only once sexually aroused) reaching orgasm through PHYSICAL stimulation of the penis for men, clitoris for women.

Other sites promise 'mind-blowing' orgasms. **Ways Women Orgasm** takes a more pragmatic approach and offers the chance to compare notes on how to make female orgasm more likely through an appreciation of the facts of female sexuality.

## Investing in your sex life

Many couples, both men and women, find any discussion of their sex life intensely embarrassing. This lack of discussion leads to difficulties in enjoying sexual pleasure and exploring sexual fantasies. Physical intimacy may be lost if the couple has not invested in learning about enjoying sex play together.

*"What's the one thing that differentiates good friends from lovers? Sex...*
*Stop having good sex and you stop feeling connected to your partner." (Tracey Cox; Hot Relationships; 1999)*

The discussion of **investing in your sex life** covers the following:

- **ENJOYING SEX PLAY**: especially over time, a woman can enjoy her own arousal through erotic sex play even if orgasm is missing.

- **EMOTIONAL INTIMACY**: a woman is more likely to feel amenable to sex if her partner invests in the companionable and loving aspects of the relationship.

- **PHYSICAL INTIMACY**: given that the immediate rewards of a sexual relationship have a strong male bias, a man needs to invest effort in making sex more rewarding for his partner.

The term emotional intimacy equates loosely to the word LOVE. The term physical intimacy equates loosely to the word SEX.

A man's desire for physical intimacy (male sex drive) leads to commitment to each other over a lifetime (emotional intimacy). A woman's sexuality works quite differently. Her pleasure comes from being able to excite a man. She learns that sex motivates a man, initially perhaps to pay for dinner or buy her jewellery, but later to support her in the immense task of raising children.

Young women may enjoy exploring sex with different partners but ultimately most women want to be more than a notch on a man's bedpost. They hope for companionship, through sharing interests, a sense of humour and common life goals. So a woman offers sex to a man over the longer-term because she identifies him as a worthy mate and a supportive companion.

## Long-term sexual relationships

Sex is relatively straightforward in the first 10 years or so. In long-term relationships, sex can become limited in imagination and spontaneity, partly through habit and partly through poor communication.

Over time, any couple who cares about their sex life will need to find new ways of enjoying sex play. This may involve investing in other areas of the relationship first.

If your sexual relationship has broken down, you need to start right back at the beginning. No one is likely to engage in sex as a loving act if there are issues in the wider relationship.

The first step in revitalising any couple's sex life is to talk through the general issues with a neutral third party (therapist). Relationships only survive through a willingness to give, on both sides.

Events in the past cannot be changed but it can help if each partner acknowledges what has happened and appreciates how the other person felt about the situation. Once the big issues have been resolved, decide together to invest some effort in the time you spend together generally.

Put off addressing any change to your sex life until there is a firm foundation for the wider relationship. Wait until you feel some sexual anticipation returning to the relationship.

*"It's important to see three points: (1) change is possible; (2) it isn't his fault that he is the way he is; and (3) there is no better alternative." (Kramer & Dunaway; Why Men don't get enough Sex and Women don't get enough Love; 1994)*

I realised that if I wanted my partner to support me in my ambitions for family (which naturally included plans for his money and efforts) then it was reasonable that I should be willing to contribute towards his ambition for enjoying sex play with a partner.

It's important to recognise that men do not gain the same emotional intimacy from family life that women typically do.

# Enjoying sex play

Women do not seek out relationships with men purely to enjoy orgasm. This is just as well because women's sexual arousal tends to be elusive, especially with a partner. What a woman does with this knowledge is up to her.

*"Most women who masturbate experience orgasm. More have orgasm with masturbation than in sex with a partner and these orgasms are often much more powerful than those experienced with lovemaking." (Sheila Kitzinger; Woman's Experience of Sex; 1983)*

The most positive attitude is to approach a sexual relationship with enthusiasm and a sense of fun. Trust is needed for both partners to be able to talk about their sexual fantasies.

Orgasm is only one aspect of enjoying sexual pleasure together and is much less rewarding if other sensual and loving sex play is missing.

*"Most couples who rate their sex lives highly say they are proactive in sex. They think about when, where and how they'll have it and think up new things to try." (Tracey Cox; Hot Relationships; 1999)*

**Ways Women Orgasm** is for couples who want to share ideas on enjoying sexual pleasure together, within the context of a healthy relationship and appropriate contraception.

Good sex relies on the willingness of both partners to invest effort in open communication and contemplating new ideas. It is assumed that couples are informed about the basic sexual facts.

*"In summary, since intercourse has been defined as the basic form of sexuality, and the only natural, healthy, and moral form of physical contact, it has automatically been assumed that this is when women should orgasm." (Shere Hite; The Hite Reports; 1993)*

## How women can enjoy sexual pleasure

Consider new ways of enjoying your own sexual arousal. Forget about the goal of orgasm and focus on erotic and sensual sexual pleasure.

Here are some suggestions:

- Take your man shopping and get him some sexy clothes. Book an evening out together and have sex before you go out.

- Prepare for sex by having a towel and waterproof sheet to protect the bed. This means that you don't have to worry about marking the sheets and you can also use baby oil or other lubricant freely.

- Offer your man a 'quickie' now and then (standing up or bending over perhaps in the shower or by the bed). This is pure male gratification but he can always pay you back later!

- Turn the tables on the sexual stereotypes. Think of your man as your sex toy. What would you like to do with a man who was at your beck and call? Do things the way you want to and just call on him when you feel you need him.

Many women never discover how to orgasm so be grateful for what you have! I had always assumed that sex should be, at least eventually, comparable with female masturbation. I have since concluded that for me the two are quite separate experiences.

During sex, I enjoy the eroticism of penetrative sex and the opportunity to explore with my partner how we can bring some variety to our sex life. When I am in the mood, I enjoy the pleasures of my own sexual arousal as my partner stimulates me.

During masturbation, I enjoy the eroticism of sexual fantasies and the sensations of release and relaxation that come with orgasm.

I make the best of the pleasures that there are. Both experiences are very pleasurable; just in a different way. It may be that how we enjoy our best orgasms is unique to ourselves.

It is worth mentioning that I only became aware of my own physical sexual arousal during sex from around my mid-thirties when my body reacted more favourably to being stimulated by my partner.

# Emotional intimacy

Enjoying sex for life involves continuing to be thrilled by each other's company in a broader sense than just sex. It involves demonstrating affection by reacting sensitively to each other's needs.

The physical intimacy of sex (because of its highly personal nature) leads to emotional intimacy where there is trust and respect.

Women perhaps focus on these aspects of sex more than men tend to given that female sexual arousal is more elusive.

Take a look at Luke Wilson's role in the film 'The Family Stone' (2005), which portrays emotional intimacy very effectively and that's without sex! At its best, sex can be a connection between two people.

*"Men, remember, feel good as a result of having sex.*

*Women want to feel good before having sex."*

*(Kramer & Dunaway; Why Men don't get enough Sex and Women don't get enough Love; 1994)*

Given that a woman is unlikely to orgasm during sex:

- Relationships involve giving your woman some of the things she wants outside the bedroom if she is to be willing to pleasure you inside the bedroom. Emotional intimacy involves investing in the companionable and loving aspects of the relationship. Have fun together but not just in the bedroom!

- Pleasuring a woman involves less focus on the goal of orgasm and more focus on general sensual pleasuring including clitoral stimulation. Mutual enjoyment of physical intimacy means listening to your partner and responding to her desires.

**Sex tips for men**

Intimacy can be lost in longer-term relationships if a man interprets every show of affection as a sexual invitation.

Your woman wants to kiss you because she feels loving and caring towards you not because she has a hard on.

A man's sexual arousal can be very flattering but not when his own orgasm is so obviously his main objective in love-making.

Here are some suggestions if you are aiming for sex for life:

- When you have family, insist on some privacy in the bedroom early on and be prepared to arrange and pay for regular evenings out together. Spend some quality time together but avoid looking for an immediate payback.

- Be ready to acknowledge the effort your partner makes for your benefit by offering sex and be ready to give her some space from time to time. Look at the balance between who gives and who receives (a higher pay check is not enough).

- She will not want to 'make love' to you if she is angry or exhausted. You can't expect her to be amenable in bed if you are inconsiderate outside the bedroom. Decide which chores you can take on and do them without needing to be asked.

- Be the devoted admirer: charming, companionable and have a laugh together. For a woman to be amenable to sex she needs to feel good about herself (sexually attractive) and good about you (wider relationship).

Apply the kiss test: full French kissing (sensual and loving) can be the sexiest part of sex. If you have stopped kissing as a couple, then revitalise your relationship and sex life by re-introducing some passion.

*"Just as a man forgets feelings, a woman forgets her sensual desires and longings*

*The practicalities of day-to-day survival and living take precedence over their deeper and more sensual desires." (John Gray; Mars & Venus in the Bedroom; 1995)*

*"This does not mean that every time I do the dishes, she is supposed to have sex with me.*

*That would not be romance. That would be a business deal." (John Gray; Mars & Venus in the Bedroom; 1995)*

# Physical intimacy

In the film 'Basic Instinct' (1992) Michael Douglas, playing the detective, asks Sharon Stone, playing the millionairess, whether she enjoyed having sex with her ex-lover.

She replies that she liked having sex with him because he was 'good with his hands'.

Pleasuring a woman is more likely to involve a man using his hands during sex than his penis.

Pleasurable touching includes sensitive stroking, gentle licking and light teasing caresses.

Men need soft hands and the use of a specialised lubricant from a sex shop will help.

*"Keep things slippery with your favorite lube and spend the evening at home with your sweetie 'watching a video'." (Rachel Venning & Claire Cavanagh; Sex toys: a playfully 101 uninhibited guide; 2003)*

As a first step, put a ban on intercourse for a month or two and focus on other forms of mutual pleasuring. Remember intercourse is good for two things: making babies and facilitating male orgasm. So even when you return to intercourse, use it towards the end of love-making.

Think of penis/vagina sex as 'intercourse-to-male-orgasm' to emphasise that a generous lover offers to pleasure his woman BEFORE taking his orgasm.

Other sexual pleasuring could involve the man offering: sensual bathing followed by fantasy role play (whatever appeals to your woman – bondage, spanking etc.), oral sex, stimulation with a vibrator (wherever you fancy), sex talk and sensual massage, leading to erotic massage: including clitoral stimulation by hand (probably not all in one session!).

## Sex tips for guys and girls

If you're aiming for 'quality sex' by sharing the pleasures of physical intimacy, then you need to invest in enjoying sex play together on a more mutual basis.

Once in a while make a special effort to bring some variety to sex by spicing up your sex life. Forget the holy grail of female orgasm and aim for giving her some sensual pleasure.

Talk to your partner.

Romance involves getting your woman into the bedroom. For sex tips on keeping her there see below:

- Make sure that you always offer some pleasure for your partner as well as for yourself. Have champagne by the bath. Spend some money on your intimate time together. Basically – live the fantasy!

- Sex sessions with a partner that include a sensual massage can be enjoyable for a woman even if orgasm is missing.

- Try something new. Visit a sex shop! Then plan with your partner to introduce something new – anticipation helps!

- Allow her some space for her orgasm even if that means being supportive of her time alone to enjoy female masturbation. It may make her more supportive of the times when you are the only one having an orgasm.

Sex shops are no longer sleazy or embarrassing places. The atmosphere is casual and relaxed and shop assistants are always happy to give help and advice. More women are shopping for toys and many shop assistants are female.

The easy way out for a man to appease his sexual frustration is to put pressure on his partner without considering how to make sex more rewarding for her.

A man can learn to enjoy arousing his partner while the woman enjoys being pampered. The woman needs to support the man's initiative by reacting encouragingly!

# Stories: Sexual desire

# A sexual relationship

Judy married in the late 1950s; well before the average woman was informed about what a sexual relationship might involve. Judy's aspirations were to provide a comfortable home for her family and to enjoy being a wife and a mother.

When I talked to her, Judy was in her mid-sixties with grown up children and a relationship of over 40 years. It was always doubtful whether she would understand a smutty joke but she had a wonderful giggle.

On the subject of female masturbation Judy commented: "I am a little bit shocked... I have always thought (totally without any proof) that young men masturbated more than young women. The reason I thought this would be that their thoughts and urges were much stronger in general towards sex."

It is often mistakenly assumed that all young women today masturbate. Whatever the social fashion most (if not all) men masturbate but even in our 'modern' times female masturbation is relatively uncommon.

Young women often don't know how to orgasm and why should they? There are few sources of information to help younger women learn how women's sexual arousal works or how they can go about enjoying sexual pleasure.

Also it can be difficult to find explanations for women's sexual experiences given that sex advice for women is often misleading.

*"It is obvious that neither younger girls nor older women discuss their sexual experiences in the open way that males do." (Alfred Kinsey; Sexual behavior in the human female; 1953)*

A sex therapist in her late fifties was totally over-awed by the modern talk of vibrators and orgasm. She was happy to admit that young women today are much more experienced than older generations (my view – it depends on the woman).

Nevertheless she was confident to advise (presumably from the book) that clitoral stimulation solves all difficulties with orgasm during sex.

I question this advice. Clitoral stimulation by itself has certainly never produced miracles for me during sex. The truth is that even during masturbation, clitoral stimulation only works when combined with the use of highly explicit sexual fantasies.

## Women have lower sexual desire

It may have become fashionable (not only acceptable but also actively encouraged) that women should be as positive about sex as men but, whatever the fashion, we cannot change our fundamental biological responses.

Flattered by male attention, young women naturally respond by appearing to be 'more sexual' than their elders. Unfortunately, society rejects a more representative picture of women's sexuality because of the cultural pressure to promote young women as sexy.

In fact the young women I spoke to were just as embarrassed about sex as their elders despite the liberalisation in sexual attitudes. Few women of any age identify with concepts as sexually explicit as clitoral stimulation or female masturbation. The conclusion must be that it is natural and normal for women to be less motivated than men to explore their own sexual arousal.

In any event, lack of orgasm is only a problem if a woman feels that she should have one in the first place. This is likely to be one reason why the scale of the 'problem' is rarely acknowledged because, as long as a woman is ignorant of what she is missing, she can happily go through life without ever knowing what an orgasm feels like.

Judy told me how, without preconceptions, a woman simply accepts her experience of sex at face value. Many women, of any generation, never read erotic novels or sex manuals. Being unaware of other women's experiences, either real or imaginary, they have nothing to reconcile their sexual experiences to. At least Judy was brave enough to comment.

*"Sexual decisions, in the final analysis must be personal." (Masters & Johnson; Human Sexuality; 1995)*

Lack of understanding about female sexuality means most women prefer to say nothing at all. It has certainly made me wonder: if the 'normal' experience is to orgasm with a partner then why do so few women positively promote the joys of sexual pleasure?

## Understanding female sexual desire

One of the misconceptions of the sexual revolution was the proposal that, for men and women to be equal, they had to be the same. But testosterone is the sex hormone. Men's bodies are full of it but women have much lower levels of testosterone.

Attributes traditionally considered feminine (e.g. being passive or accommodating) were thought to be signs of weakness or inferiority. Whereas traditionally masculine attributes (e.g. being assertive or dominant) were thought to be signs of strength or superiority.

This is a very natural male view of the world but many young and independent women also identified with the masculine perspective.

So it was implied that all women, whatever their aspirations or experience, should aspire to these more masculine characteristics and goals.

Sex is fundamentally about male sex drive. A man's erect penis is the symbol of this hormonal drive to thrust until ejaculation. If women have a reproductive drive at all then it is an emotional drive to raise their children. They certainly do not have the same biological drive to reach orgasm during sex that men experience.

Boys learn during puberty to enjoy their own sexual arousal and orgasm through masturbation. A girl also finds a new interest in the opposite sex but this interest revolves around a self-consciousness about how desirable she might be to men. Consequently, we frequently confuse women's sexual desire with a woman's ability to provoke a sexual response in a man.

Women's sexual fantasies often include an element of domination. It is fashionable to interpret such negative images as indicative of guilt or inhibition. I see it differently.

When a sexual partner takes control we have the pleasure of feeling that we are the object of their desire. Many men would not object if their woman took a more assertive role by indicating her sexual desires.

I am told that women 'enjoy' sex or even 'love' sex (and why not for heaven's sake?) but then they talk of affection. It is not clear much of the time whether women understand that true sexual arousal has to stem from some 'naughty' thought or act.

One female sex expert explained her belief that 'good sex' relies on emotional and sensual (rather than directly erotic) criteria:

"…What I know about how people get turned on and have great sex together that includes orgasm is their connection, their emotions, and sensual experiences whether it's visual looking at each other, enjoying various physical sensual activities."

True sexual desire involves our motivation to enjoy our sexual arousal and orgasm by appreciating aspects of eroticism, by discovering masturbation alone and by initiating sexual activity with a partner.

Women have lower sexual desire (sex drive) and experience much lower levels of sexual arousal than men which is why many women dislike eroticism and never masturbate.

The vast majority of women find almost any form of eroticism objectionable. Equally a woman has much more conscious control over whether she indulges in the erotic thoughts that might lead to enjoying her own sexual arousal and orgasm.

Initially, a young man is so driven by his own need to bring his state of sexual arousal to orgasm that he has little bandwidth for concerns about his partner's arousal.

The truth is that men often assume that their partner experiences orgasm: either they rely on their partner's say-so or they assume that women's minds and bodies respond to sexual stimuli much as men's do.

More experienced men come to appreciate that having an engaged sexual partner who is able to enjoy her own sexual desire through fantasies and sexual arousal can be the most arousing aspect of sex over the longer term.

My appreciation of eroticism has encouraged me to explore my own sexual arousal both alone and with a partner. Women who object to eroticism often comment that sex scenes potentially violate women or defile their bodies.

Such women must have very different reactions to a woman who is more at ease with eroticism. There is no judgment here – simply a desire to differentiate.

# Young and sexy

A young and sexy woman complained about the male attention she got every time she left the hostel on 42nd Street, Manhattan, dressed in her high heels and low cleavage. Yes, well... It is relatively easy for a woman to attract a man's attention by enhancing her looks.

It is more difficult for her to cash in on the advantage by enjoying orgasm during sex. Women are not automatically aroused as men are and so do not have the same sex drive to orgasm during sex. A woman is rarely seeking sex in the sense that a man does.

Naturally a man assumes that a woman who has made herself attractive must be interested in sex. Since men never put on make-up or dress provocatively we might think they are never interested in sex.

Of course this does not follow. The sexes have complementary roles. Women attract attention and then men make an advance. So women's bodies are a sexual commodity in a way that men's rarely are.

Men want control in sexual situations because (1) intercourse relies on their sexual arousal and (2) their performance (ability to orgasm and ejaculate) ultimately leads to reproduction.

A man selects a woman he finds attractive (which explains why some women encourage male attention) but a woman chooses the man she wants. These behaviours are fundamental to our dating and mating rituals.

Rich men prefer young and sexy women over successful women. So our heterosexual society tends to judge women by their looks before their achievements.

## Women have lower sexual desire

One year at college I lived with six other female students. Two of them were always entertaining young men in their rooms. The rest of us assumed that they must have been having sex with at least some of the stream of men who came through our flat.

My conclusion was not that they achieved sexual satisfaction with these men but that they enjoyed being so popular.

Most women need a stable relationship in which there is a high degree of trust and good communication if they are to orgasm during sex.

Young women often lack confidence and being promiscuous is an easy way to be popular, with men at least.

*"Although it is commonly believed that most males prefer sexual relationships with distinctly younger partners, and although most males are attracted by the physical charms of younger females, data which we have on our histories show that many of them actually prefer to have coitus with middle-aged or older females. ...*

*Older females ... often have a better knowledge of sexual techniques."*
*(Alfred Kinsey; Sexual behavior in the human female; 1953)*

Women's difficulties with sexual arousal and orgasm are often blamed on low libido but women naturally feel lower sexual desire than men as evidenced by:

- our enthusiasm for eroticism, either visual pornography or erotic stories;

- our willingness to indulge in sexual fantasies;

- the pleasure we obtain from admiring the sexual attributes of the opposite sex;

- how frequently we masturbate and our motivation to initiate sex with a partner.

The oldest profession (prostitution) says it all: a relatively few women provide sex for many more men. Of course the women are shamed for making money out of men's need.

Yet men often compensate women financially for sex – not an indication of equal pleasure. Even in our supposedly liberated times over 90% of the Internet provides some form of sex for men.

Inevitably there must be some women who are sexually insatiable and some men who are unmoved by sex but these individuals do not represent the 'norm'.

Most women never talk about lost sexual opportunities. They talk about commitment and trust. This enormous gap between the sexes means that most women remain terribly naïve about men's sexual desire.

## Women who fake orgasm

Men tell me how convinced they are that ALL their partners orgasm during sex. But that's kind of what faking orgasm is about, isn't it?

If it wasn't convincing then what would be the point? Men should sleep with women who are less sexually experienced.

Virgins are much more likely to admit that intercourse does not lead to female sexual arousal.

Very few virgins approach sex realising that a woman might need to exaggerate her true sexual arousal during sex.

Women learn over time to fake orgasm because men expect them to be moved by their love-making.

If my partner is keen but my mind is not tuned into erotic thoughts enough for me to want to engage on anything naughtier then we 'make love'.

My partner enjoys vaginal intercourse for the full-frontal access to my body and the turn-on of penetration. Mostly we use the missionary position.

Sometimes I lift my legs up and hug them around his back. Occasionally we use other positions for intercourse, such as, woman on top or doggy style from behind.

We both enjoy intimate kissing and sensual touching. I run my hands over his back and squeeze his buttocks perhaps pulling him towards me.

I tense my pelvic floor muscles to squeeze his penis inside me, which increases the stimulation of his penis.

I enjoy mild sensations of arousal, especially when my partner's groin grinds into my clitoris. I accept that intercourse is not arousing enough for orgasm.

It is simply a loving and sensual act that I share with my partner primarily for his sexual pleasure.

*"Sometimes they can choose to take a long time so that she gets her orgasm, and at other times, when she is not in the mood for an orgasm, he can enjoy the unrestrained freedom of just going for his orgasm." (John Gray; Mars & Venus in the Bedroom; 1995)*

## Men's expectations cause women to fake orgasm

It is men's modern expectation that female orgasm should occur during intercourse that causes women to fake. After all, the phenomenon of faking has only arisen since the sexual revolution that said that all women should orgasm during sex.

Rachel Swift explains the problem:

*"There are many reasons. By far the most common is that we fear to display our so-called 'inadequacy' in not being able to climax. We are afraid of being labelled 'frigid'." (Rachel Swift; Women's Pleasure; 1993)*

Rachel adds:

*"Another important reason why women fake their orgasm is the fear of upsetting their partner. Many men anxiously insist that the woman must have satisfaction." (Rachel Swift; Women's Pleasure; 1993)*

The trouble with faking is that it is a one-way street. Once you have led a man to believe that sex is orgasmic it's a little difficult to make a confession. If a woman hasn't the guts to admit it first time around then she is unlikely to confess later on.

*"The male obsession with orgasm leads 50% of women to fake it ..." (Marina Muratore; The Bluffer's Guide to Women; 1998)*

Even if a woman wanted to be honest, she still has the problem of how to respond during sex. Men want a partner to be enthusiastic for them to enjoy sex. A willingness to engage on fantasy sex play is what makes a woman 'good in bed'.

If a woman just lies there then sex is likely to last longer, which is not necessarily in her interests if she knows that intercourse does not lead to sexual arousal. Many men assume that women will assist with their sexual arousal as a matter of course.

Women are likely to need to fake orgasm during intercourse because the vagina (as part of the birth canal) has very few nerve endings.

The clitoris (as the female sex organ) is much more sensitive. Basically, you have to touch what works.

# The sexual politics of female sexual desire

Although the modern day hype about female sexuality was in part sparked off by the work of Alfred Kinsey, the facts he reported have long since been lost in the rush to sensationalise female sexuality.

Kinsey's report clearly set out the much lower sexual response of the female (as measured by the incidence of orgasm) and the incredible range in sexual responsiveness reported by women.

*"While it was 25 per cent of the females who had never reached orgasm by the end of the first year of marriage, it was 17 per cent who were not reaching orgasm in the fifth year, and 11 per cent who were not reaching orgasm in the twentieth year of marriage.*

*On the other hand, 39 per cent of females were reaching orgasm in all or nearly all of their marital coitus during the first year of marriage. This percentage had gradually increased over the years. By the end of twenty years of continuous marriage, the number so responding had risen to 47 per cent - nearly half! - of all the females in the sample."*

(Alfred Kinsey; Sexual behavior in the human female; 1953)

The Kinsey report was co-authored by four men. Imagine first four women reporting on male sexuality! Then think to yourself just how impartial most men are likely to be over female sexuality. No wonder they never considered that women might fake or simply be mistaken.

Even today, women who claim easy orgasm with a partner can rarely explain how they orgasm during sex. Orgasms 'just happen'.

Very few women appreciate the eroticism that leads to sexual arousal, which explains why even today female masturbation is relatively uncommon.

Sure there are women who enjoy adventurous sex play with a lover. I know because I'm one of them. Sure there are women who enjoy their own sexual arousal and orgasm through masturbation. But this is very different to saying that all women are as sexual as all men.

The young men I have been with seem to live in a permanent sex fantasy and masturbate up to two or three times a day. I only masturbate that much per week maximum and can happily go a week or two without orgasm.

To compete with 'male sex drive', modern women are assumed to have an equal 'female sex drive'. Yet prostitution and pornography still thrive as much as ever. Insistence on political correctness means that no one can explain these anomalies.

## Sexual desire versus sex drive to reach orgasm during sex

Female orgasm is not required for a woman to become pregnant. Consequently women do not have the same biological drive as men to orgasm during sex so sexual relationships favour male orgasm.

The aim of **Ways Women Orgasm** is not to dwell on the difficulties but to accept that they exist and suggest how couples can improve on what they already have.

Some women suggest that any presentation that does not portray sex as 'wonderful', 'orgasmic' etc. will 'put women off sex'. This is ludicrous. Women know what they want and what they enjoy as much as men do.

Feminist beliefs about sexual equality with men (how can we be equal when men don't have babies?) prevent women from learning the facts of their sexuality.

Many women never orgasm by any means and most of the stories of female orgasm during sex come from women who don't even know how to masturbate to orgasm. It is quite normal for a woman only to orgasm through masturbation alone.

Sadly, because so few women can masturbate to orgasm, this experience is categorised as sexually dysfunctional by experts today.

The pressure on women to be sexual equals with men means that women's difficulties with sexual desire are hushed up. Instead of sex becoming more open it just got a whole lot more embarrassing. Most sources never even admit the facts.

Our definition of female sexuality should reflect the experiences of ALL women whatever their age, attitudes or politics. Only then can we hope to gain a more realistic understanding of how the average woman can hope to achieve true sexual arousal and orgasm.

The truth is that female orgasm during sex is much more difficult to achieve than is ever acknowledged.

# Sexual promiscuity

Renate, a student of twenty-six, liked to be affectionate with her male friends but then was bewildered when they interpreted her hugs as a sexual advance.

A man tends to assume that physical intimacy is a given as soon as a woman shows him any affection. A woman needs time to build the emotional intimacy that causes her to be amenable to sex.

*"Women associate affection with love. ... Men associate affection much more directly with sex. ... Men see affection of any kind as a sexual invitation. Many women find this bewildering." (Kramer & Dunaway; Why Men don't get enough Sex and Women don't get enough Love; 1994)*

This explains in part why women can happily kiss each other, touch and go to the bathroom together without any sexual implication.

It is much more difficult for men to engage in the same kind of innocent intimacy with others of the same sex because men's intentions when seeking physical intimacy are often sexually motivated.

One evening Renate invited some friends around for supper and after the others had left, one young man simply went upstairs and got into her bed. Renate did not know how to ask him to leave and so she had sex with him.

After having sex with a number of her male friends, Renate found that even some of the men started to treat her disrespectfully.

## Men are rarely called sluts

We accept men being promiscuous because of their sex drive but women do not have the same excuse. This is why we can admire James Bond's light-hearted sexual exploits but all three women in Charlie's Angels are engaged in committed relationships.

The truth is that most women are naturally more selective about who they have sex with.

*"Among all peoples, everywhere in the world, it is understood that the male is more likely than the female to desire sexual relations with a variety of partners.*

*... it seems probable that these characteristics depend upon the fact that the female is less often aroused, as the average male is aroused, by the idea of promiscuity." (Alfred Kinsey; Sexual behavior in the human female; 1953)*

Teenage girls should never feel bulldozed into sex by the popular view that sex is always easily pleasurable for women. True sexual liberation means girls having control over their own body and the confidence to hope to enjoy arousal from their sexual relationships.

Most women who learn how to orgasm during sex do so only after many years with the same man.

In the 'Fifth Element', Bruce Willis kisses the alien beauty assuming that she is unconscious. Jumping up, she points a gun at him and gabbles unintelligibly. Later, he asks for a translation: "Not without my permission". He smiles wryly, "I thought so".

Whatever taunts are thrown out by men looking for a frivolous lay, in the longer term men respect a more picky woman.

This is why many people believe in sheltering young women from eroticism because it is generally much more difficult for women to enjoy the same sexual pleasure that men do, especially from casual sex with an unfamiliar partner.

In fact, a sexually demanding partner can be a turn-off for a man. Simply put, men prefer to be the ones chasing women rather than the other way around.

Nevertheless, a man is unlikely to see the contradiction in wanting his woman to be enthusiastic about sexual opportunities with him even when he knows that she is less driven by sex in general.

*"When men see an attractive woman, they fantasise about sex.*

*When women see an attractive man, they fantasise about a relationship – charming, agreeable company over dinner, friendship and comfort.*

*Sex does not necessarily come into it." (Marina Muratore; The Bluffer's Guide to Women; 1998)*

# How female sexuality differs to male sexuality

Many heterosexuals like the fact that the opposite sex is fundamentally different. Both our sexuality and our emotional responses differ.

Men are macho, sometimes a little insensitive, largely disinterested in how they look, social issues or children. Women are pretty, sometimes a little controlling, largely disinterested in getting dirty, doing battle or anything remotely technical.

When we generalise we need to be careful not to imply that everyone is completely categorised by their gender. Gender and the associated hormone drives need not always totally determine our individual priorities in life.

*"Both men and women seem to accept that gender differences will remain." (Anthony Mason; The Bluffer's Guide to Men; 1998)*

We accept that men still fight and play sport separately from women but the issue of sex drive or sexual desire is a more sensitive topic. My mission has been to try to get acknowledgement of the different emotional drives that influence our lives.

The defensiveness surrounding the sexual politics of heterosexual society means that no one wants to admit what we stand to gain from the other sex. So no one questions why women spend so much time on their looks and why men subsidise women's lifestyle. Women's financial dependence on men is taboo because of the social custom of women trading sex for money.

Have you ever wondered why only women are called 'whores'? The fact is that men rarely need a financial incentive to have sex. Yet even a man would struggle to orgasm with any woman regardless of age or attractiveness. Women are able to have sex with a conveyor belt of partners because they DON'T orgasm during sex. Men don't lack stamina; they just orgasm easily.

Even today female sexuality is associated more with women's role in providing men with sexual pleasure through intercourse than in enjoying their own sexual arousal and orgasm. Even a man would struggle to reach orgasm with the amount of genital stimulation that women get from intercourse. Yet such is the confusion over female orgasm that even women themselves insist that they can orgasm from vaginal intercourse despite the fact that it provides insufficient clitoral stimulation for orgasm.

If we understand what makes each other tick, relationships and family life could be more harmonious. There needs to be more honesty about pornography – what is exploitative and what is simply innocent eroticism. Women also need more information to learn how an appreciation of eroticism can lead to enjoyment of their own sexual arousal through female masturbation.

Men's subconscious sexual desire is generally aligned with their conscious mind. I find that it takes a considerable effort to get my conscious mind in gear. So I often go along with sex more in response to my partner's initiative than my own desire even though sex can be very pleasurable. It would seem that physical pleasures do not motivate me as they appear to motivate men.

I don't remember ever being aware of my own physical arousal (erection) when I was younger. When I came off the pill at 35, intercourse became much more comfortable and naturally lubricated. Before we always used an artificial lubricant (e.g. KY jelly).

My physical arousal (erection) is often linked with seeing my partner's penis or by giving him fellatio (oral sex). The swollen pubic area is very noticeable both to touch and to the eye. Sometimes I also have a heightened awareness of my arousal.

Stand by the bath with one foot on the floor, the other on the side of the bath, and place your fingers down over your vulva. Place your middle finger on the skin (hood) over your clitoris and rest the two other fingers either side of your labia. If you have an erection, you should be able to feel the solid bulge of your erection since the erectile tissue either side of the labia protrudes.

Although I experience my most satisfying orgasms through masturbation alone (when I can focus fully on fantasy), I am never aware of any degree of clitoral erection when I masturbate. Perhaps, for women, an erection is simply another evolutionary redundancy? Even with my partner, an erection does not mean that my mind is consciously tuned into sexual activity at all.

I would say that this is one of the main sexual differences between male and female sexuality.

# Women's sexual desire

Women who live alone or do not have an active sex life with their partner sometimes perceive themselves to be sexually needy because they start to doubt their ability to attract men.

Margaret (early fifties, children, relationship 30 years) was confident that she was highly sexual and interested in sex. However, her sexual relationship with her partner had broken down and she admitted that she did not consider female masturbation remotely interesting.

Given that she made no mention of a lover, I found it difficult to see that she had any outlet for her sexuality. When Margaret described herself as sexy, it was in terms of looking attractive, being young-at-heart and being physically active at her local tennis club with like-minded women.

*"Nearly all (but not all) younger males are aroused to the point of erection many times per week, and many of them may respond to the point of erection several times per day.*

*Many females may go for days and weeks and months without ever being stimulated unless they have actual physical contact with a sexual partner." (Alfred Kinsey; Sexual behavior in the human female; 1953)*

Women often define their sexuality by their emotional sense of well-being and their attractiveness rather than by any 'sex drive'. A man's sexual arousal can be very flattering and women enjoy the compliment.

As they grow older men worry about impotence; women worry about losing their attractiveness. Female sexuality is often defined in terms of young women's attractiveness to men.

## Men hope for sex for life

Older women often imply that marriage involves both sides 'putting up' with a non-ideal compromise. Today couple's expectations have increased.

In the past men may have been grateful for sex of any description but now they hope that their woman will engage on a variety of sexual activities and even that she will be enthusiastically orgasmic.

*"Married women are facing more sexual problems than single girls, with problems ranging from a lack of interest in sex to failure to reach orgasm. What a surprise!" admits Linda Kelsey in her article 'The truth about Married Sex.' Linda acknowledges that "For married women today it's difficult to square our expectations of sexual fulfilment with the realities of long-term relationships."*

*She suggests that the influence of the modern youth culture means that middle-aged women today "still feel like a woman with sexual needs, or at least a woman who wants to feel she's still sexually attractive." (Daily Mail UK newspaper Thursday, October 6th 2005)*

One summer's evening at a barbeque, a man in his fifties commented that he had almost forgotten what sex was because it was so long since he had had any. Understandably everyone was embarrassed, including his wife, and a few years later I heard that they had divorced. I assume this stand-off explains why so many married women prefer to say nothing about sex.

The proposal of the sexual revolution was that modern sexual relationships should be mutually pleasurable. So we blame the wife for being 'unloving' even though we all know that he probably has an orgasm during sex every time and she quite possibly has never had an orgasm in her life. A man needs to compensate a woman somehow for the sexual pleasure he enjoys.

Men enjoy sex fairly spontaneously but it is much more difficult for a couple to find ways of including some pleasure for the woman. In the marriage scenario, all pretence of romance or affection leading to 'making love' can be lost. Everyday pressures and routine reduce sex to the minimum required to keep a man's sex drive at bay, satisfying neither party.

Long-term sexual relationships involve making effort from time to time and a man needs to ensure that he is not the only person enjoying sexual pleasure from the couple's sexual relationship.

**Ways Women Orgasm** would like to hear success stories from couples who have overcome these pitfalls in longer-term relationships.

# Female orgasm is not required for reproduction

We have known for decades that intercourse doesn't provide sufficient PHYSICAL stimulation (of the clitoris) for orgasm.

But even more fundamentally, how do women achieve the PSYCHOLOGICAL arousal needed to orgasm during sex?

Over the years, I have found very few women who seem bothered that sex is unlikely to provide female orgasm. I understand that women who never masturbate are not motivated by orgasm.

I am targeting women who are familiar with orgasm from masturbation and who are interested in experiencing something similar with a partner.

Women do not become aroused enough for orgasm simply by looking at the naked male body. If we did, then we would also pay to enjoy the bodies of the opposite sex as men do through lap-dancing and pole-dancing bars.

Equally, women would buy pornographic magazines to enjoy their own arousal from looking at men's naked bodies and genitals.

Men learn from masturbation that their sexual arousal arises from looking at pictures of naked women, especially their sexual attributes.

So men find it natural and easy to become aroused during sex through kissing and caressing the body of a sexual partner.

Women learn from masturbation that their sexual arousal arises from an appreciation of eroticism, through sexual fantasies. These are surreal psychological scenarios involving highly taboo sexual acts (such as rape) and unrealistically assertive men.

To reach orgasm from sexual fantasies alone a woman has to achieve an intense mental focus. Not only is this difficult in the presence of another person, even a lover, but such a mental block-out is frankly incompatible when 'making love' with a partner.

Intercourse (at its best) provides a woman with a loving act through which she can encourage her man's commitment to the relationship by facilitating his orgasm.

Men naturally find vagina intercourse a fulfilling sexual act since it provides both the physical stimulation (of the penis) and the psychological arousal (by penetrating a woman's vagina) that they need for orgasm.

This explains the contradiction of rape. How can an act that is supposed to be mutually pleasurably also inflict so much misery on women?

Men are not victims of rape (through vaginal intercourse) because intercourse is an act of male sexual dominance. A woman's natural instincts are to accept a man making love to her only once she has identified him as a potential mate.

Women's sexual role (during sex with a partner) remains what it always was:

- To accept a man's desire for physical intimacy as his sign of devotion to her;

- To provide a man with sexual pleasure by facilitating male orgasm; and

- By appreciating a man's love-making, to provide the emotional intimacy that motivates him to support a family.

Men's psychological arousal is almost instant partly because their bodies are full of the sex hormone, testosterone.

Sex has been designed to facilitate male orgasm and this emotional payback helps in part to motivate men to support a family.

Whether we like it or not, orgasm represents a much smaller part of the wider picture of female sexuality.

Women may be unhappy about a lack of orgasm during sex but they are able to put up with it. Very few are motivated to find answers.

Women today who hope for orgasm have been given unrealistic expectations by the modern drive for sexual equality in all things.

This has also increased the pressure from men who have always hoped that women might be as enthusiastic about sex as they are.

# Women have a lower sex drive

Men's sexual arousal is usually easy whereas women's sexual arousal and orgasm are not automatic so unsurprisingly sex tends to focus on male sexual arousal.

A man's orgasm (since it is usually co-incident with ejaculation) is critical to reproduction and so it makes sense that men are motivated by eroticism and able to reach orgasm easily.

Female orgasm, on the other hand, is not required for a woman to conceive. Even the wonders of modern contraception cannot change women's sexuality from what Nature intended it to be.

*"...men and women are manifestly not the same. And nor are their responses to one another." (Anthony Mason; The Bluffer's Guide to Men; 1998)*

The fact that women masturbate less frequently than men (if at all) is rarely acknowledged. Even when it is, women are reluctant to accept that this fact indicates men's higher sex drive.

Despite the contrast with male sexuality, where boys learn to masturbate in their pre-teens and where men orgasm easily (most of the time) with a partner, many women cannot accept that men's sex drive might be stronger. The male and female experiences are so different that it makes it very difficult for men and women to understand the other gender's perspective.

*"We have pointed out that ... the incidences of responding males, and the frequencies of response to the point of orgasm, reach their peak within three or four years after the onset of adolescence.*

*On the other hand, ... the maximum incidences of sexually responding females are not approached until some time in the late twenties and in the thirties, although some individuals become fully responsive at an earlier age."(Alfred Kinsey; Sexual behavior in the human female; 1953)*

## Male sexual arousal is much more automatic

Unlike boys, girls do not experience spontaneous sexual arousal and so they have no similar natural motivation to investigate how their genitals might respond to stimulation. If she is to discover how her sexual arousal works, a girl has to make a much more CONSCIOUS decision to explore her enjoyment of eroticism and develop her fantasies.

So while most young men are quite naturally motivated to explore their own sexual arousal and to reach orgasm through an appreciation of eroticism and genital stimulation, most young women are, just as naturally, more focused on exploring their emotions and relationships with others. As a consequence, men and women approach sex from very different perspectives.

*"...many boys, and nearly all girls, are taught that masturbation is evil, ... This is nonsense, of course; masturbation has several very positive values, especially for women....*

*In childhood and adolescence it teaches a girl to explore her body and not to be ashamed of its shape, its texture, and its surfaces. It teaches her, especially, not to be ashamed of touching and playing with her genitals.*

*It does more. It helps a girl become aware of her response to sexual stimuli and to recognize the stages of sexual arousal. And it enables a girl to develop her own sexuality – to know what she enjoys and what she dislikes – which is important if she is to be fulfilled sexually later." (Derek Llewellyn-Jones; EveryMan; 1980)*

Relatively few women masturbate and even fewer learn how to apply their orgasm techniques to sex. A woman who does not masturbate cannot know that she reaches orgasm with a partner because she has no way of knowing what orgasm is.

This probably also explains multiple orgasms. Unless a woman knows what orgasm feels like (from masturbation) she can easily confuse sensations of sexual arousal (or thrills of muscle spasms) with orgasm. My body's reaction after orgasm is similar to a man's. I feel completely relaxed and I do not have the ability to arouse myself immediately due to clitoral sensitivity.

If a couple has some understanding of the different rewards that men and women obtain from sex, they can make sure that there is a balance of giving and receiving in their sex life. If we understand how our partner's responses differ to our own, the modern couple can aspire to 'quality' sex within the context of a positive and mutually supportive relationship.

# Stories: Female masturbation

## Female masturbation is relatively uncommon

Carolyn, a relationship counsellor in her fifties, told me she thought it unwise to positively encourage female masturbation. She did not give her reasons.

*"Many women think of masturbation as unnatural and disgusting and a complete waste of time, and don't understand why anybody does it and are unsympathetic to the view that people might continue to do it even though they have sexual partners. The majority of men, though they may keep their feelings to themselves, don't agree." (Miriam Stoppard; Healthy Sex; 1998)*

It is often implied that for a heterosexual woman, sex is an emotional experience and that orgasm (if acknowledged at all) comes from simply loving her partner. The unspoken fear is that any activity as sexually explicit as masturbation might interfere with the more acceptable loving experiences that a sexual relationship can provide.

Carolyn knew that I masturbated and she asked me, rather tactlessly I thought, whether I had ever had any lesbian tendencies. It reminds me of the joke told by a character in the film 'Flashdance'. A male chef asks, "What's this?" and sticks his tongue out flat. The answer – "A lesbian with a hard on!".

Lesbian women are seen to enjoy explicit sexual arousal (involving the clitoris). For heterosexual women, enjoying sexual pleasure is primarily associated with immoral behaviour. Within loving relationships heterosexual women usually settle for vaginal intercourse, which can be justified morally on the grounds of reproduction.

*"Although 58 per cent of the females in our sample were masturbating to orgasm at some time in their lives, it was a much smaller percentage which had masturbated within any particular year or period of years.*

*Because of the considerable discontinuity of most of the masturbatory histories, it is probable that not more than a fifth - 20 per cent - of the females were masturbating within any particular year." (Alfred Kinsey; Sexual behavior in the human female; 1953)*

We like to underplay the physical aspects of heterosexual women's sexual arousal. Even though women do have 'hard-ons' we rarely acknowledge this fact. We prefer to attribute strong physical responses to male sexuality. I enjoy my own sexual arousal and orgasm but my focus is on what is happening in my head rather than to my body. In general, men are more tuned into the physical side of sex (genital focus) but a woman appreciates the sensuality of her whole body (her power to arouse a man).

When a man masturbates, he uses firm and sustained stimulation of his penis from the outset. When I first masturbated a partner, I was surprised by how vigorous I could be when stimulating his penis with my hand. A man can expect the reverse: he will need to use much more subtle stimulation on a woman's clitoris than he is used to when masturbating himself.

When I masturbate I don't even consider clitoral stimulation until I can feel some stirrings of arousal (by tuning into an effective fantasy). Even then I only rub my vulva (stimulating the clitoris through the surrounding skin) relatively slowly and gently with physical stimulation focused mainly on the peak of orgasm itself.

Our interpretation of women's sexuality is faulty. We assume women are sexual if they support the view that intercourse is mutually orgasmic (despite the known facts). Women who masturbate are dismissed as sexually dysfunctional (pre-orgasmic). In fact such women are more sexual than average because they learn how to orgasm through genital stimulation as men do.

*"Masturbation is a normal sexual outlet, which is most common in adolescence, but which is practised at all ages, by people with and without sexual partners. Masturbation is a healthy way of learning to explore your body, of developing your sexuality and your sexual fantasies. All of these are important for a fulfilling sexual life." (Derek Llewellyn-Jones; EveryMan; 1980)*

One disadvantage of masturbation and learning how to give yourself an orgasm early on in life is that your expectation is set much higher than a woman who does not know what an orgasm is. You are then sure to face disappointment if you assume that a sexual experience shared with a lover will necessarily be as easily pleasurable.

# Women's sex drive to orgasm during sex

Becky explained via e-mail: "I had my first orgasm at 26 during masturbation – pretty late I know & since then no stopping me with the sex toys : ) . Plenty of my girlfriends have not though – and like you say, don't seem too bothered about it which I can't understand."

Despite this evidence Becky was convinced that every woman must be interested in orgasm. Many women dislike the eroticism that helps a woman develop the sexual fantasies that lead to female sexual arousal. Consequently female masturbation is relatively uncommon.

Ironically Becky's experience of sex was more miserable than most. "I'm 31 & have had pretty non-orgasmic experiences to date! Issues with vaginismus & then guys who can't get their heads around that, hormone stuff, dry years & mostly casual relationships."

As a sex writer, Becky got to explore sex with different men: "I've been seeing an escort for various treatments – yoni massage, spanking, fantasy play etc, which has really helped & just started seeing a guy who I think will be good for me so we'll see."

As they become more financially independent, more young women explore how they can enjoy physical intimacy through dating men. Even so women stand to gain less from sexual promiscuity than men.

All the evidence indicates that most women who learn how to orgasm during sex do so only after years of investment in a sexual relationship with the same partner.

Becky told me: "I had a breast orgasm at the weekend – interesting as it's never happened to me before : ) " Becky still did not know how to orgasm during sex and had to masturbate herself to orgasm after her boyfriend reached his orgasm from their sex play.

Regardless of her own real life experiences, Becky would not accept that men might have a stronger sex drive.

Women can be terribly naïve about men's sex drive, despite the evidence. One young woman was passionate in her conviction that "women enjoy sex like men do".

So I suggested: "Presumably you masturbate regularly, get erections throughout the day and are always hassling your partner for sex?" She replied: "No, and I have never met a man who does all these things either."

*"Male masturbation has always been a secret from which women have been excluded. Even in marriage, few women are given the opportunity to witness it." (Miriam Stoppard; Healthy Sex; 1998)*

It is really quite disturbing that young women today are so unaware of the facts about male sex drive. Every man knows that past a certain point it is difficult for a man to hold back on his instinct to follow through on his sex drive.

This is why women who 'lead a man on' may find it difficult to convict a man of rape and, in the UK, rape within marriage has only been a crime since 1991.

Society in our age of information claims to want to protect young people but there is a lack of willingness to be honest about sex. Women's sexuality has been hyped so much that women often believe that they get as much out of sex as men do.

A woman may want to have sex for emotional reasons (such as a subconscious desire to get pregnant) but this is very different to the male drive to orgasm during sex.

From their teens men have little conscious choice over their sexual arousal and they easily orgasm during sex whereas Becky did not discover orgasm by any means until her mid-twenties.

Male sexual dysfunction involves loss of sexual pleasure (through problems with arousal) but female sexual dysfunction often involves painful sex.

Nevertheless it is implied that sex is always equally pleasurable for men and women. Women need reassurance that pain, discomfort or undue pressure from a partner are unacceptable as part of healthy relationship sex.

It is certainly possible for a woman to enjoy the physical intimacy of a sexual relationship with a man but it is much more difficult for a woman to enjoy orgasm with a lover.

A woman needs to accept investing in her sexual relationship for her lover's benefit especially over the longer-term. It would be nice to have this effort that women make in sex more formally acknowledged.

# Women's sexual arousal and orgasm are not automatic

Almost complete mystery surrounds women's sexual arousal. Women's PHYSICAL arousal is rarely acknowledged and our understanding of women's PSYCHOLOGICAL arousal is very vague. No wonder many of us gain the impression that female orgasms simply mushroom up out of nowhere.

Explanations for women's sexual arousal often defy belief. It is suggested that women, unlike men, can reach orgasm in response to many different sources of physical stimulation – even amazingly from a woman brushing her hair!

This is just one example of how we are asked to believe that women can achieve what even a man would find difficult. It is worth bearing in mind that the majority of men generally know what an orgasm is.

Many women are unfamiliar with real female orgasms and are more likely to be talking about sexual arousal.

Of course male orgasm does not occur automatically either, for the most part. Male arousal happens fairly spontaneously but men usually have to work at achieving orgasm.

It is men's ease of arousal that explains why every boy discovers masturbation and makes it inevitable that boys learn how to use what turns them on (fantasy aided by pornographic images) enough to reach orgasm.

Shere Hite found that women, who reach orgasm during intercourse, either ensure that they obtain DIRECT clitoral stimulation by applying orgasm techniques to sex (by masturbating themselves during sex or having their partner masturbate them) or they find ways of maximising INDIRECT clitoral stimulation by finding suitable positions and techniques for sexual intercourse.

### Sexual arousal originates in the brain

Female orgasm is one of Nature's optional freebies – take it or leave it. But just to state the obvious: if anyone is to experience orgasm, they must first be motivated to do so and secondly they must know how to become aroused enough to reach orgasm.

Physical stimulation is all very well but before that, something has to be happening in the brain.

A physical and psychological build up is required to generate the consequent sexual release that we call 'orgasm'.

Rather like climbing up the steps of a slide in order to enjoy slipping down the other side, it seems unlikely that even women can reach the peak of orgasm without a build-up of any kind. In other words, a woman is not going to discover orgasm while doing the ironing!

*"The more you fantasise, the higher your libido.*

*... it's pretty well established that the more you think about sex, the more you want it.*

*That makes fantasies the cheapest, most effective sex aid around." (Tracey Cox; Hot Sex; 1998)*

Since female arousal is not required for intercourse women can engage in sex through intercourse without the need to be aroused or orgasmic. This is a major advantage in relationships where a woman can focus on facilitating male orgasm (which, when co-incident with ejaculation, leads to reproduction) rather than aiming for her own (which is not involved in reproduction).

Very few women are familiar with how true sexual arousal is achieved. Unlike male masturbation, which happens fairly naturally, a woman only discovers orgasm through masturbation as a result of consciously choosing to explore her sexuality.

Women have to learn about their sexual arousal and a woman needs to be open-minded enough about eroticism to be able to overcome any moral objections she might have to indulging in the sexual fantasies which lead to orgasm.

*"Approximately 30 percent of women don't have sexual fantasies. For some, it's a vestige of the old notion that fantasy is something only men do.*

*Others are embarrassed by the harshness of their sexual inspiration and quickly squash it." (Rachel Swift; Satisfaction Guaranteed; 1996)*

# Women have to learn how their sexual arousal works

Some women appear to be so sheltered from the world of adult eroticism that one wonders if they have ever experienced sexual urges of any kind.

Nancy, a recently widowed woman in her seventies became acquainted with John, a man of the same age, during a stay in hospital. On the grounds of friendship, they met once for lunch and then Nancy invited him to her house. On admitting John to her home, he took the sexual initiative by giving her a tongue-in-mouth French kiss.

Nancy contained her revulsion at the uninvited physical intimacy until John left but resolved that she would never see him again. Nancy told me that even her husband of fifty years had never kissed her 'like that'. Men never seem to lose their enjoyment of physical intimacy with the opposite sex whereas women do not necessarily appreciate the physical side of sexual encounters at all.

On the other hand Nancy has already had her chance in life. As a teenager in the early 1940s, she was sheltered by her family and society from any knowledge of sexual pleasure. Young women were simply not equipped to know how to respond to their lover in bed. This was a sad loss for Nancy as well as for her husband.

The phrase 'lie back and think of England' came from Lady Alice Hillingdon who said (1912): "I am happy now that George calls on my bedchamber less frequently than of old. As it is, I now endure but two calls a week, and when I hear his steps outside my door I lie down on my bed, close my eyes, open my legs and think of England."

*"Sex is the price women pay for marriage. Marriage is the price men pay for sex." (Allan & Barbara Pease; Why Women can't read Maps; 1999)*

### Women need the facts to enjoy sexual pleasure

It is often asserted that women's sexuality can be re-engineered simply by changing attitudes. Sadly, regardless of the social fashion, all women have the same fundamental sexual responses and these are quite different to men's.

Society today encourages women to behave in a sexually provocative manner. However since young women often don't know how to orgasm it seems unlikely that women who engage in casual sex are enjoying sexual pleasure. In any event, it is worth questioning the value of a relationship for either side that starts by bartering sex for a meal or a couple of drinks.

*"The percentages of females who had experienced orgasm (the accumulative incidences) had risen steadily during pre-adolescence, .... but less than a quarter (23 per cent) of the sample had had such experience by fifteen years of age.*

*A little more than a half (53 per cent) had had orgasm by twenty, three-quarters (77 percent) by twenty-five, and about 90 per cent by thirty-five years of age. ... there appear to be some 9 per cent who would probably not reach orgasm in the course of their lives." (Alfred Kinsey; Sexual behavior in the human female; 1953)*

Some women never tune into eroticism and never learn about their own sexual arousal. Marriage used to be about women 'putting up with' sex but increasingly, if they are to keep a family together, a couple needs to invest in their sexual relationship. Marriage is not just about family; it also involves a man and a woman being companions and hopefully lovers for life.

Sex and love are often confused for women and, even today, many people believe that knowledge of sexual pleasure is 'inappropriate' for young women. Knowledge does not force a person to make certain choices – it gives them a choice. There is no reason for sheltering young women from eroticism. Teenage girls should be told how couples can enjoy sex for life.

Regardless of a woman's ability to enjoy her own orgasm or her attitudes towards eroticism in general, a woman needs to be prepared to invest in her sexual relationship over the longer term. This is fundamentally about give and take. A man needs to acknowledge the fact that women do not enjoy the same orgasmic pleasure from sex. He needs to appreciate the female perspective by responding to a woman's enjoyment of the more sensual and companionable pleasures of sexual intimacy.

Long-term relationships are not only about sex but also about enjoying each other's company over many years.

# Women have to learn how to orgasm

In the film 'Shirley Valentine' (1989), Pauline Collins plays Shirley, a middle-aged housewife. Shirley comments:

"I'm not particularly fond of it – sex. I think sex is like supermarkets, you know, overrated.

Just a lot of pushing and shoving and you still come out with very little in the end." (Note: this film was set in the days before supermarkets sold everything from clothes to microwaves!)

Shirley reminisces about a conversation where one of her friends comments on their youth:

"In those days everyone thought it was a case of – in out, in out, shake it all about. Stars would light up the skies and the earth would tremble."

Shirley laughs at the ignorance of her generation of men who were unaware of the fact that clitoral stimulation is required for female orgasm.

The implication is that younger generations of women expect to have orgasms either through female masturbation or with the assistance of a more knowledgeable lover.

It is assumed that men in more modern times are well-informed about foreplay techniques as well as positions and techniques for sexual intercourse.

Shirley comments: "They think they know it all – the clitoris kids I call them!"

We may have more knowledge today but our expectations are correspondingly higher.

Young women often don't know how to orgasm until they try masturbation and learn how to use a vibrator to discover orgasm.

## Modern hopes for fantasy sex

Women of an older generation often mistakenly assume that younger women have perfect sex lives simply because they live with a man before marriage.

That's just like assuming that all married women enjoy sex. Otherwise why would they be married?

It is evident that women seek relationships with men for reasons other than the 'success' of a sexual relationship.

*"In reality, the more sexually active you are, the more likely you are to masturbate, regardless of whether you do or don't have a partner.*

*... Of the women who have discovered its joys, virtually all can masturbate to orgasm ...*

*On the opposite side, if you're a female who has never masturbated, statistics indicate it's quite likely you've never had an orgasm in your life. Pretty strong support for solo sex!*

*The truth is good girls do do it and if you never have and won't try, give up now on ever having a fulfilling sex life.*

*Masturbation is a sure way (and often the only way) to discover what turns you on sexually, and unless you know how to excite yourself, you've got zero chance of telling your partner how to." (Tracey Cox; Hot Sex; 1998)*

Women are likely to find transferring orgasm techniques to sex much more difficult than the experts imply.

Although it is a popular suggestion that clitoral stimulation solves any problem with orgasm, the truth is that some completely normal women never orgasm with a partner by any means.

Female sexual arousal is much more difficult to achieve with a partner.

Surrounded by unrealistic portrayals of female sexuality in the media, women often conclude that they are abnormal when they are, in fact, facing a very normal dilemma with sex and their relationships.

Women's use of sexual fantasies for sexual arousal is the most likely explanation for the different experiences of sex and masturbation.

# Techniques women use to reach orgasm

I'm sure that men will understand the point. We express our sexuality through two basic phenomena:

- Firstly, enjoying our own PSYCHOLOGICAL arousal by appreciating eroticism; and

- Secondly, bringing our sexual arousal to orgasm by PHYSICAL stimulation of the genitals.

Yet many women are shocked by eroticism (whether visual or verbal pornography, erotica or the concept of sexual fantasy) and equally shocked by the idea of explicit clitoral stimulation (either female masturbation or oral sex – cunnilingus). So how is it that they reach orgasm by any means?

Of the women who responded to Shere Hite's questionnaires (1976), 82% said that they masturbated and yet I have found very few women who masturbate. Most are offended by the suggestion that any woman would want to engage in clitoral stimulation under any circumstances.

Shere Hite was asking detailed questions about how women reach orgasm. Naturally this biased the results of her surveys because it is only through female masturbation that a woman has the confidence to answer detailed questions about orgasm.

A general failing of surveys is that they ask closed questions like: Do you masturbate? Any woman who has ever put her hands anywhere near her genitals can justify ticking the box.

Masturbation as an adult activity involves knowing how to become sexually aroused enough so that genital stimulation leads to orgasm. Female sexual arousal has to be CONSCIOUSLY generated.

## Most women are unaware of the need for orgasm techniques

As a woman who has questioned a lack of female orgasm during sex, I am told that other women find orgasm easy. The trouble is that the facts stand against this claim.

Common sense tells us that (compared with the genital stimulation that men need) the clitoral stimulation provided by vaginal intercourse is likely to be insufficient for a woman to reach orgasm.

Women, whose sexual experiences are based purely on sex with a partner, often interpret sex in the light of emotional criteria. They are confused by other women's questions about orgasm because they think it is easily achieved.

They believe that all you need is loving feelings for your partner and then you reach orgasm the first time and every time from vaginal intercourse.

BUT we are mixing apples with pears here.

Women who do not appreciate eroticism, do not explore their sexual fantasies, do not masturbate and think that vaginal intercourse is the only acceptable sexual activity are unlikely to be able to advise women who, having explored their sexual arousal both alone and with a partner through a variety of activities, question a lack of orgasm during sex.

The phrase 'orgasm techniques' sounds fancy but only means getting turned-on and then knowing how to orgasm by stimulating our genitals. Men also use orgasm techniques because (even for men) orgasm does not simply drop out of a tree.

A woman, who can masturbate to orgasm, may advise other women to learn how to masturbate because masturbation is the starting point for understanding our own sexual arousal and how to achieve orgasm.

Many of these women might hope that they will learn one day how to do the same with a partner but this is very different to saying that it is easy to achieve.

*"... the fact remains that the techniques of masturbation usually offer the female the most specific and quickest means for achieving orgasm.*

*For this reason masturbation has provided the most clearly interpretable data which we have on the anatomy and the physiology of the female's sexual responses and orgasm." (Alfred Kinsey; Sexual behavior in the human female; 1953)*

Men's sexual experiences are much more straightforward. Women's experiences are taboo because of lack of understanding.

Women rarely compare notes even on masturbation let alone how they succeed with transferring orgasm techniques to sex.

# How a woman can learn how to masturbate

If a woman is open-minded to the idea of exploring eroticism, she should start by reading some erotic literature. I suggest:

- 'Emmanuelle' by Emmanuelle Arsan: relates the sexual adventures of young women;

- 'The Happy Hooker' by Xaviera Hollander: describes the author's experiences of pleasuring men as a high-class prostitute and the madam of a brothel; and

- 'The Story of O' by Pauline Reage: describes a fantasy castle setting where men use women for their pleasure (includes sadism). Remember not to judge – this is fantasy!

I read these books while still a teenager and I am confident that any heterosexual woman should be able to enjoy at least some of the explicitly sexual scenarios.

Read these books in private; preferably when the house is empty. After reading a book, return to the sections that you found most arousing. Try to imagine yourself in the title role.

Then spend some private time perhaps on the bed gently touching your clitoral/vulva area while reading the most arousing passages or while re-living them in your mind.

Forget about your body to start with and focus on what is happening in your mind. Physical stimulation is used to bring a mental state of sexual arousal to orgasm.

So if you are not mentally turned on then don't bother with any physical stimulation. There's no point.

*"To masturbate, fantasizing, or getting into an aroused state mentally is important. Also, for me, being alone is important.*

*I use the tips of my fingers for actual stimulation, but it's better to start with patting motions or light rubbing motions over the general area." (Shere Hite; The Hite Report; 1976)*

Find a comfortable position (women masturbate in various positions) and explore gently stimulating your vulva and over the clitoral hood. Some women use a pillow, or other object or just their fingers.

When I first learned how to masturbate, I would rub my vulva through my underwear. Later I enjoyed more focused clitoral stimulation by using my fingers directly on the skin.

Lying face down, with my eyes shut, I move my hips gently from side to side with my fingers positioned over my vulva. I tense my pelvic muscles slightly. As the intensity of focus on fantasy increases my sense of arousal, my fingers press more firmly into the clitoral area.

If all else fails then buy a vibrator.

A man needs to allow his woman privacy and to avoid interrogating her afterwards. To enjoy our own sexual arousal we need to feel free to explore our sexual fantasies. This is difficult if we have to justify them to someone else later. Just think how you would feel!

Remember also that a man would probably always choose sex over masturbation. It's different for a woman who only enjoys orgasm through masturbation alone: she doesn't necessarily want to be interrupted by an enthusiastic partner!

The women who replied to Shere Hite's questionnaire in 1976 described their experience of female masturbation as follows:

- 73% – stimulate their clitoral/vulva area with hand while lying on their back
- 5.5% – stimulate their clitoral/vulva area with hand while lying on their front
- 4% – press their clitoral/vulva area against a soft object e.g. pillow
- 3% – press thighs together rhythmically
- 1.5% – water massage of clitoral/vulva area
- 11% – women who masturbate in more than one of above ways

So once again, I'm a freak – well in the 5% category! Why be like everyone else? Women are most usually depicted masturbating on their backs so that any audience can see what they are doing.

So, is it that most women say they masturbate on their backs because they do or is it that they imagine that this is how a woman should masturbate? One wonders…

## How to use a vibrator to discover orgasm

Laura was educated and cultured but she also had a worldliness and the classy sex appeal that attracts the most ambitious men. In her early thirties, Laura told me that she had always been confident that she had orgasms during sex.

*"...in regard to sexual responsiveness the female matures much later than the male." (Alfred Kinsey; Sexual behavior in the human female; 1953)*

When she was twenty-eight, a liberated friend told her how to use a vibrator to enjoy orgasm through female masturbation. Her friend was so convinced that Laura should try the experience that she took her to a department store to buy the gadget.

If only we all had friends like this!

Laura admitted that this piece of equipment sat in her bedroom drawer for some time. Eventually when she was brave enough to try it, she learned for the first time what orgasm was. Laura masturbated as a means of going to sleep as well as enjoying orgasm.

Tracy Cox gives ten good reasons to masturbate including:

*"It releases tension and helps us sleep – a secret sleeping pill without any side-effects!" (Tracey Cox; Hot Sex; 1998)*

In over ten years of sex with different partners, Laura had always assumed that she experienced orgasm during sex. It was only once she discovered masturbation that she found out what real female orgasms felt like. Despite the evidence of her own experience, Laura still believed her friends when they said that they had orgasms during sex.

Laura even believed her mother who said that she had never had a problem with orgasm. We now have more information and more opportunity to explore our sexuality but our expectations are correspondingly higher.

Thanks to the pill, women today come to question their sexual experiences in a way that women who had children earlier in their lives probably had little time for.

## Great sex even when female orgasm is missing

Having told me that she had never had an orgasm with a man even now, Laura went on to describe some of her sexual encounters as 'totally amazing'. Laura did not see any contradiction because, for her, sex with a man was about personal chemistry. Laura got a great ego boost from the sexual power of being pursued by men.

It is easy for a woman to pleasure a man and the fantasy leads us to assume that it ought to work the other way around. When it doesn't, both partners can end up feeling inadequate. Laura admitted that she felt selfish in asking a man to spend longer than a few minutes on pleasuring her as she knew it would take far too long for him to be able to arouse her sufficiently.

*"During 'sex' as our society defines it both people know what to expect and how to make it possible for the man to orgasm. The whole thing is prearranged, preagreed.*

*But there are not really any patterns or prearranged times and places for a woman to orgasm – unless she can manage to do so during intercourse.*

*So women are put in the position of asking for something 'special', some 'extra' stimulation..." (Shere Hite; The Hite Reports; 1993)*

Laura still hoped that one day she might discover how she could orgasm during sex. Despite Shere Hite's suggestion that nature never intended women to orgasm from intercourse, women today still have the strong impression that they should.

The advantage of masturbation is that a woman at least knows what orgasm is. Whether this helps with orgasm during sex is another matter. The only disadvantage of masturbation is that a woman is likely to realise that something is missing from sex.

It is wrong that women, who have explored their own arousal sufficiently to have discovered masturbation to orgasm, are described as sexually dysfunctional (pre-orgasmic). The truth is that they are only unusual for being more sexual than average.

What man ever concludes that he is dysfunctional because he masturbates? Yet we are told that female masturbation prevents women from enjoying orgasm during sex. This is rot. Masturbation is the first step in anyone learning how to orgasm.

## Comparing orgasm from female masturbation and with a partner

Graphs are not very exciting concepts but nevertheless they can be useful. Imagine the male orgasm graph which looks a little like a vertical phallic symbol. Then imagine the female orgasm graph which looks like the outline of a woman's vulva.

The male experience is shorter but more intense. The female experience is longer but lower overall. My experience of female masturbation is that the initial phase can be horizontal – nothing happens. I lie there waiting for the inspiration of an effective fantasy.

But once that spark takes light, my experience is similar to a man's. Within a minute or two the whole thing is over. The build-up is quick and the sensations of release are sexually satisfying. The aftermath of orgasm involves a sense of release followed by blissful relaxation.

Build-up with a partner takes much longer than a couple of minutes. But also the sensations are more pleasurable and physically intense as he stimulates me. My mind has no conscious focus except the sensations of my partner touching me and thinking about his erection.

For me, orgasm with a partner includes pelvic contractions but there is not the same sense of release.

Using fantasy allows me to be the woman but also to identify with the man at the point of orgasm as he thrusts and ejaculates to orgasm.

Perhaps this ability to superimpose the act of male ejaculation on my orgasm produces my sense of release.

During female masturbation, whatever sexual activity I am imagining (usually anal sex or occasionally fellatio), my focus at the point of orgasm is thinking about the man's orgasm. Male ejaculation, for me, is highly graphic and the greatest turn-on.

When women ask about lack of orgasm, experts often suggest that inhibition or psychological trauma may cause a woman to view sex as 'dirty' or as a 'violation' rather than as a loving act involving mutual sexual pleasure. I challenge this suggestion.

Women who masturbate to orgasm are in fact much LESS sexually inhibited than other women. Not only do they appreciate eroticism enough to enjoy their own sexual fantasies through masturbation when alone. They are also more willing to engage on a variety of sexual activities with a partner to explore how they might enjoy their own sexual arousal during sex.

If men want to enjoy sex in the longer-term they need to find a woman who cares about them enough to invest in their sex life together.

In a positive relationship, where there is a willingness to give on both sides, a couple can enjoy sharing emotional and physical intimacy by being more honest about the rewards.

In the longer term, a man hopes for a partner who is positively enthusiastic about their intimate time together. For example, a man hopes for a lover who:

- has some appreciation of sexual pleasure and eroticism;
- is willing to explore a variety of approaches to enjoying sexual pleasure with a partner;
- understands a man's desire to live out his sexual fantasies; and
- takes an active role in responding as a lover.

I approached sex initially as a man must. I hoped to feel sexual arousal and that I would be able to reach orgasm during sex.

I was bitterly disappointed, as many women are who are familiar with orgasm from female masturbation, when they first come to sex.

I concluded that the female mind and body simply do not respond to sex as a man's mind and body do.

I also concluded that the idea that women respond similarly to men is based on sexual fantasies not reality.

Since talking to other women, I now know that women interpret emotional sensations as if they represent true sexual arousal and orgasm.

# How we enjoy our best orgasms

Shere Hite identified two main approaches that women used to increase clitoral stimulation and their chances of orgasm during intercourse. They either maximised DIRECT clitoral stimulation by using masturbation during sex or they used positions and techniques for sexual intercourse that maximised INDIRECT clitoral stimulation caused by the penis thrusting into the vagina.

*"... orgasm is most likely to come when the woman takes over responsibility for and control of her own stimulation. You always, in essence, create your own orgasm." (Shere Hite; The Hite Reports; 1993)*

Since direct clitoral stimulation is likely to be more effective, sex experts will often recommend applying orgasm techniques to sex learnt from masturbation. Evidently some women do succeed with transferring their orgasm techniques from masturbation to their sex life but **Ways Women Orgasm** asks women to comment on how successful this approach is for them in practice.

*"For many women intercourse is not the best way to get the type of clitoral stimulation needed to have orgasm. In these cases manual or oral stimulation of the clitoris combined with intercourse and other pleasurable activities usually leads to orgasmic response." (Michael Carrera; Dictionary of Sexual Terms; 1992)*

## Hoping for someone else's sex life

It is sometimes implied that because someone else has succeeded with a certain technique that we might all be able to use the same orgasm techniques with the same success. Unfortunately there are no guarantees. What works for one woman will not necessarily work for another because we all have different personal backgrounds, personalities and attitudes.

The overwhelming reaction I have had when asking experts about lack of orgasm is that I am expecting too much. Essentially, if you can orgasm ever then you are luckier than most women out there. The fact that a woman can't orgasm when she wants (e.g. during sexual activity of any description with a lover) is just plain spoilt.

Others appear to assume that a woman who knows how to orgasm one way (e.g. through masturbation) should be able to orgasm in any other situation (much as a man can).

Men's innate level of arousal is usually so high (especially when younger) that they orgasm no matter how they are stimulated. So masturbation works (either alone or with a partner), oral sex works, intercourse works etc. etc.

Equally, although standing can be the most natural position for masturbation alone, a man easily adapts to sitting or lying when with a partner. Women's minds and bodies are not as flexible in the way they respond to stimuli – often we only orgasm in specific circumstances.

*"Many males, projecting their own experience, are inclined to overestimate the incidences and frequencies of masturbation among females.*

*For the same reason, they poorly understand the techniques by which females masturbate, the anatomy which may be involved, the nature of the female's physiologic responses and the part which fantasy plays in her masturbation." (Alfred Kinsey; Sexual behavior in the human female; 1953)*

Explanations for female orgasm are often too vague to be useful but even when they are specific it is not clear why they do not work for all women. For example, Shere Hite catalogued a variety of positions/techniques that women use for masturbation including legs apart/together, rubbing against pillow/object, on front, on back etc.

I have always masturbated on my front using my fingers to stimulate the clitoris. Despite trying other positions and vibrators none of them has worked for me.

Likewise even though many women say they get their best orgasms from oral sex, I have never found oral sex arousing enough for orgasm. Interpreting our sexual experiences in a way that can be useful to others is difficult and it may be that each woman learns differently how she can orgasm.

This makes it difficult to pass on sexual experiences to others because in the end we all have to learn what works for ourselves. Perhaps a woman learns only one way to enjoy the best orgasms.

# Stories: Sexual arousal

# Women's sexual arousal

Published in 1972, 'Joy of Sex' by Alex Comfort MD was revolutionary at the time because it suggested a new openness and a sense of fun in modern sexual relationships.

Liberal-minded couples welcomed the idea that it could now be considered normal and 'uninhibited' to enjoy sex as a natural part of an adult relationship.

Drawings, as opposed to photographs, portrayed the physical intimacy between two lovers sensitively. This tasteful presentation of a couple's sex life avoided any potential concerns that the book might be pornographic in nature, making it attractive to women in particular.

In fact, Alex Comfort never ran a sex therapy practice and so he was not presenting a heavily researched view of sex. He was offering suggestions, based on his own sex life (with his much younger mistress – not his wife), for how other couples might bring some variety to sex. 'Joy of Sex' documents a man's appreciation of eroticism and the activities that he found pleasurable.

The book is not explicit about the woman's arousal and my mistake was to assume that the relationship illustrated was based on equality between the sexes.

I assumed – wrongly as it happens – that other women would also be looking for a sexual (rather than an emotional) payback from their sexual relationships involving similar levels of sexual pleasure that men enjoy.

A woman can have sex for years without ever experiencing sexual arousal or orgasm. This explains why the average age to come out is 17 years old for gay men but 40 years old for gay women.

Of course, a woman's sexual fantasies might cause her to suspect she is lesbian earlier than this. But a lesbian woman can marry and have children just as a heterosexual woman does because female orgasm is not required for her either to participate in a sexual relationship or for reproduction.

## Sexual relationships are not based on equal sexual pleasure

In general sex manuals can be misleading because they tend to describe the physical activities of intercourse, or masturbation for that matter, without simultaneously discussing what is happening in the person's head.

The implication is that the physical sensations of sex fully occupy the woman's mind throughout and create by themselves the level of sexual arousal required to experience orgasm.

In other words, the assumption is that women respond sexually just as men do.

The fact that women are much slower to arouse may be acknowledged but it is rarely explained why this should be or what the consequences might be for a sexual relationship.

Any difficulties with female orgasm are often dismissed as insignificant.

*"Frigidity – This does not mean failure to enjoy sex when one is dead with fatigue... Nor does it mean failure to get a mind-blowing orgasm on every single occasion. If it does mean these things, every woman is frigid. ..." (Alex Comfort; Joy of Sex; 1972)*

Perhaps all that is missing from 'Joy of Sex' is simply an acknowledgement of how much more difficult it is for a woman to apply her sexual fantasies to sex with a partner.

Ironically, although it may suit men to have the visual benefits of covers off and lights on, women may be the opposite. I close my eyes during masturbation to focus on fantasy and during sex I also prefer subdued lighting to blot out the everyday world so that I can fully absorb myself in enjoying my physical arousal.

Even today the average person does not associate women's sexuality with the capacity to enjoy sexual arousal and orgasm. When I asked a young female doctor for information about female sexuality, she was embarrassed. The sexually responsive woman is more often associated with women in erotic fiction and pornography, providing men with a sexual turn-on, than with women's real life experiences.

An older male doctor referred me to a family planning library in London that provided information about contraception and childbirth. Sexual pleasure is associated with the sex industry where women are either being exploited or are exploiting men for money. Since the sex industry is fuelled by men's interest, not women's, it is difficult to find un-biased sources of information about female sexuality.

## Sexual arousal during intercourse

When I had sex for the first time, I was disappointed because I had hoped that sex would be spontaneously arousing enough for me to orgasm. I didn't have any clear idea about what I would do during sex except perhaps to respond affectionately to my lover's love-making.

It's amazing when you think of it. I was eighteen years old and a virgin so my vagina was as tight as it was ever likely to be. Yet I couldn't feel a thing from thrusting, not even when my partner's penis initially penetrated me. I was waiting for something to happen and suddenly it was all over.

Even subsequent times I was none the wiser. Naturally, we experimented with oral sex as well as different positions and techniques for sexual intercourse but nothing worked. I was so far off feeling any sexual arousal that it was difficult to imagine what could possibly make a difference.

Although I knew how to orgasm from masturbation, this was of little use to me. Masturbation was a solitary experience relying on being highly focused on sexual fantasies. Sex with a partner was completely different. The emotional environment was incompatible with the use of fantasies.

Erotic literature had given me absolute faith that foreplay and vaginal intercourse would provide guaranteed spontaneous sexual arousal and orgasm. So I just lay there, like a lemon, waiting to be transported to the heights of sexual pleasure assuming no need to contribute in any way.

Despite talking to experts about my experiences, so far no one has been able to explain them at all. When I have told them that my boyfriend remarked that other virgins had made the same comment, the most usual reaction is silence.

I am told that if I read so-and-so I would realise that my experience cannot be. They imply that no one else has the same experience.

Therapists conclude that since other women say nothing they must be happy with sex. There is little acknowledgement of just how embarrassed most people are about discussing their sexual experiences.

I can vouch for the fact that even when a person is relatively relaxed about sex (as I have been) the humiliation of the implied sexual inadequacy is a very effective silencer.

So women learn to accept their sexual experiences for what they are. They make the best of it for the sake of their partner. Sex becomes an activity to be 'gotten over with'. Sexual arousal is implied or faked depending on pressure from the man.

As a more experienced woman I now know that a woman plays along with men's sexual fantasies, in part, to minimise her own effort in an activity that is not designed to provide women with an equal sexual pleasure. After all, it's human nature...

Why spend half an hour when you only need to spend a couple of minutes? It's not only prostitutes who know the value of time. It is much easier for a woman to play along with a man's fantasies of arousing a woman so that he orgasms quickly.

In the British film 'Saving Grace' (2000) two women (wife and mistress) compare notes after years of sex with the same man. They don't talk about the sexual pleasure they enjoyed, they giggle about how much noise he made when having his orgasm. Men never appreciate that a woman's role in intercourse is often that of a spectator: simply waiting for the man to come.

If sex provides men and women with equal pleasure, why do women so often want to obtain a financial advantage from their sexual relationships with men?

For women, sex is always a trade: either for MONEY or for LOVE (companionship, mutual support and possibly family) because women do not experience the same delirious pleasure from sex that men do.

The issue of clitoral stimulation is a red herring – women aren't that timid and neither are their partners. If women could orgasm as easily as men they would simply use another approach to sex e.g. oral sex or mutual masturbation rather than intercourse.

The problem is that women don't approach sex turned on enough in their minds for clitoral stimulation to lead to orgasm.

Men look to sex for sexual pleasure (orgasm in particular) but women have to settle for the emotional aspects of sexual relationships. Sex can be a sensual pleasure and over time an erotic pleasure as a woman's clitoris becomes less sensitive.

# The mystery of female sexual arousal

In the film 'True Lies' (1994) Jamie Lee Curtis, as the dowdy housewife turned spy in the role of a prostitute, performs a sexy pole dance for her screen husband Arnold Schwarzenegger.

It seems so natural that a man's arousal comes from admiring a woman's body. Yet we never question why a man's foreplay techniques do not include him using his body to provide a woman's arousal. For example, a man's foreplay techniques do not typically include wearing exotic underwear, clothing that accentuates his sexual attributes or moving his body provocatively.

Throughout history, a woman's priority has been to ensure that she had a man who could protect her (and her children) rather than help her orgasm during sex. So a man's body is not a sexual commodity to women in the way that a woman's body can be to men.

*"The truth is that, just as women have spent centuries being selected by men for their desirability as sex objects. Women have been evaluating men as success objects. By this we mean that women evaluate men both as successful protectors, particularly in violent times, and as successful providers." (Kramer & Dunaway; Why Men don't get enough Sex and Women don't get enough Love; 1994)*

## Women's sexual arousal is not automatic

Unfortunately, there is nothing either easy or automatic about female orgasm, especially during sex with a partner. Not only do we lack men's spontaneous sexual arousal, women are also not turned on by the sexual attributes of a lover as men are. This explains why most women do not seek to enjoy the male body through pornography, lap-dancing or pole-dancing.

Nevertheless, it is implied that female sexuality involves women achieving similar levels of sexual arousal as a man without the same natural advantages. A woman who describes herself as 'turned on' is more likely to indicating that she is amenable to sex than that she is close to orgasm.

Female sexuality is often defined in terms of a woman's attractiveness to men rather than her own true state of sexual arousal. It is easy to confuse women's own sexual arousal with their ability to arouse men.

*"Many men believe that if a woman excites them sexually and looks sexy, she must be experiencing sexual feelings – in other words, if she looks sexy she must feel sexy; if she's exciting me, she must be excited, too. The man projects his own excitement onto the woman." (Kramer & Dunaway; Why Men don't get enough Sex and Women don't get enough Love; 1994)*

Men's sexual arousal is usually easy and, since men hope a lover will enhance their sexual arousal, women often have sex with men for reasons other than their own orgasm:

- In the shorter term, a woman can find sex fun and even exhilarating without orgasm if she appreciates being able to excite a man sexually and if her ego is flattered by the sexual compliment;
- In the longer term, a woman may find other life priorities (such as children) but she still needs to offer a mate enough sex to stop him wandering off with someone more amenable.

It is vital to appreciate that men need a sexually responsive partner to enjoy sex fully. Sexually experienced women, including those who engage in casual sex, learn that they can facilitate a man's orgasm by faking their own arousal and orgasm.

This 'responsiveness' as a lover does not necessarily indicate that a woman knows how to achieve her own orgasm by any means.

*"Most... males do not realize that it is only a select group of females, and usually the more responsive females, who will accept pre-marital or extra-marital relationships.*

*Some ... will fail to take into account the large number of females who... never become involved in the sort of non-marital relationship from which these males have acquired most of their information about females." (Alfred Kinsey; Sexual behavior in the human female; 1953)*

Some women might hope for an adventurous sex life (or even for sexual arousal and orgasm during sex) but, luckily for all of us, most women do not approach their relationships with men demanding 'success' in their sex life.

Since women have lower sexual desire they tend to settle for companionship, love and affection, which depend on knowing and liking a person.

# Confusion over female orgasm

When they talk about their sexual relationships with men, women will often refer to love, trust and commitment.

These factors are obviously important for the stability of long-term relationships that family life depends on.

But they are not factors that will help a woman learn how to enjoy orgasm during sex.

Many women see sex as an emotional and loving experience. Either they have no expectation for orgasm or they assume that their loving emotions result in the phenomenon that other people call orgasm.

This is fine and no one wants to upset other people's sex lives if they are happy with them. Many women enjoy sex as a sensual and sexy physical act with a partner regardless of their own sexual arousal.

But women who ask about female orgasm need to know the facts.

Loving emotions do not lead to true sexual arousal. Just as men have to (usually very willingly!) focus on eroticism if they are to become aroused, women also have to accept that enjoyment of sexual arousal depends on having 'naughty' thoughts.

Guilt about sexual fantasies is misplaced because our ability to enjoy our own sexual arousal is part of the human experience.

Such feelings occur naturally and as long as we enjoy them alone or with a consenting adult partner, are quite harmless.

The degree to which we are able to enjoy our sexuality depends on the balance between our desire to enjoy sexual pleasure and our need to satisfy moral constraints.

It is the taboo nature of sexual activity that causes us to feel sexually aroused.

## Why women still prefer 'making love'

Men tend to become defensive when it is suggested that vaginal intercourse does not facilitate female orgasm.

One reason is that embarrassment about sex causes many less adventurous couples to limit their sex life to intercourse.

Nature's fault again but women do not find the kind of physical sex play that men enjoy arousing enough for orgasm.

More than that, many women are actually disgusted by the idea of any activity more sexually explicit than 'making love'.

But we are talking about quite different women and attitudes here. A woman only asks about female orgasm because she already knows how to achieve it from masturbation.

Such women are likely to be more open to exploring sex with a partner, including a wider variety of physical sex play and techniques, because they enjoy eroticism through fantasies.

Women need to stimulate their clitoris for orgasm just as men need to stimulate their penis. Intercourse does not provide enough clitoral stimulation for female orgasm no matter how long and enthusiastically a man keeps thrusting.

What is confusing, for women who masturbate, is that clitoral stimulation can only lead to orgasm once a woman has achieved the necessary psychological arousal through fantasy.

Women do not become aroused enough for orgasm by looking at the naked male body. If they did, then women would enjoy pornography, lap-dancing and pole-dancing bars as men do.

Women's sexual arousal depends on sexual fantasies with a complex psychological context (often BDSM) that can be tricky to combine with a real life sexual relationship.

Many women do use fantasy during sex but others find that their mind-based fantasies are ineffective with a partner.

A woman may need to learn other ways of incorporating her fantasies into her sex life.

This may include reading some erotic fiction immediately prior to sex and during foreplay (man doing all the work!) or bringing some ideas from her fantasies into physical sex play (activities other than intercourse) that may be combined with intercourse.

# Some women never tune into eroticism

Angela, a woman in her early twenties, was having relationship problems with her boyfriend of six months.

She was upset that he enjoyed looking at other women. She got him to agree to stop buying pornographic magazines, which she found demeaning.

*"Porn to men is not a big deal. They honestly can't see how watching a sexy film can be any sort of reflection on their love for their girlfriend.*

*Most don't understand why she takes offence because, as far as they're concerned, every guy does it. They're right.*

*Research shows the infrequent porn user is your average guy – 90 per cent of them. He's not a deviant, he just likes looking at sexy pictures. It's got a lot to do with what turns each sex on.*

*Usually, men are turned on more by pictures and visual images, women are turned on more by words. Now, that's a massive generalisation, but true in a lot of cases." (Tracey Cox; Hot Relationships; 1999)*

She believed that if he loved her, he would only want to look at her body. Angela was also disgusted by the idea that men can enjoy eroticism outside a loving relationship.

I was surprised by her reaction because it has never occurred to me to place limits on my partner's enjoyment of eroticism. Equally, I cannot imagine limiting my own thoughts at his request.

Angela, still very much in love, was confident that she experienced orgasm with her partner but told me that she did not use fantasy.

## Emotional orgasms

Angela was sure that the arousal she gained, although driven through her emotional psychology, resulted in real female orgasms. Even the first time and every time afterwards, intercourse was orgasmic for her.

Angela thought that her sexual arousal stemmed from the idea that her partner found her sexually attractive. She said that she needed to be 'on top' to orgasm. Who knows?

Some sources suggest that women who orgasm during intercourse have a more prominent clitoris or, perhaps, it is simply that their sexual fantasies (or expectations?) map more easily onto reality.

I asked Angela how she knew that she was not having 'emotional orgasms' (peaks of sexual arousal).

Angela was confident of her interpretation of her experiences. Growing up reading Cosmopolitan magazine, she called herself a 'Cosmo Girl' who was well informed about female masturbation and orgasm.

Of course, just because a woman has read about other women's experiences of orgasm this does not necessarily mean that she knows how to achieve the same for herself.

Angela had disliked eroticism ever since puberty when her father, brother and their friends made her feel degraded by their lewd sexual remarks.

It's a shame that some women are so sensitive to men's sexual remarks, which are more often than not intended as a compliment.

The problem arises because many women associate eroticism with being considered 'dirty'.

Women are not even generally attracted by nakedness and especially not genitals whether those of a man, another woman or even their own. In fact, they go to great lengths to beautify their sexual attributes by covering up with pretty lingerie.

A young American woman, who had only twenty four hours in Rome, felt so threatened by the young men of Rome that she vowed to spend her whole trip in the women's hostel.

Admittedly, Italian men are the most voluble and persistent of any nation that I have been to! I have always accepted male heckling with a smile and interpreted any sexual innuendo as a compliment.

# Women often assume sexual arousal during sex

Unless they masturbate, most women are unaware that clitoral stimulation is needed for female orgasm. Equally, they are unaware that before genital stimulation can be effective, a person needs to know how to achieve true sexual arousal, which depends on an appreciation of eroticism (images for men; scenarios for women).

From puberty onwards men's sexual arousal (as evidenced by an erection) makes regular masturbation inevitable. Since women do not experience erections (of the clitoris) in the same way, most never learn how to achieve sufficient sexual arousal for orgasm either alone or with a partner. Consequently even those professing enthusiasm for sex are rarely able to display any real knowledge about how to reach orgasm.

After decades of marriage one woman told me: "I have to disagree with the comment of a woman's arousal and the ease of achieving orgasm. Maybe I am one of the lucky women out there that is in touch with her sexual being. I get sexually aroused by my husband just by looking at him without his shirt, the words that he uses with me, and by the attention that he gives to me. Also I have I believe an easy time in obtaining an orgasm or two with my husband."

Most men can orgasm within a few minutes. So is this woman claiming to be able to match her partner's speed of reaching orgasm?

Perhaps her partner is one of those one-in-a-million men who is willing to continue pleasuring a partner after he has come?

Anyone who suggests that it all happens 'naturally' or that women's arousal is as easy as men's is, frankly, mistaken.

Women's minds and bodies simply do not work the same way as men's. If they did then women would pay for sex as well as lap- and pole-dancing as men do.

The sight of a man's sexual attributes do not cause us to become aroused enough for orgasm. Also women do not approach sex already fully aroused because our bodies are not full of testosterone.

Women who discover orgasm through masturbation in their twenties or thirties will often admit that they had always been utterly convinced that they did orgasm during sex when it turns out they didn't. How can women not understand that orgasm is a significant pleasure? Not only do you definitely notice orgasm but also you set out with the intention of achieving it.

The facts of female sexuality are:

- Women do not have the same levels of testosterone (the sex drive hormone) as men;

- Women do not buy erotica or pornography as regularly as men do;

- Women do not masturbate anything like as much as men do; and

- Not every man pays for sex but many evidently do – most women never pay for sex.

When I talk about the fact that sex tends to be much more important to most men than it is to most women, I am talking about how we enjoy our own sexual arousal and orgasm.

Women who disagree with me are only talking about the emotional (loving and affectionate) aspects of their relationships with men. They are rarely interested in orgasm at all.

A popular suggestion is that a woman needs a truly loving partner who knows how to 'give a woman an orgasm'. Wouldn't that be nice! It is a fallacy to think that anyone else can give us an orgasm.

Even men have to learn about their own sexual arousal through masturbation. So how do women experience orgasm as men do without the same knowledge or practice?

I would love to believe that women understand how their sexual arousal works but the evidence stands against this. Most couples today clearly continue to base their sex life on vaginal intercourse despite the fact that intercourse provides insufficient clitoral stimulation for orgasm.

Yet very few women question a lack of orgasm during sex. Equally, society still censors eroticism to protect women's sensitivities but without sexual fantasies women are unlikely to discover orgasm by any means.

## Sexual arousal from romantic emotions

Many women talk about sexual arousal and orgasm in terms of their relationship. They describe their loving feelings for their partner and explain their sexual arousal in terms of the idea that their partner finds them attractive.

Masturbation has no meaning for them because, for such women, sex focuses on the emotional benefits of sharing physical intimacy with their man.

It's important not to judge other people's experiences and, as long as women are content with what they have, I don't want to cause them to feel that their experiences are lacking in any way.

Women who are unfamiliar with orgasm are simply placing a different interpretation on their sexual experiences. They accept their sexual experiences for what they are because they never know what they are missing.

Women are told that orgasm occurs easily and naturally during sex so many believe that they orgasm when, in fact, they don't.

Such women will describe their sexual experiences, even in terms of arousal and orgasm, as if they arise from their feelings for their partner. They interpret orgasm as an accumulation of emotional sensations rather than as a true sexual release.

One female sex expert told me: "Relationship of course, also plays a big role and impacts how and whether women will climax during love making – whether as a result of intercourse or other forms of stimulation."

Women often assume that female orgasm relies on a good relationship (quite how I'm not sure) and so they never understand how a woman masturbates to orgasm.

Remember that you are never too old to learn about enjoying eroticism and orgasm through female masturbation. It's all about having an open mind.

A woman who has explored her own sexual arousal through an appreciation of eroticism and through developing her own sexual fantasies is better placed to make the investment in exploring sex with a partner.

A woman who finds sex and eroticism disgusting or morally offensive is likely to be less willing to be adventurous in bed. If a woman has these attitudes but is willing to consider a change, I would suggest starting by reading some innocent romantic stories.

I read 'Catherine' by Juliet Benzoni as a teenager. Then you can build up to reading some more directly erotic stories.

Portrayals of women as sexual beings are not negative or disgusting. Women just find the raw crudity of sexual activity less appealing than men tend to but with fantasy you can gloss over these practicalities.

Women need to approach sex through the mind and through imagining sexual scenarios where the woman is in control (at least as the director of the fantasy!).

Imagine yourself as the object of a man's sexual desire. This in part depends on a woman being able to see herself as desirable. She may have to work on her self-image.

Remember that beauty is in the eye of the beholder and for every woman there's a man who will find her attractive. Not every man wants a blonde bombshell anorexic model in order to enjoy his sex life.

In the end women stand to lose out if they do not explore activities other than vaginal intercourse with a partner. Most women who do experience orgasm do so through direct clitoral stimulation – either oral sex or female masturbation.

The early years of any relationship are relatively easy as a couple explores ways of enjoying sexual pleasure together. Long-term relationships (over 10 years) are more challenging because a couple needs to open up to each other on a different level.

My partner and I have found talking to other people, relationship counsellors and sex therapists, very useful and more couples (especially men) should be brave enough to try this.

If you really care about your sex life, you may need to re-think some basic attitudes and behaviours. No one is going to force you into anything and it's totally up to you how you choose to change things.

# Male nudity does not cause female sexual arousal

The naked male body can be a beautiful sight and yet our heterosexual society is dominated by images of women's bodies. The ancient Greeks were more relaxed about homosexuality and statues indicate their appreciation of the sensual male nude.

Gay men certainly appreciate the naked male, including male genitals but women are often offended by nudity, especially genitals, and so nudity is censored in our society.

Andrew Stanway's film 'The Lover's Guide' (1991) was a breakthrough in British censorship of films for general release. He was allowed to show the erect penis for the first time but only because his films were intended for educational purposes.

The film 'The Wedding Date' (2005) includes a scene where Dermot Mulroney is relaxed about appearing naked in front of a woman (as if!). The woman's horrified reaction to a man's genitals not only indicates how female sexuality differs to male sexuality but also provides a clue as to why women's sexual arousal is much more elusive with a partner.

Men have more to lose by appearing naked because an erection betrays their intimate thoughts. Men don't want to expose themselves for fear of being sized up or becoming aroused under scrutiny. 'The Full Monty' (1997) indicates men's insecurities over nudity.

Men's sexual arousal arises from looking at images of the naked body of a sexual partner, which explains the daily sales of pornographic magazines.

Women, who have learned about their own sexual arousal through female masturbation, know that women do not use images of naked men for arousal. Women have to take a much more conscious approach to sexual arousal through highly explicit sexual fantasies.

As always, someone will disagree: "For instance, I'm an XX female, and yet am extremely visual and highly aroused by the nudity and genitals of partners of all genders, including men." This woman was happy to admit that she was bisexual but she was not willing to say whether she could masturbate to orgasm. So who knows whether she has ever had an orgasm.

Regardless of these claims, there are few pornographic magazines for heterosexual women. 'Playgirl' is an exception but presumably has another audience. Even the UK magazine 'Scarlet' marketed for sexual women, avoids images of couples engaged in explicit sexual activity.

*"Many females consider that male genitalia are ugly and repulsive in appearance, and the observation of the male genitalia may actually inhibit their erotic responses.*

*... there seems no doubt that these reactions largely depend upon the fact that most females are not psychologically stimulated, as males are, by objects which are associated with sex.*

*... only a small percentage of homosexual females is ever aroused erotically by seeing the genitalia of other females." (Alfred Kinsey; Sexual behavior in the human female; 1953)*

My own nakedness has never bothered me but men's interest in women's bodies teaches us to become self-conscious. Women's bodies are constantly being scrutinised not only by men but also by women. Any woman with a less than perfect body is ridiculed because the assumption is that a woman only displays her body in public to attract male attention.

'The Calendar Girls' (2003) tells the story of a group of middle-aged women who posed naked, but tastefully, for a calendar. It caused uproar because they were not young women with flawless bodies but women who had given birth or grown old.

Nudity causes men to think about sex even more than usual and they mistakenly assume that women have the same sexual motivations. While I was sunbathing on a nudist beach, one woman bent over to get sun cream out of her bag and my partner suggested that she must have done so deliberately so that the men on the beach could enjoy looking at her genitals.

The fact is that she was much more likely to be just getting sun cream out of her bag! That comment made me aware of needing to keep my legs firmly together on the beach. I have been most relaxed when on a gay nudist beach in Mikonos, Greece because I didn't have to worry that anyone might assume that I was sunbathing nude as a means of making a sexual invitation.

# Why sexual arousal is more elusive for women

Sexual desire is associated with 'sex drive'. The male sex drive is a man's biological drive to procreate by thrusting into a woman's vagina until ejaculation (usually co-incident with male orgasm).

Before the sexual revolution a woman was seen to have a complementary (not identical) sexual role to men in terms of accepting a man's sexual advances. So a woman could be the object of a man's sexual desire but it was rare to describe a man as the object of a woman's desire.

*"Among single females who were actually masturbating, the average individual was reaching orgasm about once in every two and a half to three weeks. ... We shall find that this is more or less true of the frequencies of several other types of female activity and of the total sexual outlet of single females.*

*This is one of the most remarkable aspects of female sexuality, and one which most sharply distinguishes it from the sexuality of the male. Hormonal factors may be involved. (Alfred Kinsey; Sexual behavior in the human female; 1953)*

Kinsey's report in 1953 highlighted that women were capable of orgasm. His report also concluded that women were less sexually responsive than men. Nevertheless, it became popular belief that women experienced sexual desire, sexual arousal and orgasm as naturally and easily as men.

This conclusion led to increased pressure on women to fake orgasm. It also led to the modern so-called female sexual 'dysfunctions' such as anorgasmia, preorgasmia and difficulties with low sexual desire, lack of sexual arousal and lack of orgasm during sex.

Sex has been designed physically and psychologically to favour male sexual arousal and orgasm. This is no accident.

The key reproductive act is male ejaculation (usually co-incident with male orgasm) inside a woman's vagina. So Nature ensures that men have the best satisfaction from penetrative sex and through penile thrusting to orgasm.

Men are bigger and stronger than women because Nature intends our roles to be complementary not the same. Nature also ensures that, at the end of the day, men can win the sexual game. Women's sexual role is to attract a man and cause him to become sexually aroused. The man is then able to use his resulting erection to impregnate a woman through thrusting. The woman's sexual role is to assist with the man's sexual arousal and to accommodate his needs to allow him to orgasm.

Vaginal intercourse is designed for making babies not for maximising women's chances of enjoying sexual pleasure. However, many women still prefer vaginal intercourse because it allows them to participate in sexual activity with a partner without any explicit sexual engagement e.g. oral sex and mutual masturbation not only involve more work but are more explicitly sexual.

Female orgasm is irrelevant to reproduction so it is likely to be counterproductive for women to be actively insisting on their own sexual arousal during sex. Nature's design is for a man's orgasm to be his top priority but for orgasm to be much less vital to a woman. This explains why most women are shocked by eroticism and almost never pay for sexual pleasure.

Orgasm advice for women today is not only vague but also falls back on suggesting that women are trying too hard or that orgasm is not important. This advice is hardly intended for men.

The fact is that the majority of women are not motivated to enjoy their own orgasm either alone or with a partner because they never discover how their own sexual arousal works.

Sexual arousal occurs when the mind tunes into erotic thoughts or images and is accompanied by an increase of blood flow to the genitals. The erectile organ for a man is the penis and for a woman it is the clitoris.

Men become easily erect when aroused but even when masturbating to orgasm a woman has much less conscious awareness of her erection.

Sex, vaginal intercourse in particular, has not been designed to facilitate women's psychological or physical arousal. So women with stronger sexual instincts make use of sexual fantasies to allow them to experience their own sexual arousal and orgasm.

Unfortunately many women find that the emotional environment of sex is incompatible with using sexual fantasies.

# Understanding women's sexual arousal

Sex is associated with reproduction and with pleasure. Male orgasm is usually co-incident with ejaculation which leads to reproduction but female orgasm is not required for a woman to become pregnant.

So it's at least possible that women may experience sexual pleasure (including sexual desire, sexual arousal and orgasm) differently to men.

Men discover orgasm at a young age but women have no way of knowing what orgasm is or how to achieve it – either alone or with a partner.

One woman learned to masturbate at the age of 28. Up until then she had always assumed that she experienced orgasm during sex but, in fact, she never had (See 'How to use a vibrator to discover orgasm' – p66).

It is difficult for men to appreciate that women do not have the same level of familiarity with their own sexual arousal and orgasm that men do. Women are certainly capable of orgasm but it does not happen spontaneously. Women have to learn how to orgasm.

*"The average male is aroused in anticipation of a sexual relationship, and he usually comes to erection and is ready to proceed directly to orgasm as soon as or even before he makes any actual contact.*

*The average female, on the contrary, is less often aroused by such anticipation, and sometimes she does not begin to respond until there has been a considerable amount of physical stimulation."*

(Alfred Kinsey; Sexual behavior in the human female; 1953)

Unlike men, women rarely experience erections and even if they do, they are much less conscious of them. The clitoris may have millions of nerve endings but physical sex play does not lead to sexual arousal as easily as for men. So a woman can certainly enjoy passionate kissing but, even as a lead into sex, kissing does not cause a female genital erection (of the clitoris).

Very few women masturbate regularly to enjoy orgasm. They have no experience of enjoying true sexual arousal, which starts when the mind tunes into sexual fantasies and leads to orgasm through clitoral stimulation. Women today are told that female orgasm occurs naturally during sex so even sexually experienced women assume that they orgasm during sex when they don't.

This is why some women, often quite innocently, mislead others about how easy it all is. Such women explain their sexual arousal in terms of their relationship and so they never understand why anyone would masturbate. Most women who claim to orgasm with a partner are talking about emotional sensations. Hence the term 'emotional orgasm' coined by Shere Hite.

It's important not to be judgmental about other people's sexual experiences. But it can be misleading when we try to compare different women's explanations for orgasm because we are not necessarily talking about the same thing. An orgasm, in the sense that men would probably understand the term, involves a release of sexual feelings not loving feelings.

Women who do not appreciate eroticism can completely miss the point of sexual pleasure. Women who learn to enjoy orgasm from female masturbation use highly explicit sexual fantasies. These orgasms involve a release of sexual emotions. They are not necessarily any better than the 'emotional orgasms' women get from loving emotions – they are simply different.

Sadly the aversion that many women have to eroticism actually prevents younger women learning how to orgasm. Also given vaginal intercourse continues to be promoted as the only proper sexual activity, despite the fact that it provides insufficient clitoral stimulation for orgasm, means that women often never learn how they can enjoy true sexual arousal with a lover.

In case you doubt how common it is for women to have difficulty with orgasm during sex, just take a look at the thousands of articles on the web offering advice on this very topic! Of course, these articles always promise 'easy orgasms', 'multiple orgasms' or 'mind-blowing orgasms' just so couples don't give up trying!

There is not even one article promising men easy orgasm because male orgasm is most usually a given.

## Stories: Clitoral stimulation

# Enjoying sexual pleasure

When it was suggested recently that UK schools should explain the role of the clitoris, mothers were up in arms. They objected to their daughters knowing that a girl might find it pleasurable later in her life to touch her clitoris.

There was no uproar over boys' genitals. Were the boys also told that their willies might give them pleasure later on?

Boys discover their sexuality 'naturally' and many people believe that girls should be left 'naturally' not to discover theirs.

I suspect very few mothers ever talk to their daughters about enjoying orgasm through clitoral stimulation. But then how many fathers talk to their sons about their enjoyment of orgasm through penile stimulation? They don't have to because it's so obvious.

Male sexual arousal and orgasm happen fairly spontaneously but many women never orgasm throughout the whole of their lives.

One mother believed that her five-year-old should be left alone in childish innocence happily 'pushing her dolly around in a stroller'.

It's questionable whether children as young as five would be able to make much of this information even if they could comprehend what they were being told.

But what about that dolly in the stroller? To have a real baby, male ejaculation and orgasm are essential but many people do not see that an explicitly sexual phenomenon such as orgasm is relevant to women.

*"Intercourse is necessary for reproduction, and sexual pleasure and orgasm are involved with reproduction. But exactly how? Looking closer, one sees that only male orgasm during intercourse is necessary for reproduction." (Shere Hite; The Hite Reports; 1993)*

Many women relate to their role as a mother (the reproductive aspects of female sexuality) but are less comfortable with the idea that women can enjoy sexual pleasure through their own arousal and orgasm.

Since the concept of female sexuality (in terms of their own arousal) is alien to them, many women are never even interested in discovering orgasm.

## Women have to learn to appreciate eroticism

Girls need information and encouragement if they are to experience what boys learn more spontaneously.

If girls explore sexual activities other than intercourse, not only might they discover orgasm but also ways of enjoying sex with a partner with a lower risk of pregnancy (oral sex, for example).

But you can't make girls as interested in orgasm as boys naturally are.

A fascinating collection of letters by two literary men, who correspond with each other between 1955 and 1962, provides some enlightenment. Rupert Hart-Davies explains his extra-marital affair, which came about after his wife lost interest in sex:

"She is one of the (I suspect) many women whose sex instincts are in fact wholly directed to the production of children, and when their quiver is full they want no more (as they say in the courts) intercourse." (The Lyttelton Hart-Davies Letters; 2001)

Even in 2009, a major UK bookseller told me they remove the women's erotic fiction before a head office audit. Many women are offended by books such as those in the 'Black Lace' range and yet for me they are so mildly erotic that I can rarely use them for orgasm.

I go to London for erotic literature with any bite (e.g. book stores along the Charing Cross Road).

Many people believe in sheltering young women from eroticism and yet enjoyment of eroticism is fundamental to a long-term sexual relationship.

A loving partnership involves supporting each other's life goals of both family and an active sex life.

*"The person who said that the way to a man's heart is through his stomach was aiming too high" (Allan & Barbara Pease; Why men don't listen; 1999)*

# The 'non-genital' orgasm

In response to my suggestion that it was ridiculous to suggest that a man can give a woman an orgasm, a man wrote:

"My wife is consistently orgasmic. They are obviously not faked. She can't fake the cries, the involuntary movements, the demands for more stimulation, and everything else that goes with orgasm.

I've offered oral and manual stimulation. She rejects oral because she considers it unhygienic and a short cut for those who lack skills to do it the regular way. She demands my penis as soon as I have an erection. She orgasms through penile thrusting. ...

I admit I have not had as much variety as a lot of men have had, but the three women with whom I have had sex have demanded a penis. Judging from the intensity of their orgasms, they've been very satisfied and would have it no other way.

My wife tells me she lets me caress her to orgasm with my fingers only for my enjoyment. She prefers an orgasm with my penis."

Why is a man with this experience reading my stories in the first place? I am not doubting that men have these experiences that read like erotic fiction.

I am interested in discussing any LOGICAL EXPLANATIONS for how women are supposed to achieve female orgasm given the FACTS of female sexuality.

Even men need psychological arousal and genital stimulation for orgasm.

*"In most females the walls of the vagina are devoid of end organs of touch and are quite insensitive when they are gently stroked or lightly pressed. For most individuals the insensitivity extends to every part of the vagina. ...*

*This insensitivity of the vagina has been recognized by gynaecologists who regularly probe and do surface operations in this area without using anaesthesia." (Alfred Kinsey; Sexual behavior in the human female; 1953)*

## The clitoris is the female sex organ

The vagina (as part of the birth canal) has little sensitivity. To come across even one woman who can feel sensations in a part of the body with few nerve endings would be weird but to come across three such women is positively suspicious.

Why would anyone who is hoping for orgasm ignore their own sex organ? It doesn't make sense.

Why are men so ready to accept that although they need penile stimulation in order to orgasm, women easily orgasm without any genital stimulation?

A woman's sex organ is the clitoris (which has many nerve endings) and if women experienced true sexual arousal then they would want to stimulate their genitals (through clitoral stimulation) just as men do.

Women approach sex with a focus on the penis and penile thrusting because male sexual arousal is much easier to achieve.

For years I was convinced that vaginal intercourse MUST work. Even though my own experience told me that it did not.

Even knowing that clitoral stimulation is required for female orgasm did not help because nothing seemed to work with a partner.

*"During eighteen years of marriage, we did everything but stand on our heads, but there were few orgasms for me ... Masturbation has always worked." (Shere Hite; The Hite Reports; 1993)*

Clitoral stimulation alone does not guarantee orgasm because genital stimulation is only effective once a person is mentally aroused. Anyone who is familiar with orgasm will appreciate this point.

If you cannot get turned-on in your mind then it doesn't matter how much you stimulate your genitals – nothing will happen.

This is why men need an erection before they can orgasm.

Even when I knew how to orgasm from female masturbation, I did not consider using the same orgasm techniques during sex. Many women find that sex with a lover is incompatible with using sexual fantasies.

# Real female orgasms

In the film 'Private Benjamin', a group of female army recruits sits around a campfire during an overnight exercise.

One of the women says: "I had an orgasm once..." and the others giggle. She goes on to say in a disappointed tone "...but I was alone!" Her girlfriends laugh sympathetically.

In the film, Goldie Hawn plays a spoilt young woman approaching thirty who has been married twice. Happily stoned from smoking marijuana she continues the theme:

"Well, ... once when I was with my first husband I got to this place ... that was kind of nice and tingly and ... I don't know if this was an official orgasm ... but I counted it as one for five years."

She laughs, presumably at her own naivety. Later in the film, she appears to genuinely orgasm during sex with a new lover.

She comments: "Well, now I know what I have been faking all these years!"

*"Orgasm is not just a vague feeling." (Sheila Kitzinger; Woman's Experience of Sex; 1983)*

Many women never orgasm during sex: not because women are dysfunctional but because sex is not designed to facilitate female orgasm either physically or psychologically.

Unlike men, women are much less versatile in how they are able to orgasm. A woman often finds only one way to orgasm and unfortunately the easiest way is through masturbation alone.

## Women who think they orgasm during sex when they don't

To a man, it must be incomprehensible that a woman of thirty can be unsure about whether she has ever had an orgasm.

For vaginal intercourse to be possible, a man has to be aroused in order to have an erection.

Women, on the other hand, attribute a whole range of feelings to sexual arousal in the absence of the knowledge of what real female orgasms feel like.

*"When you have an orgasm the pelvic floor muscles always contract. If that does not happen you are not having an orgasm." (Sheila Kitzinger; Woman's Experience of Sex; 1983)*

When I orgasm with a partner (by combining clitoral and anal stimulation) he can definitely feel my pelvic contractions.

During masturbation, when using fantasy I would describe orgasm as losing full consciousness of your immediate physical surroundings. As a guide, if you are not sure then it has probably not happened yet.

Female masturbation is relatively uncommon and so most women have much less familiarity with their own sexual arousal and orgasm than men typically have.

One of the key mis-understandings is that vaginal intercourse is a reproductive act whereby the male impregnates the female.

The vagina, as part of the birth canal, has very few nerve endings and so intercourse by itself is unlikely to lead to female orgasm, which is not required for reproduction.

Female orgasm represents one of Nature's redundancies.

Of course, the converse also follows. Just as vaginal intercourse is not designed to facilitate female orgasm, women are also not as strongly motivated by orgasm as men tend to be.

Orgasm represents a relatively small proportion of women's total sexuality. A woman who has never had an orgasm thinks of sex as 'making love' without necessarily even hoping for orgasm.

There is nothing wrong with this and many women are content with what they have. However, this makes it difficult to compare notes with others because women account for their sexual experiences so differently.

Even well-informed and mature women can believe that they orgasm (when they don't) simply because they do not know what real female orgasms feel like.

# Understanding the G-spot

The Gräfenberg Spot, or G-Spot, has been surrounded by controversy ever since its 'discovery' only decades ago. Some women may have one about an inch or so (2-5cm) up in the front wall of the vagina.

The G-spot is believed to be an erogenous zone which when stimulated can lead to high levels of sexual arousal and powerful orgasms. Despite all the hype many couples struggle to find any evidence for its existence.

A recent (2010) study of 1,800 women in the Journal of Sexual Medicine has found no proof for it. The research team at King's College, London suggest the G-spot may be a figment of women's imagination, encouraged by magazines and sex therapists. So what does that leave us with?

Let's take a look at our pelvic anatomy by focusing on the similarities between men and women. First, let's tick off the anus. Men and women are identical here and both sexes can enjoy anal stimulation, given appropriate lubrication and a sensitive lover.

Next, we both have genitals (penis/clitoris) so oral and manual masturbation techniques can be effective for both sexes (note: mental arousal is needed before physical stimulation can lead to orgasm – this is crucial to understanding female sexuality since women's sexual arousal is not as automatic as men's tends to be).

There is also a difference in size of the genital organs. The male genitals – at least the parts we can see outside the body are much bigger. A man's penis (when erect) must be a hundred times bigger than a woman's clitoris...

Of course, inside is a different story. Both organs reach back into the pelvis and include muscles of the pelvic area of the body (basically in between the hips).

When you are sexually aroused, the external organ becomes erect but also you have an erection of the muscles internal to the body (erectile tissue) that become engorged when a person is sexually aroused.

If you were to stimulate the person in this pelvic area when they are already engorged and physically aroused, this would stimulate their internal erection. For a man you have to stimulate his internal erection through the anus because there is no other opening.

In fact, there is also a male G-spot, which is the prostate gland and accessible by penetrating a man anally. Some women do enjoy sharing physical intimacy with a partner but even so I wonder how many women explore that one…

For a woman, you have two options. The anal option is similar to that for a man except women don't have a prostate gland. There is also the option of stimulating her internal erection through her vagina.

The vaginal opening is the one absolute difference between the sexes. However, unless you want a baby there is no need to be overly distracted by the vagina.

*"The vagina of the female is not matched by any functioning structure in the male, but it is of minimum importance in contributing to the erotic response of the female. It may even contribute more to the sexual arousal of the male than it does to the arousal of the female." (Alfred Kinsey; Sexual behavior in the human female; 1953)*

The vagina is part of the birth canal and so it has very few nerve endings. A woman is unlikely to be able to feel a man's penis inside her even if he is built like a horse.

I have only become aware of my own physical arousal (swollen and moist) since around my mid-thirties. I have also around this time experienced physical orgasms from vaginal fisting and from anal sex.

Both would stimulate an internal erection and these experiences are the closest I have ever come to what other people may be calling a G-spot orgasm.

Vaginal fisting is a misleading term since, for me at least, it does not necessarily involve putting the whole fist inside the vagina. My partner uses the fingers of one hand to penetrate my vagina.

Some women orgasm during childbirth, which is presumably a similar experience to vaginal fisting.

The success of the G-spot myth is not simply down to men's enthusiasm for intercourse. To explain their orgasms during intercourse, women have also leapt on an alternative to the clitoris. This illustrates just how few women identify with clitoral stimulation and female masturbation.

## Most women are not aiming for orgasm though genital stimulation

Some women refer to 'making love' because the term more accurately describes their motives in terms of loving emotions rather than as an explicit sex drive.

Modern expectations cause some women to talk about their sexual experiences (whatever they are) in terms of arousal and orgasm.

Some women knowingly fake orgasm but there is almost a sense of bravado associated with faking.

We assume that women only fake part of the time or are sexually experienced enough to know how to fake. Many others interpret sex as a loving act without needing to talk about orgasm at all.

The resulting confusion leads many people to believe that women orgasm during sex despite their own experiences (that women are much less driven by sex) and despite the fact that intercourse provides insufficient clitoral stimulation for female orgasm.

As in the fable 'The Emperor's New Clothes' it takes great courage to question 'truths' that the majority consider indisputable.

Any woman brave enough to question is labelled 'sexually dysfunctional' and this humiliation alone is enough to silence most people.

Women who question are confident of their experience of orgasm from masturbation. Sadly the majority of women do not understand this interest in orgasm though genital stimulation, which is more readily associated with men and with gay women.

### Intercourse was never intended to lead to female orgasm

Confusion over female orgasm arose during the sexual revolution, which discovered that women were capable of orgasm.

It was mistakenly assumed that female orgasm must naturally occur during the core heterosexual love-making act of vaginal intercourse.

Consequently although men and even lesbian women use genital stimulation to reach orgasm, heterosexual women get away with claiming that they orgasm during sex without any clitoral stimulation whatsoever.

Vaginal intercourse is a reproductive act whereby the male impregnates the female. Male orgasm (since it usually involves ejaculation of sperm) is required for reproduction but female orgasm has no role in reproduction.

Therefore women do not need to be as sexually driven as men nor do they need to become aroused or to reach orgasm as easily as men.

Some women are motivated to explore their sexuality and do discover orgasm. However, there is no reason for Nature to ensure that this experience of female orgasm occurs during sex.

Relatively few women masturbate but, even if they do, sex with a partner does not naturally provide women with the sexual arousal that causes genital stimulation to be effective.

Since women's sexual arousal is not needed for reproduction, there is no natural phenomenon that causes female arousal. Some women make a conscious effort to become aroused but it does not happen spontaneously as it tends to with men.

Women's use of fantasies may work well when masturbating alone but during sex, male orgasm needs to be centre stage.

Not only is female orgasm more elusive but also women generally are not as strongly motivated by sex as men are. So, for example, when I have offered my partners oral sex (fellatio) they almost swoon with pleasure and yet I rarely find oral sex (cunnilingus) arousing enough for orgasm.

Even women who orgasm from cunnilingus need the circumstances to be just right and I suspect that few women would be willing to pay for the pleasure as men do.

Women's 'sex drive' is much more likely to revolve around ensuring the welfare of their children. Equally, their sense of their own sexuality or sensuality is much more likely to involve an ability to make themselves sexually attractive to men than to involve them actively seeking sex with the aim of enjoying their own sexual arousal and orgasm.

# The facts of female sexuality

Shere Hite pointed out in 1976 that intercourse does not provide the specific clitoral stimulation that women need to orgasm.

So, it is very likely that any woman who claims easy orgasm during intercourse is mistaken.

Especially given so few women masturbate and so most do not know what orgasm is. Women's talk of the relationship and loving emotions also indicates a misunderstanding about the nature of orgasm.

The light-hearted book 'Bluff your way in sex' (1987) lists women's sexual anatomy as: breasts, vagina and internal organs.

The clitoris is completely omitted. This reflects how little interest most women have in the clitoris.

So even though women are likely to find orgasm much easier through oral or manual stimulation of the clitoris, most women are shocked by the idea of masturbation and oral sex. Female sexual arousal is so obscure that many women never discover the joys of the clitoris.

Hite suggested that EITHER women masturbate themselves during sex OR they find a suitable position for intercourse to maximise the indirect clitoral stimulation.

Yet few couples today appear to be aware that clitoral stimulation is required for female orgasm. Most couples still base their sex life around 'making love', that is vaginal intercourse.

If women orgasm as easily as men through oral or manual stimulation by a partner why would they EVER opt for intercourse, which provides insufficient clitoral stimulation for orgasm?

Women settle for 'love-making' BECAUSE other activities with a partner do NOT lead to female orgasm. Intercourse facilitates male orgasm, which is a much easier goal than female orgasm.

## Male nudity does not cause female sexual arousal

Understandably, it is difficult for a man to know what it's like to be a woman. Men naturally hope that women respond sexually just as men do but experience of real women should help them realise that women's sexuality is quite different.

As long as we expect women to respond as men do then we will always conclude that women are dysfunctional.

The underlying assumption is that women approach sex from a similar standpoint to men – just short of an orgasm.

But women are not full of testosterone (the sex hormone) and so they do not experience daily genital erections as men do.

Sadly (for matching heterosexual partners' sex drives) female sexuality involves women being much less highly sexed than men.

Personally I have never found that clitoral stimulation helps with sexual arousal during vaginal intercourse. This is because sexual arousal depends on what happens in the brain and does not arise purely from physical stimulation. Women do not approach sex with sufficient mental arousal for genital stimulation to be effective.

Men enjoy their fantasies and arousal through regular use of porn and masturbation. Women do not use images of naked men for orgasm during female masturbation (women use an intense mental focus on sexual fantasies).

What psychological stimuli do women use to help them become aroused enough IN THEIR MINDS to reach orgasm during sex?

Women use fantasy because they have to raise their arousal levels from a much lower base level than men do at the start of any sexual activity (masturbation or sex).

I am asking women whether they have been able to use fantasy during sex and, if not, what they use for sexual arousal with a partner.

**Ways Women Orgasm** has one key aim: to highlight just how few women are confident about discussing orgasm in any context and how even fewer are able to explain convincingly how they reach orgasm with a partner.

The current state of mystery and ignorance evidently suits many people but others would benefit from a more reasoned account of female sexuality.

# How to orgasm

Shere Hite explained how women apply orgasm techniques in order to orgasm during intercourse. Women's sexual arousal and orgasm are not automatic and so women have to learn how to orgasm. Inevitably, such techniques take time to develop.

*"... the two reasons women don't orgasm during intercourse are:*

*(1) they are given false information, specifically they are told that the penis thrusting in the vagina will cause orgasm; and*

*(2) they are intimidated from exploring and touching their bodies... They do not control their own stimulation." (Shere Hite; The Hite Reports; 1993)*

Research indicates that masturbation is innate but sex itself is learned. We know that vaginal intercourse is reproductive and so we assume it also leads to sexual pleasure.

Unfortunately, female orgasm is not required for reproduction and so vaginal intercourse is not designed, either physically or psychologically, to provide a woman with orgasm.

Luckily other sexual activities can be just as enjoyable as (if not more than) intercourse.

Intercourse naturally allows a man to control his own physical stimulation (of the penis) through thrusting. Even if the woman takes the initiative and 'rides' her man from on top, she is still stimulating his penis with her vagina.

A couple needs to build into their sex life the same freedom for the woman to obtain the clitoral stimulation that she needs.

## Clitoral stimulation is not everything

If a woman knows how to masturbate to orgasm, she may be able to obtain the additional clitoral stimulation she needs by applying her orgasm techniques to sex while her man penetrates her.

Usually a woman will masturbate herself during intercourse using a rear-entry position e.g. in the spoon position (imagine spoons lying side by side in the drawer).

*"Forget the missionary position. Most men think that if they stick it in you you'll be screaming with orgasm, just as long as they keep at it enough" says Ruth, 30.*

*"It's just not so. No matter how much you pump, nothing is going to happen, apart from her writing a mental shopping list for Tesco.*

*Unless, of course the clitoris is involved. And that's physically impossible if you're lying on top." (Men's Health magazine Jan/Feb 1998)*

Over time a man can learn how to stimulate his partner but this kind of sensitive technique is difficult to acquire as a man relies on his partner's feedback.

The likely areas, equivalent to the erogenous areas in a man, include the labia themselves (the length of the penis), either side of the labia (the testicles), the entrance to the vagina (base of the penis) and around the anus.

Porn movies are based on male fantasies and are not intended to be educational. So most real women do not relish the thought of gulping down unreal amounts of gelatinous spunk or having it sprayed all over their bodies.

I also wince when I see women apparently built like horses the way they can withstand such vigorous clitoral stimulation as if they have male genitals.

A much gentler approach is to be recommended in real life, at least to start with. A man needs to learn how his partner reacts when stimulation is pleasurable.

Signs of sexual arousal in a woman are subtler than for a man but include the degree and consistency of her vaginal fluids, the extent that the vaginal entrance and labia are swollen and the degree of clitoral erection.

Transferring orgasm techniques from masturbation to sex can be difficult for a woman because some sexual fantasies are more difficult to use during sex with a partner. Unfortunately not every woman is able to focus on fantasy during sex.

# Women's sexual dysfunction

Although many sources refer to women's 'sexual dysfunction', it is rare to find a definition of what is supposed to be sexually 'normal' for women in the first place.

Sex involves both reproduction and sexual pleasure. So in reproductive terms, a man could be described as sexually dysfunctional if he cannot impregnate a female (male orgasm required) and a woman if she cannot conceive (female orgasm not required).

Enjoyment of sexual pleasure certainly includes sexual arousal and orgasm for men. However, many women are unconcerned about a lack of orgasm during sex.

Men can usually enjoy orgasm through masturbation alone, masturbation with a partner, oral sex or intercourse. Many women limit their sexual experiences to 'love-making' despite the fact that intercourse provides insufficient clitoral stimulation for orgasm.

Even if a woman is willing to try more direct ways of stimulating her clitoris during sex with a partner, the fact is that she is unlikely to be aroused enough for clitoral stimulation to lead to orgasm. Many women are only able to orgasm during masturbation alone because this allows them to generate sufficient arousal for orgasm by focusing on their sexual fantasies.

Around 10% of women are estimated to be 'an-orgasmic', that is, they never experience orgasm ever. Women who only orgasm from masturbation are referred to as 'pre-orgasmic'. The number of men who cannot orgasm during sex throughout their lives is negligible whereas, for women, the figure is around 50% (including an-orgasmic and pre-orgasmic women).

*"Only about half of all the women who have told me about their sexual experiences say they usually have orgasms during lovemaking. The others either do not have orgasms, or find that they usually have an orgasm only when masturbating." (Sheila Kitzinger; Woman's Experience of Sex; 1983)*

### Lack of female orgasm is not a sexual dysfunction

It is unreasonable to categorise such a high percentage of women as having a sexual dysfunction. So there is nothing abnormal about either an-orgasmic or pre-orgasmic women. Such women do not have a 'problem' at all. They simply need to accept that this is the way things are for many women who hope for orgasm in their sexual relationships.

Even these statistics for women's sexual performance are likely to be optimistic because women who respond to surveys or talk to others about sex are already in a minority. Many other women justify their sexual relationship in terms of loving their partner or having children rather than as a means of enjoying their own sexual arousal and orgasm.

From Shere Hite's survey (1976) 30% of women claimed to be able to orgasm regularly from intercourse alone. This is quite amazing when you think that it is equivalent to 30% of men boasting that they prefer to orgasm without stimulating their penis.

An equally amazing 44% said that they masturbate during intercourse. At least this is a more realistic way to achieve orgasm but means that almost every other woman masturbates herself during sex. How likely is this? Well given that very few women masturbate at all and even fewer succeed with the same techniques with a partner, I am guessing not very likely.

Only 26% of the women surveyed were brave enough to admit that they could not orgasm during intercourse at all (only through oral sex, masturbation alone or that they never orgasm by any means). As Rachel Swifts points out:

*"Furthermore it's a pretty safe guess that the statistics are worse than that. Because if it's a volunteer sample, the women most likely to come forward and be candid about sex are likely to be those who are also successful with sex.*

*And while many people might be tempted to pretend they do orgasm when they don't, few are likely to pretend that they don't when they do.*

*That's about as probable as a woman claiming she weighs ten stone when she actually weighs nine." (Rachel Swift; Women's Pleasure; 1993)*

# Lack of arousal during sex

Intimacy with a lover causes me to feel affectionate but I am rarely conscious of any sexual arousal. Whether it's sex with a partner, or masturbation for that matter, I am usually pretty much stone cold in arousal terms at the start.

I might conclude that I am frigid if it were not for the fact that I cannot visualise other women I meet approaching sex just short of an orgasm. The female mind and body simply do not work that way.

Equally I don't see other women being more actively interested in matters sexual than I am – in fact usually the reverse.

I cannot use my sexual fantasies during sex and so orgasm with a partner has been elusive by any means, whether by using positions and techniques for sexual intercourse or through more direct clitoral stimulation, manual or oral.

The website 'Go Ask Alice!' is one of the few sources willing to admit that women often struggle with orgasm during sex. They suggest that women who are hoping for orgasm should use masturbation or oral sex because it takes women MUCH LONGER than men to become aroused.

*"The vagina itself is a muscular tube of about 8 cm that, when adequately stimulated, expands to fit any size penis with ease. When your partner initially penetrates you, the muscles of the vagina contract and grip the penis*

*As you continue intercourse and become more turned-on, the vagina expands even further – sometimes so much so, you can't feel his penis inside you no matter how large it is. This explains why for both partners the initial few thrusts are sometimes the most pleasurable because the vagina feels tighter*

*For most women, stimulation of the clitoris is necessary to orgasm. Intercourse can indirectly stimulate the clitoris through thrusting but more direct touching with fingers or a tongue is usually more effective." (Tracey Cox; Hot Sex; 1998).*

## Sexual arousal depends on an appreciation of eroticism

A person seeks to enjoy sexual pleasure, in the form of their own sexual arousal and orgasm, as a direct consequence of sexual desire.

However, women, especially if they are unfamiliar with orgasm, can enjoy sharing physical intimacy with a loving partner, including being the object of a man's sexual passion, regardless of their own ability to orgasm during sex.

Ironically the less inhibited you are the more disappointing you are likely to find real life because you overlook the simple things like nudity.

Sometimes people refer to 'sexual intimacy', which comes from a man and a woman sharing the intimacies of sex including nudity, allowing someone to touch the private areas of our bodies and the ultimate act of penetration.

If we were all nuns we could probably make do with sexual fantasies based on vaginal intercourse e.g. sex in public, sex with multiple partners etc.

The more we read and imagine beyond the everyday, the more we are likely to need to venture into less comfortable territory. If a fantasy is to help us orgasm then it needs to encompass aspects of sex that we consider to be taboo.

When we explore sexual fantasies, we tend to start on the more innocent side and build up to the more advanced or kinky. The same goes for sex with a partner. For example, most people probably make do with straight intercourse for a first date.

Ask your partner to spend some time preparing your body for sex. Get him to shave your pubic hair completely, which can feel kinky and also makes oral sex easier for the guy.

An enema can cause arousal so that even intercourse is more arousing than normal. Try a blindfold or having your hands tied during sex. Visit a sex shop for other ideas to get the brain going.

As long as you are both keen, consider working out a schedule for building up to fisting and/or anal intercourse. Remember the golden rule with these more advanced techniques: TAKE YOUR TIME.

You should expect to invest serious time in just relaxing, lubricating and exploring with a finger. Information is vital: Em and Lo's book 'The Big Bang' is excellent on both of these.

## What if female sexuality truly equalled male sexuality?

Imagine the scenario: a man and a woman facing each other, naked, in a world where men and women have an identical sex drive.

So, of course, they are both standing there with an erection. Just to be clear: the man has an erect penis and the woman has an erect clitoris.

Would they mutually choose to engage in vaginal intercourse? No because intercourse does not stimulate the clitoris enough for female orgasm. Even a man would struggle to orgasm from a partner banging her groin against his penis.

So the 'sexually equal' couple would presumably prefer oral sex or mutual masturbation. This way both sexes could enjoy equal genital stimulation.

Would Nature be happy? No because these activities are not reproductive and so the human race would die out. After all, the PRIME purpose of sex is reproduction. Sexual pleasure is merely a by-product.

In ten years of researching female sexuality very few women have been able to explain convincingly how they orgasm with a partner. It either 'just happens' or it happens 'naturally'.

Such explanations indicate how oblivious many women are to the psychological elements of sexual arousal and even to the appreciation that genital stimulation is required for orgasm.

Women claim that intercourse is orgasmic the 'first time and every time' and get away with it. We are all so totally convinced that because men find intercourse arousing so should women.

Men are lucky because they get turned on (enough for orgasm) by the body of a sexual partner and during intercourse the penis is directly stimulated by thrusting.

Women are not so lucky. They do not become aroused enough for orgasm simply by looking at the male naked body nor is the clitoris stimulated adequately during intercourse.

Women need direct clitoral stimulation for orgasm but, much more importantly, they need an intense mental focus on fantasy to achieve the kind of sexual arousal that leads to orgasm.

Such focus is often impossible to achieve with a partner and this explains why female masturbation alone tends to be the easiest source of female orgasm.

## Women who claim to reach orgasm from intercourse alone are mistaken

If women were able to orgasm through vaginal intercourse, without any direct clitoral stimulation, it would imply that women are MORE HIGHLY SEXED than men. Even men need DIRECT penile stimulation for orgasm.

So anyone who claims that women orgasm during vaginal intercourse is mistaken. Of course, women are known to fake both their own sexual arousal and orgasm. Equally many women simply assume that they orgasm during intercourse because few women masturbate so they never know what orgasm is. This explains why so few women ask about lack of orgasm.

It is only women who are familiar with orgasm from masturbation who realise that orgasm is missing from sex with a partner.

*"Nevertheless, many women prefer intercourse to masturbation because it gives them additional sensual benefits such as being held and being kissed and also makes them part of a spontaneous give and take." (Masters & Johnson; Human Sexuality; 1995)*

Vaginal intercourse, for a woman, feels like affectionate hugging since the vagina has little sensitivity to any sensation from penile thrusting. Vaginal intercourse is literally a heterosexual 'love-making' act. The difficulty over the longer-term is that a man forgets to 'make love' to his woman by including sensual petting and sex play before heading for his orgasm through thrusting.

Equally, women are not motivated to seek other more explicit forms of genital stimulation during sex because (1) they do not approach sex already aroused and (2) female sexual arousal does not arise from an appreciation of a lover's body.

Women co-operate with men's sex drive and provide men with sexual pleasure to create the emotional bonds needed for long-term relationships. Intercourse provides women with an easy way of satisfying a man with the least inconvenience to herself.

# Stories: Sexual fantasies

# Clitoral stimulation is not everything

As long ago as the 1950s the clitoris, and not the vagina, was acknowledged to be the origin of female orgasm.

So that by the 1960s when Masters and Johnson explained female orgasm from intercourse alone, it was in terms of women finding positions and techniques for intercourse that maximise the indirect clitoral stimulation (caused by the penis thrusting into the vagina).

*As sex therapist Lonnie Barbach notes: "In reality, the clitoris is the female sex organ.*

*... The vagina is comparable in sensitivity to the male testicles." (Masters & Johnson; Human Sexuality; 1995)*

By the mid-1970s though, it was accepted that this indirect action was not sufficient to enable the majority of women to reach orgasm.

It was agreed that most women are likely to find orgasm with a partner easier by applying orgasm techniques to sex learnt from masturbation or through oral sex because the clitoral stimulation is more direct.

In fact it's not just lack of orgasm during vaginal intercourse that women struggle with but orgasm by any means with a partner.

Most informed people today are aware of the importance of the clitoris and a woman can only know that something is missing from sex if she is familiar with orgasm from masturbation.

So why do women still ask about orgasm with a partner?

## Clitoral stimulation is known to help but cannot guarantee orgasm

Experts often imply that female orgasm is easily achieved but if it was a simple as pressing a button, why wouldn't we all have worked it out by now?

I appreciate that sexual ignorance is rife out there but surely it is accepted that the 'informed couple' exists?

Don't sex experts realise that couples read sex manuals and try different approaches to sex?

Clitoral stimulation is known to assist with orgasm during female masturbation but ONLY when combined with the use of highly explicit sexual fantasies.

So the suggestion that clitoral stimulation alone will lead to orgasm during sex with a partner is simply a shot in the dark.

It is a suggestion that is intended to be helpful but one that can, in fact, be quite misleading.

Despite all the limelight that our genitals (clitoris/penis) get, it is in fact the brain that is the true sex organ.

If you cannot generate some PSYCHOLOGICAL sexual arousal then you can forget about the rest.

I have certainly never been able to use my sexual fantasies effectively during sex with a partner – it just does not work the same way.

After years of researching the small print, I also know that I am not the only woman who has had this experience.

Women's sexual arousal relies on sexual fantasies during masturbation and many women are able to use the same orgasm techniques during sex.

Try bringing some sexual fantasies into sex with a partner even if that means reading some erotica while he touches you up.

This can be a very enjoyable precursor to sex if nothing else.

I find that women's erotica can be a little too 'soft porn' and overly focused on the woman's body.

If you want something a little more gutsy then try some homosexual erotica, which can be a real turn-on because it is full of male body parts, anal sex and fellatio.

Of course, there's always the more mundane domination and sadism which gets many of us going, like it or not.

# How to give a woman an orgasm during sex

The suggestion is that for the perfect sex life a woman just needs to find the right man: usually a loving and considerate partner, who will, of course, know how to give her an orgasm.

Self-evidently a woman needs a considerate lover if intercourse is to be a love-making act otherwise it is simply rape. A loving partner may cause a woman to be AMENABLE to intercourse but women cannot ORGASM from loving emotions any more than men can.

Orgasm involves a release of sexual emotions (through an appreciation of eroticism and explicitly sexual concepts) not romantic emotions. Romance may be an excellent lead in to sex but it cannot cause orgasm even in women.

Minor details are glossed over: such as the FACT that since the vagina, as part of the birth canal, has few nerve endings women typically are aware of little sensation from penile thrusting.

Equally no one worries about the FACT that most women need direct clitoral stimulation for orgasm and the clitoris is only stimulated indirectly during vaginal intercourse.

Never mind. A man's fantasy of providing female sexual pleasure remains intact. Through intercourse a man can enjoy his partner's breasts and mouth while stimulating his penis.

Dream on...

Men are not alone in misunderstanding female sexuality. Dismissing Shere Hite's detailed conclusions about how women learn to orgasm, one woman said "Now we're being told how we should orgasm, holy shi-! It's much easier than the babble of a therapist: find a man who KNOWS WHAT HE IS DOING!"

Sometimes people imply that an experienced male lover knows how to use positions and techniques for sexual intercourse.

They are obviously unaware that, no matter how inventive the position, the experts concluded in the 1970s that the INDIRECT stimulation of the clitoris during intercourse is insufficient to allow most women to orgasm.

A man can provide the additional DIRECT clitoral stimulation that a woman needs for orgasm by hand or mouth. Anyone who has tried this will know that such techniques do not guarantee orgasm for every woman. It may be better if the woman provides her own clitoral stimulation during sex and many experts suggest this as if it will GUARANTEE an orgasm.

No man can orgasm without first having an erection and when was the last time you saw a woman with an erection (of the clitoris)? That's why women have difficulty with orgasm.

Women certainly do not become aroused enough for orgasm simply by looking at the naked male body. If they did, sales of porn for women would presumably equal that sold to men on a daily basis.

If a woman cannot give herself an orgasm then it is unlikely that someone else will be able to. Sexual arousal originates in the brain and no man, whatever physical stimulation techniques he uses, can control what happens inside a woman's head.

Many women assume that female orgasm arises from softer (sexually implicit) images of love and romance rather than from the cruder (sexually explicit) images that lead to male orgasm.

Shere Hite referred to women's experience of heightened arousal as 'emotional orgasms' to differentiate them from real female orgasms.

Perhaps the term 'emotional orgasm' is unhelpful. Another way to differentiate between women's experience of orgasm is to ask about the impact of the relationship.

*"In some cases, it was not even clear to the woman herself whether there had been an orgasm or merely high levels of arousal." (Shere Hite; The Hite Report; 1976)*

A woman who enjoys orgasm through masturbation can enjoy orgasm quite separately from her relationship because her sexual psychology is driven through sexual fantasies. Each of these experiences is no better than the other but simply different.

Even during female masturbation, clitoral stimulation is only effective once a woman is aroused enough for orgasm through the use of sexual fantasies.

It is rarely acknowledged that women use sexual fantasies during sex. Unfortunately the complex psychological nature of many women's fantasies makes them unsuitable for use with a partner.

# Arousal comes from appreciating eroticism

Our ability to become sexually aroused through an appreciation of eroticism is a normal as well as a necessary part of human sexuality.

Sex (male arousal and orgasm in particular) leads to family and yet hypocritically, while family is encouraged, sex remains taboo.

Young boys learn about orgasm through masturbation because an erect penis is difficult to ignore. Girls do not experience spontaneous sexual arousal and so they have no similar reason to explore how their genitals might react to stimulation through female masturbation.

*"Unlike a boy's very obvious penis, which he knows is pleasurable to touch and fondle, a girl's genitals are hidden, mysterious, remote. I find it remarkable (and disturbing) that many women have never used a mirror to see what their genitals look like and to find out where their clitoris is." (Derek Llewellyn-Jones; EveryMan; 1980)*

If men learn how their sexual arousal works through masturbation, how do women experience orgasm as men do but without any learning process at all? Surely the reasonable assumption is that female masturbation fulfils a similar role for women?

From puberty onwards, boys are fascinated by their penis: the way it grows and is pleasurable to touch. They learn that their appreciation of the sexual attributes of women or men (depending on sexual orientation) takes them from arousal to orgasm.

Women do not have the same experience. In fact, if anything the childhood message that touching around the genital and anal area is 'dirty' is reinforced by the practical necessities of dealing with the periods that signal the start of female adolescence.

More than this, women's minds are simply not wired to appreciate the physical aspects of sex. This is why many women (even those who work in the sex industry) think men are 'like animals'.

Men seem to revel in all the things that women find unappealing: the hairy skin and the musky smells associated with the genitals as well as the bodily fluids that accompany sexual activity.

As a woman who enjoys eroticism, I have been able to put aside these concerns to some degree. I never think that pornography makes the woman 'dirty'.

The key is whether a woman identifies with the positive aspects of eroticism because, even when they don't masturbate, some women are able to share their partner's enjoyment of eroticism by watching porn movies together.

Women are often blissfully unaware that men masturbate regularly throughout their lives. Men cover up the strength of their sexual urges because women can sometimes be insensitive about men's passion for sex. The daily sales of pornographic magazines are a clue.

Of course, men have a higher sex drive but also they enjoy their own sexual arousal and orgasm.

Women, who masturbate, enjoy their own sexual arousal and orgasm in much the same way. They use sexual fantasies (based on their appreciation of eroticism) to bring their sexual arousal to orgasm through genital stimulation (of the clitoris).

Many women never learn to appreciate the eroticism that leads to sexual arousal so they never explore their sexual fantasies. Without the experience of true sexual arousal, they never understand why anyone would ever want to stimulate their genitals.

Many women are shocked by any form of eroticism. This shows a lack of understanding about the nature of sexual pleasure. After all, eroticism lies at the heart of our ability to become sexually aroused.

A woman who never discovers her own sexual arousal through masturbation is likely to have difficulty generating positive associations. Such women prefer 'love-making' because it avoids them needing to engage on the crude practicalities of more explicit sexual activity e.g. oral sex.

Men do not see sex purely in terms of family or 'making love'. Men also want to enjoy sexual pleasure with a partner.

If there was more education for women to help them understand men's appreciation of eroticism, perhaps more women would be willing to explore sexual activity with a partner and then fewer men would be looking for sex with a prostitute.

## Not every woman enjoys eroticism

Most girls probably read romantic stories but not everyone is comfortable with the more explicitly sexual nature of erotic stories, which help a woman develop the sexual fantasies that lead to orgasm.

Our sexual fantasies represent the aspects of sex that we find most arousing and hence most taboo.

*"Although every child learns that pretending is an important type of play, sexual fantasies after childhood are usually not thought of as playful. This attitude may exist because sex is usually regarded as a serious matter, even in the imagination.*

*Furthermore, some religious traditions regard a thought as equivalent to an act; thus, a person who has 'immoral' sexual daydreams or desires is as sinful as a person who acts on those impulses." (Masters & Johnson; Human Sexuality; 1995)*

Even men learn to orgasm through masturbation and women have to learn how to orgasm much the same way.

Women's sexual arousal and orgasm are not automatic as a man's tends to be and so female masturbation is relatively uncommon.

Very few of the women I spoke to said that they enjoy their own sexual arousal through masturbation.

If you doubt this, just try asking the women you know, not whether they have EVER masturbated but, whether they masturbate REGULARLY as an adult.

Since many women never discover orgasm through genital stimulation they never know what they are missing. They assume that enjoying sexual pleasure relates only to the sensual pleasures of sex.

Having enjoyed orgasm throughout my adult life, it is definitely an experience I would not want to have missed but I can quite see why many women are happy to do without.

### Women have more conscious choice over their sexual arousal

A good-looking and successful guy in his mid-forties was very popular with the ladies. Despite hoping for a long-term partner, so far he had only managed serial relationships (some lasting months and some years).

He told me that not one of the women he had been with over the years was amenable to enjoying eroticism by watching porn movies together.

Since many women do not enjoy eroticism of any kind, even if they knew that sexual arousal depended on erotic thoughts they would not necessarily be tempted.

Women's lower sex drive means they have much more conscious choice over their arousal.

*" ... fantasy and sexual desire often merge together.*

*People with low levels of sexual desire typically have few sexual fantasies..." (Masters & Johnson; Human Sexuality; 1995)*

Censorship of genitalia means that films for general release limit sex scenes to intercourse. Other activities, such as oral sex or masturbation, involve the explicit genital stimulation that tends to offend women.

So that even in a film as sexually daring as 'Basic Instinct' (1992) Sharon Stone appears to orgasm without the kind of continuous genital stimulation that men need.

The only media that show heterosexuals enjoying more explicitly sexual activity is pornography.

One has to wonder (since the sex industry is paid for by men) whether such activities are, in fact, reflecting sex play and fantasies that men enjoy.

How many women enjoy oral sex, masturbation and other genitally based sex play? If most do, why is hetero sex still defined by intercourse?

In the film 'Philadelphia' (1993) Denzel Washington portrays the self-righteousness heterosexual who feels that 'love-making' is more morally justifiable than the explicit sexual pleasuring enjoyed by gays and men who pay for sex.

# Women's sexual arousal relies on sexual fantasies

Real female orgasms involve the release of sexual emotions not romantic feelings. So it does not matter how much you love your partner, orgasm will not materialise out of thin air.

Orgasm requires at least a few naughty thoughts from time to time, so if your conscience is as clear as a nun's then you can forget about ever having one.

*"Few of us reach orgasm without fantasy, so let your imagination go wild! ...*

*Don't get hung up about your fantasy; it doesn't mean you're odd, gay or secretly want to be raped.*

*Most women fantasise about things they wouldn't dream of doing in real life – that's why we call them fantasies." (Tracey Cox; Hot Sex; 1998)*

It turns out that women use sexual fantasies for sexual arousal and to generate a release of sexual emotions (orgasm) not only during masturbation but also during sex with a partner.

*"Many times sexual fantasies are used to induce or enhance sexual arousal, and while fantasies are often combined with masturbation to provide a source of turn-on when a partner is not available, fantasies are also extremely common during sexual activity with someone else.*

*For instance, one study of 212 married women found that sex fantasies help many women achieve sexual arousal and/or orgasm during sexual intercourse." (Masters & Johnson; Human Sexuality; 1995)*

## Some women's sexual fantasies do not transfer to sex

Some women find that they are not able to use their sexual fantasies effectively during sex with a partner.

It has been suggested that this is particularly true for complex and surreal fantasies (as they often are).

The presence of another person interferes with the mental focus needed to generate sufficient arousal for orgasm.

Women also have to work harder than men to generate orgasm from a much lower base level of sexual arousal.

Our sexual thoughts do not rise as readily from the subconscious to the conscious mind as men's do.

So we have to be more inventive about our sexual fantasies and their surreal nature can make them more difficult to relate to a sex life with a real life partner.

Equally the imagery of physical sex play does not assist with female arousal.

To generate sufficient arousal to reach the heights of orgasm from fantasy alone, my brain really has to focus.

Even a dripping tap or someone else's presence is enough to destroy my mental absorption in a sexual fantasy. So there is no question of being able to fantasise effectively during sex.

*"Roxanne, a forty-seven-year-old psychiatrist, explains also that 'women probably fantasize more and harder than men, because the traditional idea of feminine behaviour is a burden to a woman during sex. ...*

*Fantasy restores the balance. Add to that that women spend more time thinking up stories anyway, and read more fiction than men, and you've got a wild world in there*

*... lewd extravagances that I'll bet most men never come even close to imagining.'*

*By focusing on some aspect of sex that she finds particularly arousing, and by exaggerating it to the point of outrageousness, a woman increases her chances of climaxing." (Rachel Swift; Satisfaction Guaranteed; 1996)*

## Sharing sexual fantasies

Although I knew that women's sexual arousal relies on sexual fantasies during masturbation, when I approached orgasm during sex, I never considered using sexual fantasies to generate sexual arousal.

The presence of another person makes it impossible to achieve the mental focus needed to reach orgasm through fantasy alone.

*"Women also often find it easier to fantasise when self-pleasuring than in sex with a partner.*

*The immediacy of someone else's needs actually inhibits the expression and satisfaction of their own.*

*Some also say they have to imagine that the person making love to them is not the person they know so well."* (Sheila Kitzinger; Woman's Experience of Sex; 1983)

It takes time but it helps to understand something of each other's sexual fantasies, what turns them on and what they enjoy about sex.

As with all human communication, it is worth starting off with a low ambition level before building up to major confidences.

Some people are much more easily embarrassed than others by personal or erotic detail!

Bear in mind that women's sexual arousal relies on sexual fantasies.

So a man can encourage a partner to be in a sexy mood by buying erotic but tasteful material to be shared together or for the woman to indulge in alone.

Find out what kind of stories turn her on and buy her a couple of erotic novels as a present. Choose something mid-stream initially.

Men often worry that if a woman masturbates they will miss out on sex.

In fact, indulging in fantasies and orgasm is likely to make a woman more amenable to sex and it can be a great turn-on for a man to know that his woman has come.

If you can put your sexual ego aside, many couples find that they get the most out of sex by enjoying their sexual fantasies.

Buy some sexy movies but remember that women need more story content than men.

Consider how to combine sexual fantasy (hers as well as yours) into your sex play.

Start sex sessions with a sexy book or movie. Make her arousal the focus.

*"What women want in a sexual relationship:*

*(1) More spontaneity: all too often the sexual pattern is routine, preordained, expected.*

*(2) More passion – and less urgency to have intercourse quickly.*

*(3) Their man to have less preoccupation with his own penis." (Derek Llewellyn-Jones; EveryMan; 1980)*

Many couples get stuck in an 'intercourse-to-male-orgasm' sex life. Bringing some variety to sex takes effort.

Women can help by suggesting ideas that turn them on.

Men can explore techniques for combining clitoral stimulation with other sex play, engaging in fantasy role play e.g. some playful bondage and offering some sex talk (telling the woman what is turning him on).

*"But even when a man realizes that he should delay penetration, or that the woman may not want it at all, he sometimes makes straight for the erogenous zones or the clitoris, with a hand or mouth, ignoring every other part of the body....*

*Women need plenty of time in which to unwind and begin to feel desire and desirable." (Sheila Kitzinger; Woman's Experience of Sex; 1983)*

Once in a while, make some effort to spice up your sex life. If you are curious about sex toys, 'Sex toys a playfully 101 uninhibited guide' (2003) by Rachel Venning & Claire Cavanah (founders of Babeland.com) is an excellent book to get you started.

## Women who use fantasy for sexual arousal

I have never been a romantic. But recently, I must have gone soft in the head because I now enjoy romantic dramas.

I admire the hero's masculinity, his body (admittedly fully clothed) and his portrayal of restrained sex drive.

Romance may make a woman amenable to sex but I have not found that it helps with sexual arousal. I need scenarios that involve explicit eroticism for orgasm.

It is this huge gap between women's loving emotions and their sexual arousal that must be difficult for a man to understand.

Men have a much stronger connection between their own sexual arousal and physical intimacy with someone they love.

Consequently, men do not necessarily need to use sexual fantasies during sex with a partner, especially in the early days of a relationship.

Men's experience of masturbation leads on quite naturally to sex with a partner because men masturbate by imagining the sexual attributes of a sexual partner.

Women don't use the images of men's genitals for sexual arousal during female masturbation. Women's fantasies tend to be scenarios based on sexual situations that have a psychological context.

This style of fantasy is much more difficult to transfer to sex with a partner. Some women claim to succeed with this but I have met more women who don't.

I have not been able to use my sexual fantasies effectively during sex.

It is very natural for a man to feel insecure about a woman's use of sexual fantasies, just as some women feel insecure about men's enjoyment of pornography.

We worry that a lover uses other sources for arousal because they don't find us attractive. These are common misunderstandings about the difference between enjoying our own sexual arousal and loving another person.

An appreciation of eroticism lies at the core of understanding our own sexuality, what turns us on and enables us to enjoy orgasm. A woman who enjoys eroticism and fantasy is likely to be more adventurous in her sex life with a partner.

No doubt many women are outraged by the idea of encouraging female masturbation, oral sex or anal sex. I am not particularly trying to encourage any specific sexual activity.

I am simply saying that if a young woman wants to enjoy sexual pleasure with a partner (as opposed to get pregnant) then she may need to explore activities other than vaginal intercourse.

Like it or not, this is simply the way the facts of women's sexuality stack up.

Vaginal intercourse is unlikely to arouse a woman because the vagina is capable of expanding to allow a baby's head to pass so it's not going to feel much from a thrusting penis.

Likewise, the vagina is not designed to be sensitive otherwise childbirth would be even more painful than it already is.

Originally, foreplay was supposed to compensate for inadequate clitoral stimulation from intercourse.

Unfortunately, not only do women need clitoral stimulation to continue up to the point of orgasm but also, due to the sensitivity of the clitoris, it can be difficult for a man to provide the right kind of stimulation.

So when women ask about lack of orgasm today, experts suggest that they masturbate during sex. Little is known about how successful women are with this approach in practice.

To help improve our understanding, **Ways Women Orgasm** invites women to share how they achieve arousal and orgasm during sex.

I am asking other sexually experienced women who know about orgasm from female masturbation (so we know that we are talking about the same experience) to share notes on activities that they have found arousing enough for orgasm during sex.

# How women enjoy eroticism through sex stories

Most heterosexual women do not masturbate. They also do not find the concepts of eroticism or fantasy that appealing. So who reads all the feminine erotica out there?

Presumably some lesbian women masturbate and read erotica. In fact, female masturbation and clitoral stimulation are often associated with lesbianism.

Perhaps this is why so much female erotica focuses on women's bodies and sex between women.

No offence to lesbian or bisexual women but I am straight. I like male body parts, male psyche and sexual acts involving men.

The woman is incidental. I enjoy homosexual erotica because I imagine myself on the receiving end of fellatio or anal sex, for example.

Erotica written for women often includes humiliation, domination and sadism. The titles of women's sex stories abound with words such as: slave, chains, torture, bound, obey, submission. Do women associate sex with feeling 'dirty' or guilty about their sexual urges?

*"Men have rape and domination fantasies. Women have fantasies about BEING raped and dominated." (Sheila Kitzinger; Woman's Experience of Sex; 1983)*

I like the wholehearted enthusiasm for sex that is portrayed in homosexual erotica. There is no virginal reluctance or demure disgust. People just enjoy the eroticism of sexual activity without anyone being forced into anything against their will (not always but mostly).

I admit that domination can be arousing. Given there is so much out there I have read my share. One book of sex stories involved a series of sadistic scenarios and frankly I was quite relieved when I eventually tired of the never-ending pain.

My conclusion is that the concept of sadism may get me going but, for me at least, it does not cause orgasm.

It was a revelation to me that, unlike pornography, erotica is not intended solely for the purposes of causing sexual arousal.

Perhaps this explains why I often struggle to find sex stories for women that can assist with orgasm. I have to wonder though… what else does anyone read this stuff for?

Men might feel embarrassed (or they might not!) as they head off to buy their pornographic magazines.

Their regular need to release sexual frustration through orgasm is such that men do not have the luxury of deciding to be 'pure'.

Many women are happy with interpreting their sexual relationship in terms of emotional criteria. They never feel that something is missing from their lives.

However, women who learn how to masturbate definitely do notice that orgasm is missing from sex.

*"Most women do not orgasm as a result of intercourse per se. The overwhelming majority of women require specific clitoral contact for orgasm." (Shere Hite; The Hite Reports; 1993)*

Shere Hite was phenomenal but sadly few women relate to her findings. This is because most women approach sex through their relationship with their lover.

They have no concept of enjoying their own sexual arousal through clitoral stimulation. Equally they have never discovered the pleasures of sexual fantasies.

I read Hite when I was twenty and I understood that clitoral stimulation was critical to female orgasm from masturbation.

However, clitoral stimulation never seemed to help with my sexual arousal during sex with my partner.

The fact is that even during female masturbation, clitoral stimulation only leads to orgasm when it is combined with the use of sexual fantasies.

Men have a fairly natural transition from masturbation to sex because they use images of naked women for arousal.

Women do not use images of naked men during masturbation so it is more difficult for them to transfer their orgasm techniques including their use of sexual fantasies to sex with a partner.

# Reaching orgasm

Rose was a pretty woman even in her late forties. Despite being a mother and housewife she always achieved a classy presentation.

Rose told me: "Although I masturbated as a youngster (from 14) it was never to orgasm. My first orgasm was by accident.

It happened at 17 with a boyfriend – not during penetrative sex but as a result of my body rubbing against his body.

It was a scary experience for me and I didn't like being out of control. It wasn't until I met my long-term partner who had studied the female anatomy from books and real girls that I had another orgasm at 19.

I didn't want (for a number of reasons) penetrative sex so our initial experiments were with mutual masturbation. It was really easy then about 6 months later to transfer to penetrative orgasmic sex.

I often wonder how long it would have taken for me to discover orgasm if I hadn't met this more experienced lover."

Rose did not masturbate alone but she had succeeded in applying orgasm techniques to sex and she had learned how to masturbate herself during intercourse.

Rose agreed that a man's sexual arousal can be very flattering and that an important aspect of her own sexual arousal was the idea that her partner wanted to have sex with her.

Some couples find that the spoon position allows a woman to stimulate herself (think of spoons lying side by side in a drawer – man behind the woman).

## Sharing sexual fantasies

Rose recommended: "Men need to learn manual arousal techniques (to use on the woman) and also not to be intimidated by women using masturbation as part of the act of intercourse.

Women need to learn to combine masturbation and intercourse and feel completely free to share their fantasies and use them during intercourse."

She giggled: "I wonder if the taboo about sex is not about sex per se but about the 'naughty fantasies' that make sex so good! I also found it difficult to share fantasies as I was unsure if speaking about them might somehow make them lose their power – like bursting a bubble – thankfully it hasn't".

Rose agreed that women's sexual arousal and orgasm are not automatic and that women's sexual arousal is more consciously generated: "Men are easily stimulated by sexual thoughts.

Women's automatic trigger is (1) more easily sublimated, (2) far less frequent and (3) needs other factors present to be switched on (i.e. they need to be content with other areas of their life).

I think that they do have this automatic trigger but because of the above reasons, the choice becomes more conscious. Women usually need more artificial aids to trigger arousal.

I would also add general touching and caressing (as opposed to specifically primary erogenous zone touching)." Later she remarked:

"It's peculiar that the 'power' that women have over men (i.e. the ability to sexually arouse them) is at times really appreciated by the woman and helps with her arousal.

And at other times completely abhorrent to her or at least the effect it has is abhorrent. Unfortunately, men seem to be unable to get the timing right as to when to respond to this power.

This is not very fair for men because they really seem unable to pick up the signals and respond appropriately.

I believe that for whatever reason (upbringing, genetics) that their emotions are so controlled that they cannot read the emotional signals that women give out."

*"It's not that men are insensitive.*

*Their brains just aren't organised to notice small details and changes in the appearance or behaviour of others. " (Allan & Barbara Pease; Why men don't listen; 1999)*

# How to enjoy your sexual fantasies

Women use clitoral stimulation during female masturbation but that's just dessert. Main course is achieving sexual arousal though sexual fantasies. Many women never learn how to enjoy these.

The first step in developing sexual fantasies is for a woman to read erotic stories without any goal except relaxation and enjoyment.

I started reading erotica around the age of 14. Initially I enjoyed the stories for sex information and as a light story. I also used to imagine what the men around me in everyday life might think of me sexually.

I don't know that I would ever have considered combining clitoral stimulation (initially through my panties) with the use of sexual fantasies if I hadn't read about female masturbation as well. I don't remember exactly how I learned to bring my arousal to orgasm.

I'm fairly sure that the lights were off and that I was lying on my front, hands between my legs contemplating sleep.

It was a natural and comfortable position in which to think about some sexual scenario.

Just as not every woman has the nurturing skills to make a good mother, not every woman has the sexual skills to be a good lover. A woman needs to be able to tune into male sexual fantasies.

When it comes to her own sexual arousal, it helps if a woman sees herself as sexually attractive to men and if she takes pleasure in the knowledge that a man wants her sexually.

## Fantasies do not always transfer to sex

My fantasies are nearly always based on stories that I have read. I wonder what women did before the invention of the printed word…

One of my favourites is 'The Story of O' by Pauline Reage. The story is set in a large mansion filled with men who use it as a country club but it is a brothel.

The men are rich (of course), masculine and sexually experienced (they know what they want).

I like to fantasise about group episodes with many men who are either having sex with me or waiting their turn.

One scenario is based on servicing men while they are dining around a long table. Some ideas are not ever likely to be enjoyable in reality.

*"Women are turned on by what is done to them, men are turned on by what they see." (Anthony Mason; The Bluffer's Guide to Men; 1998)*

I have also found male homosexual erotica effective for arousal. 'The King's Men' by Christian Fall tells the story of young Ned's sexual adventures during the time of the English Civil War.

'Hot Valley' by James Lear is also an historical novel and follows the sexual exploits of Jack (who is a bit of a slut) in the New England of the 1860s.

Well, I like history…

Apparently, some women are able to use their sexual fantasies during sex. Unfortunately, other women are not able to generate the focus required to reach orgasm from fantasy when they are engaged in sexual activities with a partner.

Women who spend most of their lives in a long-term relationship (e.g. marriage) often never learn how to masturbate.

Since men's sexual pleasure is so much more easily achieved, a sexual relationship tends to revolve around male orgasm.

I found that, once I had a man in my bed, any suggestion of enjoying my own orgasm through female masturbation alone, led all too easily to my partner wanting to orgasm through sex.

A man should positively encourage his woman to enjoy her sexual fantasies (if she has any) because enjoying orgasm keeps a person feeling young and sexually desirable.

# Stories: Orgasm techniques

# Why foreplay techniques don't always work as we think they should

Foreplay has evolved as a means of compensating women for the lack of clitoral stimulation during intercourse. The concept behind foreplay techniques (including clitoral stimulation) is that a man should be able to arouse a woman sufficiently to enable him to continue stimulating her to orgasm through thrusting alone.

One problem with foreplay is that clitoral stimulation needs to continue to the point of orgasm. (Imagine if a woman discontinued penile stimulation just as a man heads for his orgasm!).

*"Our data even suggest that the use of extended and varied techniques may, in not a few cases, interfere with the female's attainment of orgasm. Most females are able to masturbate to orgasm in much less time than it takes them to reach orgasm in coitus which is preceded with extended foreplay, because masturbation is usually continuous and uninterrupted in its build-up to orgasm." (Alfred Kinsey; Sexual behavior in the human female; 1953)*

Foreplay existed well before the role of the clitoris was understood. Male love-making naturally includes manipulation of a woman's breasts and crotch to increase the male arousal needed for intercourse.

More fundamentally though, foreplay techniques do not necessarily assist with women's arousal because sexual arousal depends more on a person's psychological state than on physical stimulation.

If a man has difficulty achieving an erection, it is easy to arouse him by kissing his mouth, stroking his body or masturbating his penis (just for starters!). A man's resulting erection demonstrates his sexual appreciation for his partner. In other words, it is a compliment.

The same pattern does not tend to work for most women. Firstly, women do not have the spontaneous sexual arousal men tend to have from the start and secondly, women do not find the naked body of a sexual partner as arousing as men tend to.

As a result of these two points, a woman is not turned on enough in her mind to respond to physical stimulation in the same way that a man does.

This means that it is quite normal for a woman to experience a lack of arousal during sex.

Many women don't know how their own arousal works so small wonder that men struggle to find techniques to arouse their woman.

## Women's sexual arousal is not automatic

It is a sexual fact: women do not enjoy the same easy and spontaneous sexual arousal and orgasm that men do.

The misconception that intercourse is as easily pleasurable for women as it is for men, leads many men to hope for a long-term sex life without accepting the need to offer their partner other compensations such as more sensual pleasuring.

Women may enjoy admiring a man's body in a tight pair of jeans (or even completely naked) but not usually so much that we orgasm spontaneously. So during masturbation, while men look at pictures of naked women, women tend to use fantasies.

*"The naked truth is that women are more likely to be attracted to a man when he has his clothes on." (Marina Muratore; The Bluffer's Guide to Women; 1998)*

So most women do not tend to reach a state of sexual arousal that could lead quickly to orgasm from just looking at a man and contemplating sex.

Worse than that – when we approach sex with a partner (or masturbation for that matter) we tend to be stone cold in arousal terms. In other words, women do not start a sex session just short of an orgasm.

*"Women aren't automatically excited the way men are. But men seem to expect us to be turned on, and they're annoyed when it doesn't happen." (Kramer & Dunaway; Why Men don't get enough Sex and Women don't get enough Love; 1994)*

Men have an automatic response to the sex hormone testosterone (e.g. a younger man's early morning erection) as well as becoming aroused by seeing or touching an attractive woman.

Women do not experience the same kind of spontaneous sexual arousal. Women's sexual arousal and orgasm are not automatic.

Since they have fewer 'natural' aids for sexual arousal, women's sexual arousal relies on sexual fantasies even with a partner.

# Transferring masturbation techniques to sex

Caroline lived on a farm as a child and was fortunate in having innocent and light-hearted sexual experiences as she grew up.

Even as kids they would play the 'I'll show you mine if you show me yours' game on the bus ride to school.

Her mother insisted that Caroline went on the pill at sixteen. She was not bothered about the sex.

She simply wanted Caroline to be protected from pregnancy. Caroline had her first serious relationship soon after. The sex was adventurous and great fun.

When they split up, Caroline decided to find out about female masturbation to fill the sexual void. She discovered orgasm for the first time.

Young women often don't know how to orgasm and unfortunately sex advice for women is often misleading. The only sure way to find out about orgasm is to try female masturbation.

When Caroline went back to sex with men, she found it relatively easy to adapt her orgasm techniques so that she could masturbate in the presence of a lover.

She did not always declare her use of sexual fantasies to her lovers and some men were not happy for her to masturbate.

They insisted that they had to give her an orgasm. On these occasions, Caroline simply accepted sex without orgasm.

*"The women who had orgasm during intercourse were usually those who, in a sense, did it themselves. They did not expect to 'receive' orgasm automatically from the thrusting of the partner." (Shere Hite; The Hite Reports; 1993)*

Caroline travelled a great deal, working as a fashion model in Europe, the US and South America among other places. In the space of a few years Caroline had many lovers (she mentioned the figure 80).

Many of these were one-night-stands. She simply thought the whole thing was a laugh. As she remembered some of the more outrageous experiences, she giggled.

I asked her whether she had been worried about sexual disease. Caroline admitted that she had taken stupid risks but she had been lucky.

## Sexual arousal versus sexual ego

It made me think of 'Four Weddings and a Funeral' (1994) when Andy MacDowell enumerates her lovers.

Hugh Grant, who had thought of himself as a bit of a playboy, is quite outdone by the time she gets to 32 because he had had "nothing like that many" girlfriends. Andy MacDowell explains that she "grew up in the country – lots of rolling around in haystacks".

Caroline had sex with men for the fun of it. It was not about orgasm; it was sexual ego.

A man's sexual arousal can be very flattering and Caroline liked the fact that they wanted to have sex with her. She felt that she was the one manipulating them. It seemed quite callous to me but then I have always been a bit square.

Plenty of men screw women with shallow intentions. I guess it makes sense that women do the same. Caroline thought it was sweet that I had only had three lovers.

I was never really interested in the ego trip of casual sex. I had romantic notions of love and friendship. As far as sex was concerned, being my partner's lover and pleasuring him was how I showed my love for him.

Caroline married at 23 and has been faithful to her husband. When I talked to her she was a mother of four in her late thirties. She admitted that sex had become more of a duty over time as her priorities changed to focus on the children.

Caroline was very fortunate. Other women may find that transferring orgasm techniques to sex is not so straightforward because their sexual fantasies are more suitable for use alone than with a partner.

Many women have to learn to accept enjoying the sensual or emotional pleasures of physical intimacy with a partner rather than orgasm during sex.

# Positions and techniques for sexual intercourse

Shere Hite explained in the 1970s how the women in her surveys reached orgasm during sex. She compared women's success with orgasm during masturbation to their experience of intercourse and concluded that the difference was due to lack of clitoral stimulation.

*"To have an orgasm during intercourse, there are two ways a woman can increase her chances always remembering that she is adapting her body to less than adequate stimulation.*

*(1) First and most important, she must consciously try to apply her masturbation techniques to intercourse, or experiment to find out what else may work for her to get clitoral stimulation; or,*

*(2) she can work out a sexual relationship with a particular man who can meet her individual needs." (Shere Hite; The Hite Reports; 1993)*

Shere Hite categorised only women who did not manually stimulate the clitoris during sex as able to reach orgasm from intercourse alone.

She concluded that these women were able to orgasm during intercourse because they took steps to ensure that they maximised the effects of indirect clitoral stimulation (from the action of the penis thrusting in the vagina) by finding suitable positions and techniques for intercourse.

## Some women learn to reach orgasm from intercourse eventually

Liz, an attractive professional woman in her late forties, was confident in offering me advice. She told me to buy Alex Comfort's book 'Joy of Sex' (1972) and that "everything else would follow".

She and her partner had found a position for intercourse that made it possible for her to reach orgasm.

They had found this position after a number of years not by explicit discussion but through trial and error. Liz confirmed that she used sexual fantasies during sex for sexual arousal and orgasm.

*"For a woman to orgasm during intercourse, she must adapt her body to inadequate stimulation and so it is essential that she work out this procedure with a regular partner." (Shere Hite; The Hite Reports; 1993)*

Of the women I talked to, those who told me they experienced orgasms during sex were often dismissive of female masturbation.

Without the experience of orgasm from masturbation, a woman accepts sex without orgasm. If over time, she does eventually find a way to make intercourse orgasmic then she only stands to be pleasantly surprised.

Since these women have no other sexual outlet, if they are ever to enjoy indulging their sexual instincts it has to be during sex with a partner.

Few men would settle for the indirect genital stimulation that women obtain from intercourse alone. So why are women happy to settle for less? Possible conclusions are

(1) perhaps men have become de-sensitised through the need for prolonged thrusting or

(2) women, but only some, have evolved the ability to orgasm with less genital stimulation than men need.

A more likely explanation is the tremendous pressure that women are under to explain how they orgasm during vaginal intercourse.

*"Twenty-five to 30 percent of women climax without additional clitoral stimulation. Experts believe these women may have a larger clitoris than usual so it's more easily 'rubbed' by a thrusting penis." (Tracey Cox; Hot Sex; 1998)*

Liz was not relaxed discussing sex and admitted that she was unenthusiastic about female masturbation.

Ten or more years into a relationship, many couples will be in their thirties. The man, perhaps less trigger-happy, may be able to spend longer stimulating his partner through thrusting.

The woman may find that her body is more receptive to being aroused. A healthy amount of 'inhibited' under-the-covers sex (with the lights off) would actually facilitate a woman's use of sexual fantasies.

# Difficulties in applying orgasm techniques to sex

Women's orgasm techniques leant from masturbation (including both clitoral stimulation and use of sexual fantasies) are not always as easy to transfer to sex with a partner as experts imply.

*"Among all types of sexual activity, masturbation is, however, the one in which the female most frequently reaches orgasm.*

*Even in her marital coitus the average female fails to achieve orgasm in a fair proportion of her contacts ... but in 95 per cent or more of all her masturbation, she does reach orgasm." (Alfred Kinsey; Sexual behavior in the human female; 1953)*

My experience was that the contrast between sex and masturbation alone was so extreme that it never even occurred to me to try to combine the two experiences.

Men dislike wearing condoms because they reduce the stimulation of the penis. Imagine then the position of a woman during intercourse!

Intercourse without any additional clitoral stimulation is like wearing a rubber boot as a condom!

*"Most women conclude at some point in their lives that the female body is badly designed." (Marina Muratore; The Bluffer's Guide to Women; 1998)*

Men's sexual arousal is so much more obvious and easier to achieve: you touch them just about anywhere, wear something provocative or nothing at all.

In the absence of my own sexual arousal, it was much easier to accept my partner's love-making and facilitate his orgasm.

Women's sexual arousal and orgasm are not automatic but neither is it obvious (even to a woman) how women's sexual arousal with a partner works.

I did not know where to start to suggest what my partner might try to arouse me.

It can appear to women that men orgasm 'naturally' (without any artificial psychological aids) but even for men, achieving orgasm often involves making some special effort.

For example, most men actively seek out sources, e.g. pornography, to assist with their sexual arousal and to help develop their fantasies for use both during masturbation alone and during sex.

**Female masturbation may help but is no guarantee**

I had honestly never considered masturbation to be a legitimate part of sex. Masturbation was a mechanism for assisting me in getting to sleep and for enjoying the pleasures of orgasm.

Even though I knew that sexual fantasies worked when I was alone, it was as if it would be an insult to my partner to start reading a sexy story when his body was next to mine.

Women who say they orgasm from sexual intercourse, but do not masturbate, do not necessarily have it all figured out; it's just that they have no comparison.

There is even sometimes an implication that female masturbation may prevent a woman from having an orgasm with a partner.

This is, of course, based purely on superstition rather than logic as Shere Hite explains.

*"Perhaps if you masturbate, you can get a fixation on your clitoris and are thus unable to come during intercourse."*

*"The fact that I've been masturbating since I was ten has made it more difficult for me to orgasm vaginally."*

These two quotes came from women who replied to Shere Hite's survey. She replies:

*"The truth, however, is just the opposite: masturbation increases your ability to orgasm in general, and also your ability to orgasm during intercourse. Why not? It's the same stimulation. ...*

*Of course, masturbation to orgasm does not automatically enable you to orgasm during intercourse. There is no mystical connection between the two – just the practical experience with orgasm – how it feels and how to get it." (Shere Hite; The Hite Reports; 1993)*

# Women's psychological sexual arousal

Even today, female sexual arousal is shrouded in mystery. Female orgasm is assumed to happen 'naturally' or with the assistance of a loving partner.

No one needs to tell men how their sexual arousal works. Boys experience spontaneous erections so that male masturbation is inevitable.

Girls do not develop the same genital focus and so they end up confusing the emotions of sex with true sexual arousal and orgasm. Since many women never discover orgasm through masturbation, they have no way of knowing what it is or how to achieve it.

Men's easy arousal leads to the misconception that sexual arousal relies purely on PHYSICAL stimulation.

Yet anyone who is familiar with orgasm will know that genital stimulation only works if there is accompanying PSYCHOLOGICAL arousal.

So although it is often implied that a woman can become sexually aroused during sex through physical stimulation, it is highly unlikely that clitoral stimulation alone will lead to female orgasm unless a woman first knows how to achieve the kind of psychological arousal that causes genital stimulation to lead to orgasm.

A woman learns from masturbation that her sexual arousal arises from an appreciation of eroticism through sexual fantasies.

When her psychological state of arousal reaches a peak, synchronised with explicit stimulation of the clitoris, she is able to reach orgasm.

In other words, psychological sexual arousal is not an optional extra but a necessary prerequisite in order for a person to enjoy orgasm.

After all the role of the clitoris (as the female sex organ) was identified, not from women's experience of sex but, from their experience of masturbation.

Whereas men use EROTIC IMAGES during masturbation, women use EROTIC STORIES (involved psychological and sexually explicit scenarios) to achieve the levels of mental arousal needed for orgasm.

A woman is likely to have much greater difficulty transferring her sexual fantasies to sex with a partner than men typically have with images.

The psychological and emotional context of masturbation alone is so different to 'making love' with a partner that a woman may never even consider using fantasy during sex.

Women, whose fantasies have a relatively kinky psychological context to them (as many do – usually quite surreal), often find it difficult to relate these to real life sexual activity with a partner.

Another reason women may find it difficult to transfer their fantasies from masturbation alone to sex is because achieving the arousal to reach orgasm from fantasy alone requires a high degree of mental focus.

Not only can this be difficult to do in the presence of another person, even a lover, but such a mental block-out is often incompatible with 'making love' to a partner.

Men's psychological transition from masturbation to sex is easy because their arousal comes, in part, from an appreciation of their partner's sexual attributes, which is a natural substitute for images.

But it doesn't make sense to assume that women can find a partner's naked body arousing enough for orgasm during sex when they don't use images during masturbation.

Since relatively few women masturbate, many women are unfamiliar with orgasm through genital stimulation. They prefer to limit their sexual experiences to vaginal intercourse.

Consequently, although few men would attempt to reach orgasm without stimulating their penis, many experts still assert that clitoral stimulation is not needed for a woman to orgasm during sex.

If men need to use techniques, including eroticism for arousal and genital stimulation for orgasm, then it is highly likely that women might need to use similar orgasm techniques if they are to experience orgasm.

Conversely, if we truly believe that women achieve orgasm without the arousal techniques (psychological and physical stimuli) and learning processes (masturbation) that men typically employ then women would have to be considerably MORE sexual than men are.

# True female sexual arousal and orgasm

Any talk of sexual arousal and orgasm, usually focuses on women since men's sexual arousal and orgasm tend to be a given.

It is unthinkable that anyone needs to tell a man how to orgasm.

By the time they are teenagers, boys have discovered how to enjoy their own sexual arousal, by looking at images of naked women.

Likewise no one tells a boy that to orgasm he also needs to stimulate his penis.

Most women never masturbate and so they never learn that real female orgasms arise (just as male orgasms do) from bringing a mental state of sexual arousal to orgasm using genital stimulation (of the clitoris).

Given the popular belief that female arousal and orgasm during sex are easily achieved, many women simply assume that they experience these sensations as a natural part of their sexual relationship.

## Sexual arousal (using erotic images/fantasies)

We know that men achieve sexual arousal through an appreciation of eroticism (explicitly sexual images) and yet it is often implied that women's sexual arousal arises from their loving emotions for their partner.

As if we are all as innocent as Snow White, it is rarely acknowledged that if women are to orgasm, they need to make conscious effort to occupy their minds with erotic thoughts (a process which happens much more subconsciously for the male mind).

Men's minds become aroused so instantaneously that we gain the impression that physical stimulation alone gives them an erection (causes sexual arousal).

Young men transition naturally to sex because the body of a real sexual partner substitutes for the images from pornographic magazines.

Imagine being a woman, who approaches sex with no hint of an erection!

Women do not react as men do to the sight of naked images (even a lover's body).

This is why women don't pay men to do lap-dancing, pole-dancing or other sexually provocative teasing using their bodies.

Women's fantasies work well when alone but can be difficult to relate to day-to-day sexual opportunities because they are often based on quite surreal erotic scenarios.

## Clitoral stimulation

The only reason anyone would stimulate their genitals (casual curiosity aside) is because they know that with sufficient levels of sexual arousal, genital stimulation leads to orgasm.

The average woman does not approach sex looking for clitoral stimulation because she is unlikely to be sexually aroused enough for genital stimulation to make sense.

A woman needs to know how to become mentally aroused before genital stimulation by anyone (either themselves or a partner) can be effective.

For those women who do enjoy eroticism, there is a chance that they will explore their own sexual arousal enough to discover masturbation and to make the connection between genital stimulation (of the clitoris) and orgasm.

We know that women need clitoral stimulation for orgasm from female masturbation.

But even during female masturbation, clitoral stimulation only works once a woman has achieved sufficient MENTAL AROUSAL by using sexual fantasies.

Even if a woman knows that she needs sexual fantasies to orgasm from female masturbation, she may well struggle with the same techniques during sex because of the mental focus required to reach orgasm through sexual fantasies alone.

## The ideal male lover

Alex Comfort's book 'The Joy of Sex' (1972) documented primarily positions for intercourse that he and his mistress had found pleasurable as part of their affair. The affair was quite open and the two lovers shared the family home with his wife and son.

Don't get me wrong. What Alex Comfort achieved was amazing at the time. His book brought eroticism into respectable marital sex and promoted the idea that a woman could hope to enjoy sexual pleasure with a lover.

One has to ask though. Why could a man pleasure his mistress and yet not (presumably) his wife?

As a younger, more impressionable woman, was it possible that his mistress was impressed by more than his sexual ego?

The fact is that a successful sexual relationship is more often than not defined by the ease of the man's sexual arousal, not the woman's.

So naturally sex is easier for a younger woman. The woman's role in sex is simply to accept her lover's love-making.

Equally male sexual success is viewed through the eyes of the beholder. A wife sees only the man. The mistress (younger woman) sees a sex god.

I hate to disillusion anyone, particularly when it comes to sexual fantasy. But is has to be said that if a sexual technique was infallible then it would work with every woman. The usual explanation for women who remain unmoved is that they are frigid.

The misconception that vaginal intercourse, or any physical stimulation technique for that matter, will lead to spontaneous female sexual arousal leads to women taking a passive stance in sex.

They continue to hope indefinitely that a man, knowing how to reach his own orgasm, will somehow know how to make 'a miracle' happen for his woman too.

We all assume that a woman needs to do nothing during sex except wait for her man to deliver her sexual pleasure on a plate.

Sadly we are handicapped by our faith in the sexual fantasy that male thrusting alone will eventually lead to female orgasm.

*"... a woman's sexual fulfilment is much more complex than a man's. She requires a man with a skilful touch, lots of time, and a loving attitude.*

*For a man, once he is aroused, it is generally a given that he will have an orgasm." (John Gray; Mars & Venus in the Bedroom; 1995)*

You don't say?! The trouble is that even though experts refer to women's sexual dysfunction, no one has any answers for a lack of female orgasm during sex.

I was left with a sense of hopelessness: the implication was that lack of orgasm was abnormal and yet there was no apparent solution. At the same time, it was also implied that I was expecting too much.

This is my main gripe with 'Joy of Sex' which is still published today without any acknowledgement

(1) that intercourse is unlikely to be as easily orgasmic for women as it is for men and

(2) that physical stimulation techniques of any kind are useless without accompanying psychological arousal.

No sex manual ever talks about how women get turned on enough to orgasm.

The implication is that women can achieve the same levels of arousal from physical sex play that men do.

And yet not only do women not approach sex already aroused as men tend to be but also their minds and bodies do not respond as men's do.

For one, male nudity and the kind of physical sex play that men enjoy, do not cause a woman to become aroused enough for orgasm. So a woman needs to find a way to incorporate her fantasies into her sex life if she is ever to experience an orgasm.

Anyone, male or female, whether alone or with a partner, takes a state of mental arousal to orgasm through genital stimulation.

So, firstly clitoral stimulation is needed for female orgasm but MUCH MORE IMPORTANTLY a woman needs to be mentally aroused enough for genital stimulation to be effective. Intercourse is key to reproduction but not to women's sexual arousal.

# Women's sexual arousal tends to be assumed or overlooked

Much of what is known about female orgasm comes from women's experience of masturbation.

Shere Hite's work focused on female masturbation and the clitoris.

As a research student in the United States in the early 1970s, Shere (pronounced 'sherry') Hite circulated a lengthy questionnaire through women's magazines and to passers-by on the street.

She asked women to answer direct questions about orgasm anonymously.

Only 30% of her respondents said that they were able to regularly reach orgasm from intercourse whereas most women who masturbated found it easy to reach orgasm.

By comparing the two experiences, Shere Hite concluded that women will find orgasm more difficult to achieve through intercourse because of the reduced clitoral stimulation.

The Hite Report explained why intercourse is unlikely to lead to female orgasm but it did not explain why a woman cannot orgasm with a partner by obtaining the clitoral stimulation needed for orgasm either from manual stimulation of the clitoris or through oral sex.

In common with other sex researchers, Hite's focus was primarily on the physical aspects of sex.

Of course, the other characteristic of masturbation that is missing during sex is fantasy.

That is unless a woman finds a way to incorporate sexual fantasies into her sex life.

Later when I came across the fact that some women use fantasy to orgasm during sex, I was amazed.

I could not imagine how it was possible since my use of fantasy requires a highly focused state of mind that is incompatible with sex with a partner.

## Women use sexual fantasies both alone and with a partner

The realisation that some women do use fantasy during sex (and I was able to confirm this with a few of the woman I spoke to) allowed me to see a parallel with my experience of orgasm from masturbation.

I realised that although I used clitoral stimulation during masturbation it only worked when combined with an appreciation of eroticism through sexual fantasies.

Sheila Kitzinger made the point that sex, especially sexual arousal, arises primarily in the brain.

I then realised that most accounts of sex focus heavily on PHYSICAL stimulation techniques and that PSYCHOLOGICAL arousal tends to be simply assumed or overlooked.

I concluded that this is probably because psychological sexual arousal for men is usually a given.

My suggestion is that just as men need EROTIC IMAGES and stimulation of the PENIS for orgasm, women need EROTIC STORIES and stimulation of the CLITORIS for orgasm.

This is my explanation of how I have reached that conclusion and how it fits with men's experiences of sexual arousal and orgasm.

It makes sense that women will need to use fantasy more than men to reach orgasm during sex.

Women have much lower levels of testosterone, the hormone that boosts sex drive.

Also the naked male body does not cause women to become aroused enough for orgasm (otherwise women would buy porn as men do).

There is no logical reason why sexual fantasies should not be a part of our sex life (whether or not admitted to a partner).

This conclusion helps explain why foreplay techniques may not be as effective as we would hope because, just as during female masturbation, women's sexual arousal relies on sexual fantasies.

# Lack of orgasm is not a sexual dysfunction

It is often suggested that a lack of female orgasm during sex is a sign of sexual dysfunction but the truth is that this is simply the way things are for women who hope for orgasm from their sexual relationships.

A woman is lucky to orgasm by any means.

The belief that women orgasm 'naturally' during sex is based on fantasy (erotica and pornography) and contradicts the conclusions of the scientific researchers.

*"In fact, for over 70 per cent of women, intercourse – the penis thrusting in the vagina – did not regularly lead to orgasm. ...*

*In other words, not to have orgasm from intercourse is the experience of the majority of women." (Shere Hite; The Hite Reports; 1993)*

Some people suggest that lack of orgasm is not a problem or that it is unimportant. This may be true for women who never masturbate because they never know what orgasm is.

But for women who are familiar with orgasm from masturbation, it is frustrating to be told that female orgasm is unimportant when there is so much sympathy for men's sexual performance problems and so much insistence that women should orgasm during sex.

Women need to be told the facts:

*"This means that something between 36 and 44 per cent of the females in the sample had responded to orgasm in a part but not in all of their coitus in marriage.*

*About **one-third** of those females had responded only a small part of the time,*

***another third** had responded more or less half of the time, and*

*the **other third** had responded a major portion of the time, even though it was not a hundred per cent of the time."*

*(Alfred Kinsey; Sexual behavior in the human female; 1953)*

## Intercourse is not designed to facilitate female orgasm

Anyone, male or female, whether alone or with a partner, uses genital stimulation to take a state of mental arousal to orgasm.

So during masturbation a man stimulates his penis and a woman stimulates her clitoris.

Psychological arousal arises from an appreciation of eroticism and is the most important factor in enjoying our sexuality since without it genital stimulation is ineffective.

During masturbation a man uses EROTIC IMAGES (pornography) for psychological sexual arousal and a woman uses EROTIC SCENARIOS (sexual fantasies).

If a woman wants to experience orgasm during sex, she needs to ensure that:

(1) she obtains the DIRECT clitoral stimulation needed for orgasm (manual or oral); and

(2) she finds a way to incorporate her fantasies into her sexual relationship with a partner.

Men are lucky because (since male orgasm/ejaculation is required for reproduction) intercourse naturally provides both the penile stimulation and the visual turn-on of a sexual partner's naked body that they need for orgasm.

The surreal nature of women's sexual fantasies makes them much more difficult to map onto a woman's real life sexual relationship.

Some women find that their mind-based sexual fantasies are unsuitable for use with a partner.

An alternative is for a woman to enjoy her own sexual arousal by using her sexual fantasies to inspire a wider variety of physical sex play with a partner.

# The 10 facts of female sexuality

Beliefs about female sexuality are more often based on fantasy than facts.

These are the 10 essential facts that every sexual woman should know:

### (1) Enjoying orgasm through genital stimulation

Anyone, male or female, alone or with a partner, uses genital stimulation to take a mental state of sexual arousal (achieved by appreciating eroticism) to orgasm.

### (2) The role of psychological sexual arousal

During masturbation men use erotic images (usually the naked body and sexual attributes of a sexual partner) and women use erotic scenarios (usually stories with a complex psychological context) for psychological sexual arousal.

### (3) The role of genital stimulation

During masturbation men stimulate their penis, women stimulate their clitoris (the female sex organ) BUT genital stimulation only leads to orgasm once a person is mentally aroused.

So clitoral stimulation does not by itself guarantee orgasm.

For example, even during female masturbation clitoral stimulation leads to orgasm ONLY when it is combined with the use of sexual fantasies.

### (4) Fantasies can be difficult to use with a partner

Men's arousal mechanism of erotic images transfers fairly naturally from masturbation (pornography) to sex (the body of a real life sexual partner). Women's fantasies do not transfer nearly as easily.

Some women find that mind-based fantasies are incompatible with sex.

### (5) Clitoral stimulation can be less effective during sex

Men approach sex with a desire to stimulate their penis (via intercourse or other means) because they are already aroused. A woman's challenge is to discover how to achieve sufficient sexual arousal during sex for clitoral stimulation to be effective.

### (6) Some women do use their sexual fantasies during sex

Women do not find a man's body or his sexual attributes arousing enough for orgasm, otherwise women would enjoy pornography, pole-dancing and lap-dancing bars as men do. Some women are able to use their fantasies during sex.

Alternatively a woman may learn how to enjoy a form of physical sexual arousal and orgasm during fantasy-inspired sex play with a partner that is highly pleasurable although perhaps not as sexually satisfying as orgasm through fantasy.

### (7) Some women do use clitoral stimulation during sex

Unfortunately, intercourse alone provides insufficient clitoral stimulation for orgasm. Shere Hite explained in 'The Hite Report' (1976) how SOME women learn over time (often years) to orgasm during intercourse.

EITHER they find a suitable position that maximises the indirect clitoral stimulation OR they stimulate their clitoris directly by hand during intercourse. Naturally, any woman who can orgasm through oral sex is also able to enjoy orgasm with a partner.

### (8) Confusion over female orgasm

Many women dislike the eroticism that leads to sexual arousal and so they never discover masturbation. They never realise not only that orgasm is a significant pleasure but also that a woman needs to know how to achieve it. Orgasms don't 'just happen'.

Often it is only women who masturbate who realise that orgasm is missing from sex with a partner. Many other women assume that they orgasm from male thrusting alone even though intercourse does not provide sufficient clitoral stimulation for orgasm.

### (9) Many women never orgasm by any means

Many women never orgasm during sex: not because women are dysfunctional but because sex is not designed to facilitate female orgasm either physically or psychologically. Female orgasm represents one of Nature's redundancies.

A woman is fortunate if she discovers orgasm by any means. Unlike men, women are much less versatile in how they are able to orgasm.

A woman often finds only one way to orgasm and unfortunately the easiest way is through masturbation alone.

**(10) Enjoying sexual pleasure with a partner**

Romance does not help directly with female orgasm but it may cause a woman to be more amenable to sex. Many women enjoy sharing physical intimacy with a loving partner regardless of their own ability to orgasm during sex.

Men approach sex with a genital focus because they are already aroused so they often fail to engage on the sensual aspects of sex. A woman accepts that female orgasm is difficult to achieve so she hopes to enjoy more general pleasuring with a lover.

## Stories: Enjoying sex play

# Eroticism

Men and women live in different worlds when it comes to attitudes to eroticism. I suggested that most women today know how to pleasure a man but a British sex expert (male) disagreed:

"They haven't a clue, and even if they knew, most wouldn't do it."

A joke illustrates the point: "What is the difference between a job and a wife?" Answer "After ten years a job still sucks!".

Unfortunately many people still believe in sheltering young women from eroticism and so girls are told the basic reproductive facts but nothing of sexual pleasure.

We are confident in telling girls about vaginal intercourse because it is the means of producing children. It also happens to be one of the easiest ways for a woman to provide a man with sexual release.

Putting it crudely, masturbation by hand or mouth not only involves more work but is also more explicitly sexual.

Since women are not necessarily hoping for orgasm, they can be easily shocked by sex (in the context of sex play rather than trying for a baby). Women often don't know how to orgasm and so they associate sexual pleasure with immorality.

Men do hope for orgasm; and so eroticism and sex play, including activities other than intercourse, are more important to men.

## Women do not get the same sexual pleasure

Women have difficulty understanding men's passion for sexual pleasure. The film 'Indecent Proposal' (1993) might be a little far-fetched, but nevertheless we accept that a man might pay as much as $1,000,000 for sex.

Equally the film reflects women's aversion to non-relationship sex: why else is the idea of sex with a good-looking millionaire so repulsive?

Men experience a purely physical reaction to seeing a woman's body that has nothing to do with personal relationships. So, men engage lap dancers, visit go-go bars and watch topless reviews because they enjoy the sensations of sexual arousal that come from the physical proximity of a semi-naked woman.

Conversely, women do not tend to pay even for this relatively mild physical gratification because the female mind and body simply do not respond as a man's mind and body do.

Women's sexual arousal and orgasm are not automatic and so women have to learn about their sexual arousal. Women do experience lust (or the desire to get laid) but they often need to be enticed into sex whereas men rarely need encouragement.

*" – men wish that women's sexuality was like theirs, which it isn't. Male sexual response is far brisker and more automatic: it is triggered easily by things, like putting a quarter in a vending machine.*

*Consequently, at a certain level and for all men, girls and parts of girls are, at this stimulus level unpeople. That isn't incompatible with their being people too*

*Your clothes, breasts, odour, etc. aren't what he loves instead of you – simply the things he needs in order to set sex in motion to express love. Women seem to find this hard to understand." (Alex Comfort; Joy of Sex; 1972)*

A man's arousal and orgasm are pretty much a given during sex. But a woman can take part in sexual activity without ever becoming aroused or reaching orgasm. So even women who have sex for years do not necessarily know how to orgasm.

In order to qualify as 'sexually experienced', it is quality (breadth of experience) not quantity (years or partners) that counts. As a minimum, a sexually experienced woman should

(1) be able to masturbate to orgasm alone,

(2) have explored clitoral stimulation with a partner via masturbation and oral sex and

(3) have attempted a variety of positions for sexual intercourse.

In order to discover how her arousal works, a woman needs to be positive enough about eroticism to be willing to explore her sexual fantasies. Unfortunately the average woman (and this includes many 'sex experts') lacks this experience.

# How do women achieve sexual arousal during sex?

Some women happily accept the modern media's portrayal of women as complete sexual beings, for whom spontaneously orgasmic sex is as much of a given as it is for a man.

Other women find that orgasms do not 'just happen'.

Pressure to find answers comes not only from the woman who hopes to enjoy what is supposed to be mutual sexual pleasure but also from her partner who hopes to share his enjoyment of sex with a lover.

The big hole in all the explanations is: what do women use for sexual arousal, that is their psychological arousal, during sex?

It's fine during female masturbation alone because a woman can focus fully on fantasy. It is likely to be much more difficult for a woman to generate the same conditions during sex.

This has nothing to do with inhibition, personal embarrassment or the desire to put a man's needs first.

A woman's use of sexual fantasy is like deep meditation. It takes tremendous focus and concentration to reach orgasm from sexual fantasies alone.

After decades of trying different orgasm techniques with a partner I have not been able to replicate the kind of orgasm that I get from masturbation using fantasy.

I do get some really nice feelings from anal stimulation but these are quite different physical orgasms (not the same sense of sexual release).

I am willing to go through the personal embarrassment of revealing the exact nature of my sexual experiences in the hope that other women might be encouraged to come forward and do the same.

Naturally none of us can ever know whether our sexual experiences are 'normal' or 'ideal'. Just as, if we asked someone to say what they enjoyed about a piece of music, there would be no 'correct' answer.

Everyone is likely to enjoy different aspects of what they hear in a piece of music. Nevertheless, as a relative philistine when it comes to music, I can still aspire to understand at least some of what can be appreciated by a more informed and more experienced listener.

Likewise my sexual experiences are likely to be different to other women. I read erotic novels as a teenager, discovered female masturbation to orgasm at the age of seventeen and then spent decades trying a variety of orgasm techniques with a partner.

How many women put this much effort and enthusiasm into exploring and understanding their sexual arousal?

I have paid money and faced personal humiliation in order to have my sexuality confirmed as completely normal. Yet I have to explain to my daughters that official sex information around the world continues to set unrealistic expectations for female orgasm.

Women with my experience continue to be told that they are sexually dysfunctional. This is not the case. I want to put the record straight for future generations of women. It is wrong that couples continue to be misled by what is published about female sexuality.

It is also not right that there is so little information today to help women understand how to achieve the kind of sexual arousal that leads to orgasm through genital stimulation.

No one ever suggests that men's arousal depends on their loving emotions. Likewise it is inconceivable that anyone would suggest that genital stimulation is irrelevant to male orgasm.

My motivation to pursue this topic has been driven by the unreasonably defensive response I have had from others.

I have asked legitimate and logical questions and been totally honest about my sexual experiences.

In return, I have been patronised and given emotional answers by people who never volunteer to support their opinions with their own personal experiences.

Women need to tell men that we want different things in return for sex: companionship, mutual respect and mutual support.

Orgasm would be great but, if not, then more selfless and sensual pleasuring where they put their own orgasm to one side.

## Lust is good

I suppose that I have been lucky. My sexual desire to enjoy my own sexual arousal and orgasm is evidently unusual for a woman.

I know that this is unusual because most women talk of love, trust and commitment.

From time to time, I positively enjoy jumping on my man. But it doesn't work like that, does it?

Even if a woman climbs on top (done it many times) she's still stimulating his penis with her vagina.

I always enjoyed flirtation and provoking a sexual response in a man.

Other women often seem to be more at ease with the whole female package, including pregnancy and mothering. I preferred the image of the woman who aspired to mutual sexual pleasure with her man.

Well it's not that easy. At least I never found it easy.

I guess I was hoping for the wrong things. Women hope for babies and I got those.

Men hope for good sex. For me though, I always felt that sex was over-sold, leastways where women are concerned.

I haven't met a woman who has even hinted at lust. There's superficial bravado but no heart-to-hearts.

Not one woman has ever talked about sexual frustration. I reckon there's plenty about if you're a woman.

Someone please tell me I'm wrong and that if I were a true woman I would be happy with loving feelings from my sexual relationships.

I guess I landed on the wrong planet and out there somewhere things are more equal. Men share the babies and women share the joy of sexual lust.

Until then, dream on babes...

Images of women from pornography often define the 'sexual woman'.

Yet such women are PAID not just for being attractive but more importantly because they are talented at putting on an act. Faking arousal and orgasm keeps the customers happy.

Men also often pay for dates that lead to casual sex, which is vastly improved by the ego factor (the thrill of the chase and the conquest for both sexes).

This competition silences women in long-term relationships (who can't possibly compete) and makes it difficult to identify women's true sexual desire, including their motivation to initiate sex by enjoying erotic material, masturbating and exploring genitally based sexual activities with a partner over the LONGER term.

Female arousal is taboo because

(1) men don't want their sexual fantasies dashed and

(2) women don't want to be thought to be sexually inadequate.

Sadly male and female sexuality are different because we have complementary not identical roles.

The fact is that female orgasm is much, much more difficult to achieve with a partner than is commonly suggested.

The core of the problem is that women use sexual fantasies during masturbation but these are often difficult to use to reach orgasm with a partner especially if they are surreal or kinky in nature (which they usually are).

I am not trying to belittle men by suggesting that women deliberately deceive them (although this is sometimes true).

Equally, I'm not trying to belittle women who are convinced that orgasm happens the first time and every time during sex.

I'm just pointing out to those who know what orgasm is from masturbation that other women are, often quite innocently, mistaken.

Since they never masturbate they never learn how their sexual arousal works or how to reach orgasm by any means.

Think yourself lucky…

# Why sex is fun

If the male sex drive only involved a desire for orgasm, then men would be happy settling for masturbation instead of sex. No doubt a great deal of time and money would be saved but life wouldn't be so much fun!

Men have evolved a desire for penetration above all else because it leads to reproduction. Equally, most women have little desire to masturbate and are more likely to consider sexual activity solely in terms of their relationship with a partner.

The fun of sex for a woman is being the object of a man's desire. Her conquest is attracting his attention and causing him to want her sexually.

Having caught her man, a woman needs to keep him by accepting his love-making and playing along with his sexual fantasy of causing female sexual arousal through thrusting.

As a consequence, sex is a sociable affair and masturbation rates a poor second best. For men at least. Women who masturbate may disagree.

Men are much more easily aroused. So they have a strong genital focus in sex but a woman appreciates the sensuality of her whole body (her power to arouse a man). Women naturally have a lower desire for orgasm and ability to become aroused.

Very occasionally I experience a strong sexual urge or desire to interact physically with my partner. Sadly I am frustrated every time because there doesn't appear to be a way to express my sexuality with a partner that leads easily to orgasm.

Being the object of his desire is one thing but how does a woman use a man's body to achieve her own orgasm?

Often it is easier for a couple to accept that the man goes for his orgasm and the woman simply comes along for the ride.

Other times, when she is feeling turned on they may decide to take a different approach to sex by focusing on her sexual arousal.

## How a woman can enjoy her own sexual arousal during sex

Sex, unfortunately, is not designed to facilitate female orgasm, either physically or psychologically. So a woman has to learn how to enjoy her own arousal and orgasm during sex.

Orgasm is achieved through genital stimulation (penis or clitoris) so a woman will need to ensure that she obtains more clitoral stimulation than is provided naturally by vaginal intercourse.

Some women find a suitable position for intercourse that maximises the clitoral stimulation the woman receives during thrusting, or she (or her partner) will stimulate her clitoris by hand together with intercourse.

In order for genital stimulation to be effective (to lead to orgasm) a person must first be sexually aroused. Men achieve sexual arousal through erotic images but women use erotic scenarios.

So, if she wants to experience orgasm with a partner a woman will need to find a way to bring her fantasies into her real life sexual relationship.

Sometimes I am frustrated because fantasy seems such an artificial means of achieving orgasm. I want to get as turned on as men do by engaging in physical sex play with a lover, so that I can share my orgasm with a partner.

Sadly fantasy provides the only way for me to experience the kind of sexual arousal that leads to the most satisfying kind of orgasm.

Some women do succeed with using their mind-based fantasies during sex but others, like myself, find that the mental focus required to make such fantasies effective is incompatible with sex with a partner.

An alternative is for the woman to read some of her favourite erotica immediately prior to sex and as part of foreplay (man doing all the work!).

A woman can also enjoy her own physical arousal by incorporating some of the ideas from her fantasies into physical sex play with her partner. Sharing sexual fantasies like this often takes years and a great deal of trust between lovers.

# Difficulty reaching orgasm during sex

The website 'Go Ask Alice!' confirms that it is likely to be difficult for a woman to reach orgasm through intercourse since the clitoris is not located inside a woman's vagina. They suggest that women should aim to have their orgasm during other sexual activity either before or after intercourse.

Any woman who can climax with a partner either by using orgasm techniques from masturbation or through oral sex can at least enjoy orgasm during love-making. The problem occurs when a woman never learns how to orgasm during sex because she does not succeed with applying orgasm techniques to sex.

*"a considerable portion of the sexual maladjustment in marriage arises from the fact that the average female is aroused sexually less often than the average male, and that she frequently has difficulty in reaching orgasm in her marital coitus." (Alfred Kinsey; Sexual behavior in the human female; 1953)*

Men's sexuality is straightforward in the sense that they get turned-on, they stimulate their penis and mostly they orgasm. Men can masturbate regardless of whether they stand, sit or lie down. They orgasm from oral sex, intercourse etc.

Women's sexuality is not nearly as flexible. Most women only ever find one way to orgasm and the easiest way is through masturbation alone. Even then, most women masturbate in a very specific way.

For example, I only ever masturbate on my front with my legs mostly together and by using my fingers. I have tried a vibrator but it didn't do anything for me. I have tried oral sex and that also does nothing for me. My fingers appear to provide the best focused stimulation that I need for orgasm.

So the dilemma for the so-called pre-orgasmic woman, who can only orgasm during masturbation, is that she is never able to orgasm during sex. She has to accept that she has her orgasm during time alone and that sex with a partner involves making the most of other aspects of physical intimacy including enjoying a man's arousal and more sensual pleasuring.

## Modern hopes for female orgasm during sex

Sex with a partner can quite legitimately include activities other than vaginal intercourse but ultimately most of us end up with a pattern for sex that includes intercourse or penetrative sex at some point. This may simply be because Nature intended that men should get the best possible sexual satisfaction from orgasm achieved by thrusting during penetrative sex.

*"One thing that all words about sex have in common, the four-letter words, medical words and euphemisms, is that they include the idea of penetration of a vagina by a penis. You haven't really "made love" unless this has happened." (Sheila Kitzinger; Woman's Experience of Sex; 1983).*

So the fact that intercourse does not facilitate female orgasm is still an issue even if a woman can orgasm by other means. A woman who is familiar with orgasm from masturbation is likely to be less accepting of a role focused on facilitating male orgasm. Anyone who is familiar with orgasm is likely to struggle to see the point of sexual activity without their own orgasm.

Either way whether she is familiar with orgasm or not, in the absence of her own sexual arousal, a woman approaches her sexual relationship with a man through emotional (loving and romantic) feelings rather than sexual.

Romance does not help with female orgasm but it may cause a woman to be more amenable to sex by accepting her partner's love-making.

*"Most women want affection and closeness and they obtain great sexual enjoyment if their partner arouses them, by stimulating their erotic areas gently and seductively; but once a woman has experienced an orgasm, she wants that too." (Derek Llewellyn-Jones; EveryMan; 1980)*

What amazes me is that everyone understands immediately if a man has even temporary difficulties with arousal but my dilemma meets with incomprehension. Why are you bothered about female orgasm when other women appear content?

Sex is an unbelievably embarrassing topic and given the defensiveness and lack of sympathy I have met with I can understand why.

# Women who enjoy their own sexual arousal

Perhaps it would be simpler if I explained that I am targeting women who masturbate regularly in order to enjoy their own sexual arousal and orgasm.

Other women can be totally convinced that sexual arousal is easy and I am very happy for them. But if you do not masturbate then you cannot usefully comment on the experiences of women who do. This is simply a fact.

Imagine that, as a man, you are comparing notes with another man who has never masturbated to orgasm. Presumably he has never had the urge to masturbate or perhaps he simply lacked the curiosity to explore his own sexual arousal.

Anyway, the first time you have sex you are devastated when 'the real thing' turns out to be totally un-arousing. Then you learn that experts concluded decades ago that vaginal intercourse does not provide the PHYSICAL stimulation that a person of your gender needs for orgasm. This makes orgasm highly unlikely even if a person knows that they need to compensate for the lack of genital stimulation.

There you are, with years of experience of your own sexual arousal through masturbation, knowing that you have never experienced the same kind of orgasm with a partner. This same man assures you that orgasm during sex was always easy for him: the first time and every time. He confidently informs you that orgasm is simply a matter of finding a loving partner who knows how to give you an orgasm.

Much later, you also realise that without the ability to get yourself as aroused in your mind during sex as you do during masturbation (imagine here that instead of using erotic IMAGES you use erotic SCENARIOS), there is no means of generating the PSYCHOLOGICAL arousal that causes genital stimulation to lead to orgasm.

So how does this other man generate the sexual arousal that he has never been motivated to enjoy by himself? Especially when he appears to be oblivious to the need for psychological or physical stimulation techniques to compensate for the known facts of his anatomy and psychology for your sex. How can it be that everything works for him WITHOUT HIM EVEN TRYING?

The answer is that it doesn't because he has never aspired to the same experience in the first place.

If a woman believes she has the same kind of orgasms that men experience, then why would she not masturbate as men do? The problem with sex advice today is that women who never masturbate, advise women who are familiar with orgasm from female masturbation. This is wrong because you cannot advise someone unless you have more experience than they have.

Women who know how to achieve their own sexual arousal have an unusually high (for women) appreciation of eroticism and so they understand that orgasm involves a release of sexual feelings, not loving feelings. Consequently, true sexual arousal relies on a person's ability to appreciate eroticism (images for men; scenarios for women).

*"Human males throughout history and among all peoples have been most often concerned with the sexual activities of the female when those activities served the male's own purposes, and her solitary and even homosexual activities have often been ignored." (Alfred Kinsey; Sexual behavior in the human female 1953)*

Despite acknowledging men's biased interest in female sexuality, Kinsey does not comment on the pressure that men inherently place on women by describing them as 'sexually frigid' and in modern times as 'sexually dysfunctional', not when they do not masturbate or orgasm through oral sex, but specifically when they do not orgasm from vaginal intercourse

My aim is to reassure those women who have explored their sexuality both alone and with a partner enough to know that orgasm during sex is not easy. I am interested in whether other women, who are familiar with orgasm from female masturbation, are able to achieve something similar during sex with a partner.

It does not matter if other people believe that women can experience orgasm without learning about their own sexual arousal through masturbation as men do. Neither does it matter that women claim to experience the same spontaneous arousal as men even though the female body and mind do not respond as men's do. I am not trying to convince everyone.

If people want to learn from the experiences of others, that is their choice. If not, I am not in the least offended.

# Sexual relationships favour male orgasm

Younger women are often seen to be more sexual simply because, until they find their mate, they have more incentive to be popular with men.

Dating includes sex as part of a 'wine and dine' package fuelled on both sides by sexual ego. Sex is fun because of the chase and the novelty of an unfamiliar lover.

So, single women often struggle to understand the challenges of a live-in relationship spanning decades where sex can easily become quite mundane.

Women who have been married for decades know that it is women who make relationships work over the longer term.

When men buy women flowers etc. they are implicitly acknowledging this special effort that women make in relationships.

After the initial romantic glow any woman, to varying degrees, engages in a sexual relationship for her partner's benefit, especially once any appearance of 'love-making' is lost.

Unfortunately, the experience of the majority is overruled by the more sensational. So the idea that every woman is a secret nymphomaniac remains the popular view even though it contradicts most people's real life experiences of sex.

## Sex is important to men regardless of any relationship

Physical intimacy is so important to men that relationships with women often do not make sense without sex.

A man's sex drive has little to do with a relationship and this disconnect leads a woman to conclude that his ardour is impersonal.

Hannah (late forties, children, relationship 25 years) told me of a friendship she had had with a man when she was younger.

She enjoyed talking with him. After they had known each other a while he suggested that they have sex. He claimed that it was not a big deal to change their friendship into a sexual relationship.

However, Hannah said that she did not think of him in that way. The man concluded that if they were not going to have sex then there was no point continuing the relationship.

*"Men will do anything for sex, and will behave quite out of character to achieve it, such as spending several hours being romantic, and paying attention to what a woman says." (Anthony Mason; The Bluffer's Guide to Men; 1998)*

Hannah told me that she shared my experience of not being able to orgasm during sex. Nevertheless, after twenty five years with her partner she was still prepared to participate in sex on a regular basis (admittedly because he was paying the bills).

Instead of appreciating her generosity, her partner had complained that she made no effort to 'make sex exciting for him'. Why does a man believe that a woman should do this for him?

It is natural that men hope a lover will enhance their sexual arousal but they should consider what they can offer in return.

Hannah's partner refused to make any change. Men often want to know how to get laid: try putting your own orgasm to one side and investing some time in pleasuring your woman.

*"Men often feel very angry with women who never initiate sex and too often don't want sex.*

*But this anger has a tone of alienation, guilt, and insecurity:*

*men feel instinctively on some level that sex does not involve an equal sharing, especially when they are having an orgasm and the woman does not – and this puts them on the defensive." (Shere Hite; The Hite Reports; 1993)*

If a man wants to enjoy sex for life then, he needs to find ways to make the experience more balanced in her favour. You only achieve a good sex life over the longer-term by investing in your sex life.

Hannah admitted that, even if she did not have an orgasm, an occasional sensual massage would be a significant improvement on their intercourse-to-male-orgasm sex life.

*"Your partner's not there to service you, it's not their job to keep you sexually satisfied. You're together because you love each other and want to make each other happy. Constantly hassling them for sex does the opposite." (Tracey Cox; Hot Relationships; 1999)*

# Making the most of sex play

Overall my partner and I have been lucky to have enjoyed exploring eroticism and sex play together.

Sure we have had our ups and downs like anyone else. There have also been many positive moments.

When I am in a romantic mood, perhaps after a movie or after spending companionable time with my partner, it can be the most exhilarating experience to enjoy passionate kissing while having sex.

There are also times when I feel especially tuned into my sexual fantasies and I want to have adventurous sex with my partner.

It is a real luxury to approach sex with a man totally without embarrassment so I can ask him to do whatever I want.

We have had some sexy weekends away. One time I set out to join Peter, travelling by train from London to an Oxfordshire village.

I decided to get in the mood by reading one of my erotic novels. It was a great turn-on, reading about sex while surrounded by strangers.

Peter was happy to oblige when we arrived at the hotel. Straight intercourse can be pleasurable as a 'quickie' when I am already aroused. We knew that we had the whole weekend ahead of us so it was great to approach sex more frivolously than normal.

Another time we flew out to Prague in winter and got cosy straightaway in the hotel room. Peter ran a bath while I lay on the bed reading an erotic story.

After bathing with some fellatio thrown in, I lay on the bed still reading while Peter touched me up. I keep reading until the sensations cause me to want to focus on my own sexual arousal.

### Sharing eroticism and sensual massage

We have also had holidays (when the children were taken care of in activities) where we have retired to bed after lunch each day to have a couple of hours sleep and some sex. I relaxed while my partner gave me an erotic massage.

There was no goal of orgasm for me because at the time I only enjoyed arousal during sex. I have enjoyed the sensations of having my clitoral area (up and over the hood of the clitoris) stroked.

We would finish with vaginal intercourse: either with my partner on top or beside me so he could continue stroking my clitoris while penetrating my vagina with his penis from behind.

We spent a number of summers sailing in Turkey. Peter liked me to go topless as we sailed along the coast for lunch at a beach restaurant.

Holidays have provided an opportunity for us to spend some quality intimate time together.

We notice that other couples often go on holiday with friends: the men engage on activities while the women shop or read by the pool.

We often wondered why other couples did not appear to make time for a siesta and some sex play during their holiday.

*"Some couples find it easy to talk and share together, to explore different ways of making love and discover what each wants*

*Women who describe this kind of relationship often comment on its quality as a whole, rather than just its sexual aspects." (Sheila Kitzinger; Woman's Experience of Sex; 1983)*

Over more than twenty years of our relationship, we do not see other couples with an intimacy we envy.

No doubt there are other couples who have regular sex and enjoy talking together. But it's rare. We are happy with what we have.

So when I am told that every couple out there is enjoying an idyllic sex life, I have to wonder. Most middle-aged couples we come across are rarely even intimate with each other.

Perhaps we live a quiet life but swingers are, in any case, only on an ego trip.

## Pleasuring a woman

An erection might feel good but it is likely to be a disadvantage if a man wants to devote time to pleasuring a woman.

After all, two minutes is a typical time given for a man to reach orgasm!

A man can learn techniques for slowing his arousal and increasing the time he takes to orgasm by investing private time during masturbation.

*"Basically, a man needs about two or three minutes of stimulation to have an orgasm. It is generally a very simple process, as easy as shaking up a can of beer and then letting it pop!*

*If a woman is to have an orgasm, she generally needs about ten times that amount of time.*

*She needs twenty to thirty minutes of foreplay and stimulation of her genitals." (John Gray; Mars & Venus in the Bedroom; 1995)*

There are various ways to spice up your sex life.

Start your sex sessions with a quickie in the shower (get your partner to lather you and either masturbate or suck you off) and then retire to the bedroom to return the favour by investing some quality time in pleasuring your woman.

The worst thing that might happen is that you could come a second time but there's no pressure!

Use of fingers and some back-up sex toys will ensure that you are never caught unprepared!

If you invest in one accessory for your sex life (apart from condoms, of course, if required) then make it a professional lubricant from any decent sex shop.

Foreplay techniques are useful but remember that women's sexual arousal relies on sexual fantasies.

*"'You're a lousy lover!' she said. 'How can you tell that in two minutes?' he asked." (Allan & Barbara Pease; Why men don't listen; 1999)*

## Sexual arousal changes over time

Penetrative sex is the greatest turn-on to both sexes but relies entirely on the man's sexual arousal. If a man offers it from the first moment of a sexual encounter (or five seconds later), a woman never has time to feel that it would be nice to have.

Women's sexual arousal is less automatic and so subject to more misunderstanding than men's.

But if a woman learns how to enjoy her own sexual arousal and orgasm, it is more likely that she will be willing to invest in her sex life with a partner over the longer-term.

A man should focus on sensual pleasuring rather than insisting that his woman orgasms from his efforts.

" ... *by 50 as much as half the male population lacks the testosterone that would give them the kind of sex drive young men have early in the morning." (Duncan Gould and Richard Petty of the Well-Man Clinic London, The Times 24th March 2000).*

Sex can become more rewarding over time: just as men slow down and become slightly less preoccupied with their own need for orgasm, a woman's clitoris becomes slightly less sensitive so that her partner's touch is more effective.

*"Men are frequently unaware that, though the source of a woman's pleasure may be the size of a peanut, it is armed with all the sensitivity of a six-inch penis.*

*The degree of delicacy in approaching such a minute hand grenade can take years to get right.*

*Until that time arrives, many women would rather read a good book." (Marina Muratore; The Bluffer's Guide to Women; 1998)*

Even today people still refer to 'vaginal orgasms' as if women who experience orgasm through vaginal intercourse have a different source for their orgasms.

The FACTS are that the vagina has very few nerve endings but the clitoris has many.

# How a woman can enjoy sex play

In the novelty of a new sexual relationship, I have explored a variety of sexual activities with a partner.

So, in addition to vaginal intercourse missionary style, in the early days we tried oral sex, manual clitoral stimulation and different positions for intercourse.

I enjoyed the role of the prostitute, giving pleasure to my man, but I never experienced the sexual arousal required for orgasm.

The sensations from oral sex were too vague and my clitoris was too sensitive for my partner to be able to stimulate me manually.

For many years, our sex life settled into the usual marital rut of nothing more than vaginal intercourse to male orgasm.

It was the easiest way to provide my partner with some sexual relief and involved me in minimal sexual effort (we always had to use a lubricant).

Once we had children, we would occasionally get away for weekends. These opportunities, plus holidays (with childcare) where we had more time for sex, meant that my partner could stimulate my clitoris (never to orgasm) during rear-entry intercourse.

I took the contraceptive pill from the age of eighteen until my partner had a vasectomy after the birth of our third child.

Around this time, approximately aged 35, I found that vaginal intercourse became much more comfortable and naturally lubricated.

I'll never know whether this effect was age related or the result of coming off the pill. I found that from time to time my body felt more sensual and aroused.

As a young woman I was never aware of any sense of physical arousal. But now my mind tunes into eroticism more consciously and I am aware of having an erection of the internal clitoral organ.

## Naughtier than vaginal intercourse

When I am feeling aroused, I look forward to sex sessions with my partner. Sometimes we watch a porn movie in the living room.

We put a waterproof sheet and large towel over the ottoman. I kneel down and bend over the ottoman.

My partner sits behind me with a good view up between my legs. He has control of the baby oil and lube.

While we are watching the movie he penetrates me from behind with fingers and penis. I fast forward to the bits of the movie that I like.

Other times we have sex on the bed. As always, we use a waterproof sheet, large towel and lots of lube. We keep a bag of sex toys.

I like the lights low so that I can focus fully on the sensations of my partner stroking me. I usually lie on my front while he stimulates me from behind.

He starts with toys or fingers but ends with penis penetration, stimulating my clitoris throughout. Admittedly a man needs to be a bit of an octopus to do all of this simultaneously but practice helps!

Depending on my levels of arousal, I feel different sensations from sex with a partner. Basically the more turned on I am from the start the better the feelings.

Vaginal fisting where my partner penetrates my vagina with the fingers of one hand can give me amazing feelings.

When his fingers thrust gently backwards and forwards, I feel quite overwhelmed with waves of physical arousal.

Anal sex, starting with finger penetration, but usually ending with penile penetration has always been arousing for me. Sometimes we start a sex session with a shower and my partner gives me an enema.

It's vital to take things slowly and start with finger penetration. This is the difficult part for a man. You need to be ready to stop if your partner is not enjoying it.

It is counterproductive for the woman to be the martyr here. Keep it fun and arousing!

# Stories: Emotional Intimacy

# Female sexuality in perspective

Humans are one of the few mammals known to have intercourse even when the female is not in estrus (the fertile period in the female's reproductive cycle).

Intelligent social animals learn that cooperative behaviour can be far more successful than that of any individual alone. Thus human sexuality has evolved beyond the immediate needs of reproduction to allow for the forging of emotional bonds between partners vital to long-term sexual relationships.

We have sex for the following reasons:

- **recreation**: enjoyment of sexual pleasure;

- **bonding**: emotional intimacy to support longer-term sexual relationships (deferred reproduction); and

- **reproduction**: directly seeking to achieve pregnancy.

Individuals are motivated by each of these to varying degrees. Men are more likely to benefit from enjoying sexual pleasure. After all, only men are motivated to pay for sex.

Whereas women tend to benefit from the emotional intimacy that keeps a man motivated to support the family.

## Reproduction is the main purpose of sex

With all the hype about sexual pleasure it is easy to forget that the PRIME purpose of sex is reproduction. This involves not only a man impregnating a woman but also the provision of a home in which a child can reach maturity.

Despite drives for sexual equality, women are still the home-makers and need to identify a man dedicated to their family goals.

Even today a woman benefits from having the protection of a strong and capable man. So a woman chooses a man who is likely to be able to protect her and a family against the threat from other human males as well as other dangers.

Sex provides an emotional intimacy that makes a relationship more stable and more capable of sustaining children in the future.

If women wanted sex the same way that men do, they might be tempted to have sex with many different men even when they have children.

But who would support them while they are raising all the resulting children? A man wants to know that a child is his before he is likely to be willing to contribute towards its upkeep.

A human female has to be able to offer a mate the sexual interaction he needs so that he does not seek sex elsewhere. Now we might think that Nature would ensure this by causing sex to be equally pleasurable for men and women.

The fact is that there is no need for this because women already have enough incentive: the survival of themselves and their children.

'The Duchess' (2008) stars Kiera Knightley as the Duchess of Devonshire (1757 – 1806). The story portrays the duchess in a loveless marriage under obligation to provide a male heir for her husband.

She falls in love with another man but when she tries to leave her husband he gives her a choice. If she leaves with her lover then she loses the custody of her children.

Given the choice between sexual pleasure with the man she loves and her children, she chooses to raise her children. Many men are perplexed when women lose interest in sex once their family is complete.

Ultimately, a woman gets the emotional intimacy she needs from her children at a time in life when men are often more dedicated to their own personal goals.

Naturally there are exceptions to the dedicated mother. Generalisations are not intended to categorise people absolutely but simply to provide possible explanations for different behaviours between the sexes.

My suggestion is that the importance of orgasm and especially enjoying sexual arousal with a lover is generally lower for women than it typically is for men.

# Sex and love

A BBC documentary 'The Human Body' presented by Dr Robert Winston films a sex education class.

First the teacher writes the word 'SEX' in large letters on the blackboard and then asks the teenagers to suggest other words associated with sex.

After the standard contributions the teacher adds the word missing from the list: 'LOVE'.

Despite contraception, sex still involves a risk of pregnancy, sexual disease and much emotional turmoil(!). So we promote the link between sex and love to ensure that young people understand the responsibilities associated with a sexual relationship.

An English girl of sixteen came out to the South of France one summer. On her first night she met an Australian whose self-confessed ambition was to lay every woman in the resort.

She fell for his chat and his blond good looks and lost her virginity. The next day he moved on (mission accomplished so to speak) and naturally she was devastated.

*"Male promiscuity often depends upon the satisfactions that may be secured from the pursuit and successful attainment of a new partner.*

*... Once having demonstrated their capacities to effect sexual relations with the particular individual, they prefer to turn to the pursuit of the next partner."*

(Alfred Kinsey; Sexual behavior in the human female; 1953)

Courtship involves a man showing his willingness to engage on the loving aspects of relationships in return for sex. So any woman hoping for more than a 'one night stand' should make a man wait (at least a date or two) for sex. It won't do him any lasting harm.

Since a woman does not get the same easy pleasure from sex, she offers a man short-term pleasure in the hope of longer-term companionship and support (including family).

This highlights another difficulty in assessing women's sexual desire (and their ability to enjoy sexual arousal). Young women often make the mistake of assuming that a man will love them if they offer him sex. You can follow their logic but it doesn't work like that.

A man is more likely to marry a woman who is sexually choosy than one who is sexually easy. Not only can he be more certain that a child is his but also her willingness to have sex only with him is a compliment because it singles him out as a mate.

## Sex and love are different

In the long run, most of us find that having sex with someone we know and love adds something special to the experience. But that does not mean that sex and love are the same thing.

SEX is raunchy, exhilarating, orgasmic and fun. LOVE is caring and nurturing. The two can go together or side-by-side but they are different.

Sex education for teenagers (especially girls) should cover not only the reproductive facts but also how they can enjoy a sexual relationship. Most women who experience orgasm do so through masturbation or oral sex.

Telling teenagers to limit their sexual experiences to intercourse makes it less likely that a woman might learn how to enjoy her own orgasm.

Vaginal intercourse may lead to family but it was never intended to facilitate female orgasm, either physically or psychologically.

Not every woman is attracted to eroticism and so many women miss out on the sexual fantasies that lead to female sexual arousal and orgasm.

Many women never learn to explore their sexuality, either through masturbation or through activities other than vaginal intercourse, and so they miss out on enjoying sexual pleasure and their own sexual arousal and orgasm.

It's not just women who are unwilling to acknowledge difficulties with female orgasm during sex. It's much easier to assume female sexual arousal or overlook it than to face it because there are no easy solutions. Why admit a problem you can't solve?

Very few couples are truly honest with each other. Most men never admit to their partners that they masturbate. Some men also prefer to pay a stranger for sex than to have to face asking their wives or girlfriends to participate in an explicitly sexual act.

# A man's sexual arousal can be very flattering

In the early days of a romance, a man feels loved and needed through sex. A man's sexual admiration for a woman makes her feel cared for and appreciated.

*"Men are motivated and empowered when they feel needed... Women are motivated and empowered when they feel cherished..." (John Gray; Men are from Mars, Women are from Venus; 1992)*

Women's key family role makes them more dependent on a supportive relationship. For women love-making tends to be less about orgasm and more about building long-term emotional bonds. So women's sexuality is often defined in terms of:

- focusing their efforts on presenting the sexual attributes of their bodies to attract the sexual attentions of a man;
- preferring sensual 'love-making' to more explicitly sexual activity based on clitoral stimulation (such as oral sex or masturbation); and
- facilitating male orgasm through vaginal intercourse (including assisting with male arousal by exaggerating their own sexual arousal).

In 'The Mirror has two Faces' (1996) Barbra Streisand and Jeff Bridges star as a couple who agree to marry but not have sex. On continued sexual rejection by her husband, the wife admits "I don't do anything to you – that's the problem." She continues: "I believe in lust and sex and romance. I want someone to go crazy, out of his mind for me."

*"It cannot be emphasized too often that orgasm cannot be taken as the sole criterion for determining the degree of satisfaction which a female may derive from sexual activity. Considerable pleasure may be found in sexual arousal which does not proceed to the point of orgasm, and in the social aspects of a sexual relationship.*

*Whether or not she herself reaches orgasm, many a female finds satisfaction in knowing that her husband or other sexual partner has enjoyed the contact, and in realizing that she has contributed to the male's pleasure." (Alfred Kinsey; Sexual behavior in the human female; 1953)*

While men are valued as providers, women are valued for being attractive. A woman wants to be rushed off her feet with a man's passion for her. A woman's ability to turn her man on causes him to want her both sexually as well as to 'love and to hold'. Sometimes female sexuality is defined in terms of women's power to attract a man.

A woman can enjoy many aspects of her sexual relationship with a lover, such as sharing the sensual pleasures and emotional intimacies of sex, regardless of her own sexual arousal and orgasm.

Sex and love are often confused for women and, for many women, sex need not be about orgasm at all. 'Titanic' (1997) was one of the most popular films of all time because women love the idea that a man could be so totally devoted.

Rod Stewart's song says it all: "You're in my heart. You are my lover, you're my best friend". Emotionally, it's possible that men need women more than women need men because men don't share emotional intimacy with others as easily as women do. It is sex that binds a man to a woman and motivates him to fight to the death if necessary to protect her.

*"How to satisfy a woman every time: Caress, praise, pamper, ... die for, dream of, tease, gratify, squeeze, indulge, idolise, worship. How to satisfy a man every time: Arrive naked." (Allan & Barbara Pease; Why men don't listen; 1999)*

Like it or not, sexual relationships favour male orgasm and naturally, given their drive to reach orgasm, men hope a lover will enhance their sexual arousal. By being the appreciative female lover a woman shows that she cares about her partner.

A woman becomes less willing over time if she feels that he does not care about her priorities. Showing that you care about someone involves talking together and seeking an understanding of how the other person feels and what is important to them.

*"A man's sense of self is defined through his ability to achieve results." (John Gray; Men are from Mars, Women are from Venus; 1992)*

*"A woman's sense of self is defined through her feelings and the quality of her relationships." (John Gray; Men are from Mars, Women are from Venus; 1992)*

# Why do women not always appreciate displays of male sexuality?

I have never seen any reason to be embarrassed about my body. I am pretty. I have sensual skin that browns easily and a sexy figure. My parents were always relaxed about nudity.

So when I was eighteen, out in the South of France for the summer, I enjoyed going top-less sunbathing. Why have those bikini lines that make your breasts look like icebergs? One day, as I was lying there on the popular pebble beach desperately trying to tan, I heard... "Just look at all those tits!" as a sailor's voice carried across the water: the British Navy had arrived.

I looked out to sea and there was the naval ship. So I was less than surprised when half an hour later (they're quick, those boys!) my sunlight was being blocked by a very pleasant young sailor. Of course, he wanted to know all about me. It was my afternoon off and, since he was only in port for a few hours, I didn't see much point in getting to know him. We talked and he walked me back to my apartment. Sorry, nothing happened...

Some men like to display their male sexuality by aiming sexual remarks at women. That summer I was occasionally offended by men's appreciation of my sexual attributes. "Hey, you with the big tits!" was once shouted at me from across the road. I can't say that I've ever wanted to be singled out for my tits. It's nice to have some but how to explain to a man...

It's the way the man shouted for all to hear. It made me feel, not like a person, but like an object to be ogled at without any sensitivity and also with the implicit knowledge that I could not retaliate by shouting something similar back. How do you make a man feel like a piece of sexual meat? Female sexuality does not so naturally include such vocal displays of appreciation for the sexual attributes of the opposite sex. So it can be difficult to understand.

Imagine you had to wear your penis on your chest under your tee shirt, but essentially for the whole world to see. Would you appreciate comments from women about the merits of your sexual anatomy? Men may feel that it can never be insulting to be big. Well as a woman you can be both too small and too big. We are all sensitive about being identified as unusually different.

So when you think a woman is dying to be told how big her breasts are – give it some thought. Men perhaps feel that they would love to receive sexual heckling from women. Maybe. Just think how you would feel if a gay man made a sexual remark to you.

Well there's a parallel here. Sexual remarks are great when you are the one dishing them out. Sexual compliments are only appreciated if you find the other person sexually attractive and women often take longer to decide on this point than men. Also women are not so often in the position of singling out the man they find attractive. Women's sexual arousal is not driven by looking at naked images of men so we have less to gain from physical intimacy with the opposite sex.

For the most part, my experience is that male commentary is most often not intended to be offensive. I enjoy being whistled at by passing men and I always smile and wave back. Even quite recently, a passing French man made some remark I did not entirely understand – "Nice arse" or similar – and seemed surprised when I thanked him for the sexual compliment.

Once in informal company I used an impolite four-lettered word for a woman's private parts. I was surprised that even in this day and age the women were shocked by the mention of such a word. Of course, the men said nothing. Although rarely admitted, censorship of nudity exists because most women positively dislike looking at anyone's genitals up close (even their own).

I have always told my young daughters to use the word 'pussy' for their sexual anatomy, which I consider to be about as rude as the word 'willie'. I was really quite angry when our young nanny told them to use the phrase 'front-bottom' instead. It would seem that women are offended by almost any explicit reference to their genitals regardless of who is making the comment.

By accepting intercourse, regardless of female orgasm, women never need to engage on other more explicitly sexual activities. It's this aversion to the physical that gives men the impression that women are sexually inhibited. The facts are: female sexual arousal does not occur as easily as male but also women do not obtain the same rewards that men do from physical intimacy.

# Why do so many women dislike eroticism?

Pornography is defined to be 'sexually explicit material (verbal or pictorial) that is primarily designed to produce sexual arousal'.

Two women give their views on pornography.

Helen Longino, the American philosopher: *"I define pornography as verbal or pictorial explicit representations of sexual behavior that ... have as a distinguishing characteristic 'the degrading and demeaning portrayal of the role and status of the human female . . . as a mere sexual object to be exploited and manipulated sexually'."*

Why is it assumed that men are always the exploiters and women always exploited in sex? Is it assumed that any sexual act must always be solely for men's pleasure? Surely a heterosexual act can, at least sometimes, be as pleasurable for women as it is for men?

Susan Brownmiller, the American feminist and journalist: *"hard core pornography is not a celebration of sexual freedom; it is a cynical exploitation of female sexual activity through the device of making all such activity, and consequently all females, 'dirty'."*

Most men are not sex perverts and only enjoy positive images of women. So how do these pictures make the woman 'dirty'? Let's face it: people who have moral objections to sexual pleasure have never tried sexual activities other than intercourse. They simply cannot imagine that they would ever enjoy more adventurous sex and so they believe that no one else should.

*"Photographs of female nudes and magazines exhibiting nude or near nude females are produced primarily for the consumption of males. There are, however, photographs and magazines portraying nude and near nude males - but these are also produced for the consumption of males. There are almost no male or female nudes which are produced for the consumption of females.*

*The failure of nearly all females to find erotic arousal in such portrayals is so well known to the distributors of nude photographs and nude magazines that they have considered that it would not be financially profitable to produce such material for a primarily female audience."* (Alfred Kinsey; Sexual behavior in the human female; 1953)

Perhaps women dislike seeing themselves portrayed as sexual beings – people with physical attributes that other people find sexually arousing? Or is it just that women don't understand because they don't become aroused by looking at pictures of naked men? Answers on a postcard...

This is the apparent contradiction in our society's portrayal of female sexuality. We assume that women enjoy sex as much as men, including their own sexual arousal and orgasm during sex, and yet many women are disgusted by even a hint of the eroticism that is at the core of our enjoyment of sexual pleasure.

I am not offended by men's enjoyment of pornography because, although I don't use images for arousal, I do use stories. One might be tempted to call one: 'visual pornography' and the other: 'verbal pornography' but women prefer the term 'erotica'.

Erotica is a genre of literature that includes sexually explicit material as a primary feature. Unlike pornography, erotica is not aimed exclusively at sexual arousal (but it's not exactly art either!).

Gloria Steinem talks about erotica: *"a mutually pleasurable, sexual expression between people who have enough power to be there by positive choice.... It doesn't require us to identify with a conqueror or a victim"*.

Ironically, many erotic stories for women include more sadism and domination than is ever implied in the average pornographic magazine (at least the ones that can be bought in an everyday store – as opposed to hardcore). So why is pornography always bad but erotica is more often OK?

Let's be very clear about one thing though. Most reasonable people would consider any pornography MORALLY WRONG that is produced as a result of the real life exploitation of one being by another.

Thus any sexual act with animals, children (most usually persons under the age of 18) and anyone who has been coerced into sexual activity through emotional, physical or financial intimidation cannot be supported by a civilised society.

# Sheltering young women from eroticism

Reading the word 'sexy', a boy of nine screwed up his face in a gesture of disgust and said "Yuck!"

I asked him why and he replied, "Because my parents told me it's disgusting".

Presumably these parents are trying to warn their son away from the temptations of sexual pleasure with its associated immoral behaviour.

For women, there has always been acceptance of sex within the context of family but disapproval of sex for pleasure.

In fact where a woman's only sexual experiences are of intercourse, she is unlikely to ever discover her own sexual arousal.

Since women's sexual arousal and orgasm are not automatic many women never learn how to enjoy their own sexual arousal and orgasm (either alone or with a partner).

Women's sexual arousal relies on sexual fantasies and so women who do not appreciate the positive aspects of eroticism also have no expectation for enjoying sexual pleasure.

*"Women often feel they have no right to sexual experience apart from that which a man provides." (Sheila Kitzinger; Woman's Experience of Sex; 1983)*

Many women are disgusted by pornography, which appears to display women's bodies like a meat market for male gratification.

Women who enjoy their ability to arouse a lover learn that male turn-ons simply work differently. A woman gives to a lover through sex in return for benefits in the wider relationship.

A woman who learns how to orgasm through masturbation, also knows the humility of accepting that the adult world cannot always be squeaky clean.

Many other women (with fewer sexual instincts) can only justify sex as part of a loving relationship.

## Disapproval of sexual pleasure

Many people believe that women are always exploited through sex because men stand to gain so much more pleasure. Melanie Phillips

(Daily Mail – 24th February 2003) complains about those who want to provide young people (girls of fifteen) with the facts about adult heterosexual practices (including oral sex and anal sex).

Melanie fears (as do many others) that knowledge about enjoying sexual pleasure will damage the teenagers' emotional development and suggests that *"genital gratification separated from a permanent loving commitment is a form of degradation."* She also believes that *"spiritual and emotional meaning distinguishes human sexual activity from animal behaviour".*

The view that women's experience of sex should be restricted to marriage almost denies the fact that a woman might be capable of appreciating her sexual experiences for their own sake.

The fact is that some women do explore sexual pleasure.

*"In most cultures, throughout history, everywhere in the world, some sort of distinction has been made between the acceptability of pre-marital coitus for the male and the acceptability of such coitus for the female.*

*This undoubtedly stems from the fact that it has always proved impossible to prevent the majority of males from having coitus before marriage; while females, who are less often sexually responsive at early ages and less often stimulated psychologically at any age, have proved to be more controllable." (Alfred Kinsey; Sexual behavior in the human female; 1953)*

There is no reason why honest information about sex should encourage sexual promiscuity in girls.

Neither is it likely that knowing how couples enjoy sex in long-term sexual relationships will harm a loving relationship – in fact quite the reverse. There is a double standard here because no one worries that information about sexual pleasure will do boys any harm.

At its best, sex can be an innocent pleasure for any couple to enjoy whether they are married or not. If a woman finds a man she likes and respects, then the sex is sure to be even better. Sex is key to the emotional bonds that underpin healthy family life.

# How to get laid

Men should take comfort from the facts of female sexuality. Most women are unlikely to orgasm from intercourse alone (which provides insufficient clitoral stimulation for orgasm) and yet amazingly few women ask about lack of orgasm.

In addition to the obvious personal embarrassment, likely explanations include:

- Not every woman is interested in orgasm, whether from masturbation or from sex.

- Relatively few women masturbate and so many women never know what orgasm is.

- Some women assume that they orgasm during sex when, in fact, they don't.

- Others accept that sex involves male orgasm rather than hoping for their own.

In the film 'Erin Brockovich' (2000) Aaron Eckhart plays the free-spirited boyfriend.

Despite the cool image (tattoos and Harley Davidson), most men probably disrespect Eckhart's role because he offers to look after the children of the independent and career-focused Julia Roberts.

In fact, Eckhart is incredibly sexy in this role and many women would love to go to bed with a man who exudes such charm, affection and emotional warmth.

Regardless of her sexual expectations, any woman is more likely to offer sex when she feels good about the relationship and loving towards her partner. Romance (affectionate and companionable time spent together) can lead a woman to be more amenable to sex.

However, these stimuli are very different to those she needs to reach orgasm (sexual fantasies involve explicit eroticism). Sadly, Nature has no need to care about female orgasm. As long as a woman is amenable to having sex, the job is done!

## Emotional intimacy

The film 'Overboard' (1987) stars Goldie Hawn and Kurt Russell. Goldie plays a spoilt millionairess who loses her memory and Kurt plays the carpenter, who purely out of revenge, pretends that she is married to him with his four children.

Sexual relationships favour male orgasm and it is clear that he would have little problem having sex with this woman he hardly knows and even dislikes. It is equally clear that she would consider it out of the question to have sex with a man she cannot remember knowing.

In order to be amenable to sex, a woman needs to find a man sexually attractive. Women take longer than men to decide on this point because a woman is not looking for good looks alone but also for a man who is devoted to her.

*"Men are most comfortable expressing love through sex, through shared activities, through being a good provider, and through just being together..." (Kramer & Dunaway; Why Men don't get enough Sex and Women don't get enough Love; 1994)*

Later in the story, they get to know each other and one evening, saying it is her birthday, they go on a date. After dancing, they talk and gaze at the evening sky while romantic music plays. They kiss and, on returning home, 'make love' for the first time.

*"98 percent of the women... said they would like more verbal closeness with the men they love; they want the men in their lives to talk more about their own personal thoughts, feelings, plans and questions, and to ask them about theirs." (Shere Hite; Women & Love; 1987)*

The woman now feels affection for the man and finds him physically attractive. Of course, he always was attractive but he suddenly appeals because she respects him and cares about him.

Perhaps it is as self evident to women that relationships are about companionship as it is to men that they are about physical intimacy. In fact, both are part of a long-term relationship.

*"Men want friends to play with, ... whereas women want friends to talk to." (Marina Muratore; The Bluffer's Guide to Women; 1998)*

# Women settle for emotional intimacy over sexual arousal

On relating our experience to others, we all tend to gloss over details or not own up to difficulties that were perhaps transient.

I told Linda, a mother of three in her late forties, that I had never had an orgasm during intercourse. Linda looked at me incredulously and laughed as if I must be ignorant of the most basic sexual facts.

Naturally, I died with mortification at the implied sexual inadequacy.

*"In fact, since only about 30 percent of women achieve orgasm with intercourse but over 80 percent experience a climax with masturbation, orgasm by means of masturbation rather than by sexual intercourse, should be regarded as the normal experience." (Miriam Stoppard; Healthy Sex; 1998)*

Later when Linda joked that she would rather do her gardening on weekends than have sex, I was confused.

Although I would not go to the ends of the world to enjoy my own sexual arousal and orgasm by masturbating, it is definitely worth investing a few minutes of effort from time to time.

Women who have never masturbated presumably assume that reaching orgasm must always be a drawn out affair.

If I am already turned on and have an effective fantasy to hand, it is no trouble reaching orgasm from female masturbation within a couple of minutes.

Masturbation is very enjoyable but I have no sense of needing to interrupt other activities to engage in it. I usually consider masturbation when I am already lying in bed either on waking or on going to sleep.

*"In fact, women do not take longer to orgasm than men. The majority of women in Kinsey's study masturbated to orgasm within four minutes, similar to the women in this study.*

*It is, obviously, only during inadequate or secondary, insufficient stimulation like intercourse that we take 'longer' and need prolonged 'foreplay'." (Shere Hite; The Hite Reports; 1993)*

The only women I have found to be confident about orgasm are those who masturbate. This is because in order to aim for orgasm a person needs to know how to become sexually aroused.

I believe that many women never learn now to do this. Those who claim to orgasm the first time and every time from intercourse are simply blissfully ignorant of the facts.

The fact is that women have to learn how to orgasm. One woman told me that it had taken around ten years for her and her partner to achieve a 'good' sex life. Surely this fact is worth passing on to younger generations?

Imagine telling a man he has to wait ten years to learn how to orgasm from sex! Young women often don't know how to orgasm and older women are not always that open about their own sexual experiences.

The huge gap between how women's sexual arousal is portrayed in the media compared with reality means that sex advice for women is often misleading.

Months later, when we had talked around the subject a few times Linda told me that she did not always experience orgasm, that orgasm was not that important to her and that her partner was the prime initiator in their sex life.

So, her experience of sex with a partner was little different to my own. Linda explained that she had never approached sex expecting to experience orgasm.

Linda liked to dress provocatively and was evidently one of those women who enjoy attracting a man's attention. For her, sex was about sharing an intimate physical act with her partner and so masturbation was meaningless.

They watched porn movies together and Linda confirmed that she preferred some story content rather than the endless banging sessions.

*"For some women lovemaking without orgasm is unsatisfying and they feel they have missed out on something precious.*

*For others the journey holds more richness and delight than the getting there." (Sheila Kitzinger; Woman's Experience of Sex; 1983)*

# Intercourse does not facilitate female orgasm

Men's sexual arousal is usually easy, which gives them a natural advantage. As a consequence, while men can usually hope for orgasm from their sexual encounters, most women have to settle for the more diffused sensations of sexual arousal.

*"Sex is a very different experience for women and men. A man experiences pleasure primarily as a release of sexual tension.*

*A woman experiences sex in an opposite way. For her, the great joys of sex correspond to a gradual build up of tension. ...*

*A man's immediate desire to touch and be touched in his sensitive zones is a given. He does not need much help in getting excited. He needs help in releasing or letting go of this excitement.*

*In a sense, he seeks to end his excitement, while a woman seeks to extend her excitement to feel more deeply her inner longing."* (John Gray; Mars & Venus in the Bedroom; 1995)

Love and romance make a woman amenable to a sexual relationship but do not by themselves create orgasm.

Over time, a man needs to offer some sensual pleasuring focused on his partner's sexual arousal so that sex holds some rewards for her.

After all, not many men would be happy about not having orgasms with intercourse...

## Women need other compensations for sex

Sex is much more straightforward and easily pleasurable for men. Women's sexual experiences are more difficult to interpret especially given the belief that it is 'natural' for a woman to reach orgasm with a partner regardless of the facts.

*"Although there has been some disagreement in the past as to whether the absence of coital orgasms without accompanying manual clitoral stimulation is an abnormality per se, most sexologists today have concluded that this is not the case. ...*

*This distinction is often of little solace to a woman who is unhappy about not having orgasms with intercourse, however, even if she is vehemently reassured that she is completely normal."* (Masters & Johnson; Human Sexuality; 1995)

For a long time, I found it difficult to interpret this advice. Initially I was outraged at the implication that women are happy settling for emotional (as opposed to physical) pleasure from their sex life.

Orgasm may not be the critical goal for women that it typically is for men but any woman who is familiar with orgasm from masturbation, questions why sex does not lead to orgasm.

Apparently, some couples have the 'problem' that the woman can only orgasm from intercourse with additional manual stimulation of her clitoris.

Many men are unhappy with this because they believe that a woman should orgasm simply from thrusting. Women also feel inadequate because they feel that manual clitoral stimulation is 'cheating'.

Couples need to be much more realistic about expectations for female orgasm. Men need direct penile stimulation for orgasm so it is only reasonable that a woman will need at least as much clitoral stimulation (which intercourse does not provide).

It is often implied (wrongly) that a woman can orgasm as easily as men do via other means with a partner e.g. oral sex or mutual masturbation. Yet experts I have talked to have admitted that a woman is lucky if she finds even one way to orgasm.

Given the fact that women do not enjoy orgasm as easily through sex as men do, women settle for emotional intimacy over sexual arousal and the sensual pleasures of erotic massage.

This does not mean that women do not hope to reach orgasm in general but that they accept that it is difficult to achieve through sex with a partner.

This has certainly been my experience.

# Why sex is called 'making love'

The heterosexual act of vaginal intercourse is designed foremost as an expression of love between a man and a woman.

After all, if sex was purely about two people reaching orgasm, then we would more naturally engage in activities that involve more direct genital stimulation. Intercourse is a natural progression from kissing to a man capitalising on his sexual arousal to 'make love' to a woman.

When a woman is amenable to accepting a man's sexual initiative, intercourse allows her body to provide him with the sexual release of orgasm.

Penetration involves the maximum turn-on for a man and signifies a high level of trust and intimacy between two people.

Intercourse represents the most personal acceptance that a woman can offer that can be emotionally rewarding for a man (especially if her sexual acceptance is awarded sparingly).

*"Although we may use orgasm as a measure of the frequency of female activity, and may emphasize the significance of orgasm as a source of physiologic outlet and of social interchange for the female, it must always be understood that we are well aware that this is not the only significant part of a satisfactory sexual relationship.*

*This is much more true for the female than it would be for the male. It is inconceivable that males who are not reaching orgasm would continue their marital coitus for any length of time." (Alfred Kinsey; Sexual behavior in the human female; 1953)*

Many women see sex as a loving and sensual act with a man they love. The vast majority of women are not interested in the eroticism and physical sex play (focused on genital stimulation) that would lead to their own sexual arousal and orgasm.

The sexual revolution implied that women's sexuality could become more like men's simply as a result of a change in attitudes.

In fact, many women settled for faking orgasm to keep men happy rather than being motivated to reach orgasm with a partner.

## Female sexuality cannot change just to fit the fashion

Despite the supposed liberalisation in attitudes, men today still feel obliged to apologise to women for sexual innuendo. They appear to assume that a woman will always be offended by sexual references, which of course they often are.

But if women are so shocked by eroticism how do they achieve the sexual arousal that leads to orgasm? The answer is that they don't.

Most would be horrified at the suggestion that they could experience sexual arousal by appreciating aspects of eroticism.

Women prefer to assume that female orgasm involves loving feelings rather than crude sexual urges.

Many women enjoy the kind of romance stories that end just as the couple kiss. Although sex is implicit, there are none of the explicit sexual references that so often offend women. This is just where men would want the story to start not to end.

Women are not naturally attracted to the physical as men often are. A woman who is unable to empathise with men's enjoyment of these phenomena will have difficulty understanding the attraction of eroticism.

Women who masturbate enjoy aspects of eroticism through sexual scenarios or stories. Fantasy allows women to gloss over the crude practical details of sex.

But it is one thing to use sexual fantasies during masturbation alone or during sex, for that matter. It requires a much higher level of trust and communication to discuss ways of sharing our sexual fantasies with a partner during physical sex play.

Women may not be happy about a lack of orgasm during sex but they can put up with it. If a man ever experiences impotence, he can feel that life is no longer worth living. Women don't have the same biological drive to reach orgasm with a partner.

This means that women don't have the same motivation to explore all the options with a partner. Since intercourse has been endorsed by society as 'acceptable and proper' heterosexual behaviour, it is the default and requires minimal discussion.

# Stories: Physical intimacy

# Emotional intimacy may lead to physical intimacy

Sex does not stand alone in a relationship and in long-term sexual relationships couples need to invest in quality time together.

The candle-lit dinners, soft music and flowers we tend to associate with romance provide the backdrop for the companionable aspects of a relationship.

Emotional intimacy comes from spending intimate time together by sharing conversation, humour and friendship over dinner, while taking a walk or as you prepare a meal together.

*"Women need to feel a degree of sexual intimacy before sex becomes desirable...*

*For women, intimacy sometimes results in sex; for men, sex sometimes results in intimacy." (Marina Muratore; The Bluffer's Guide to Women; 1998)*

Men may have sex constantly on the brain but a woman's mind does not tend to dwell on her genitals (or anyone else's!) during the course of a normal day.

So women's sexual arousal is not automatic in the way that men's tends to be especially during sex with a partner.

How to get laid: you need to lead up to sex by creating an environment that will lead to emotional and physical intimacy and hopefully sex.

Men are not a sexual commodity in the way that women can be to men. So, for example, we don't refer to men as blondes or brunettes.

We want a friend, a companion and, yes, a lover but someone who is interested in us as a person as much as a body. Women don't stand in line to see a man's genitals.

*"Above all women like men who take an interest in them." (Marina Muratore; The Bluffer's Guide to Women; 1998)*

Sexual relationships favour male orgasm and yet men can be reluctant to invest effort in pleasuring a woman.

A woman is initially flattered when a man gets turned on by her body but over time she doubts that he is devoted to her personally because his sexual frustration is so apparent.

A difficult one for men but… try not to be too obvious about your own need for orgasm.

*"A woman… wants more intimacy, comprising affection, commitment, and respect for individual identity…*

*Although she knows he wants sex, she is frustrated because this seems to be the only form of intimacy he is interested in with her." (Kramer & Dunaway; Why Men don't get enough Sex and Women don't get enough Love; 1994)*

Men approach sex with a genital focus because they are already aroused so they often fail to engage on the sensual aspects of sex.

Since female orgasm is difficult to achieve with a partner, women are more likely to be looking to enjoy their own arousal through general pleasuring and non-genitally focused activities.

A woman hopes that a man will show his gratitude by engaging on the more companionable and supportive aspects of the relationship.

In essence, women want to feel appreciated in a wider sense than just as a sexual partner.

A woman is much more likely to be willing to pleasure her man when she feels good about the relationship in general.

In the longer term, a man will also need to return the favour by ensuring that the woman receives some pampering by including a more sensual massage.

Over time sex all too easily falls into the marital rut of intercourse to male orgasm.

If men want women to be more amenable to sex, then they should take the emphasis off orgasm (both their own and hers) and spend more time on sensual sex play, including touching and kissing.

Also try to have some fun sometimes by introducing a new sex toy or sensation.

## Women who enjoy sexual pleasure

Naturally, some women insist that they are just as sexually driven as men. Even today when pornography dominates 90% of the Internet, women remain incredibly naive about men's passion for sex.

One woman said: "The basics are this: men like sex and will give affection to get it. Women like affection, and get it during sex. It works out well for both. I believe women enjoy sex as much as men do."

Although the sensual pleasures of physical intimacy with a lover can still be enjoyed if orgasm is missing, men would never settle for non-orgasmic sex. Women who are familiar with orgasm from female masturbation also hope for more than affection from sex.

Women, who prior to the 1950s had been thought incapable of sexual pleasure, are now told they can 'enjoy' sex as much as men since female orgasm is assumed to occur 'naturally' during intercourse.

I have tried to imagine what it must be like for a woman to approach sex without knowing what her own sexual arousal and orgasm feels like. Even so, I have to question how a woman cannot notice a man's early morning erection.

Do they never realise that almost any intimate physical contact causes a man to be eager for sex? There are no female equivalents to these.

Equally presumably they never notice any difference between the pleasure they get from sex compared with their partner. Yet a man's drive to reach orgasm determines the pace and usually the end of any heterosexual activity. A woman has little say in the matter.

In any case, have these women never heard of rape, of prostitution, of men's use of pornography and masturbation?

Not every man is a potential rapist, has paid for sex or is a sex pervert (e.g. fetishes, peeping tom etc.). But these examples indicate how much more sexually motivated the average man is compared to the average woman.

This fact also explains why women (but not men) can hug and kiss each other without anyone assuming that there is a sexual context to the relationship.

It is important to differentiate between what women say and what women do. Women often stand to gain by professing an enthusiasm for sex. This is hardly a modern female ploy: the sexually provocative female has existed since time began.

What is much more indicative of women's enthusiasm for sex is what women actually do:

- Men masturbate regularly throughout their lives but very few women ever masturbate to enjoy arousal and orgasm;
- Men enjoy their own arousal through pornography throughout their lives but even young women buy much less erotica;
- Our culture abounds with images of women's bodies but women do not generate a demand for images of men's bodies;
- Lap-dancing and pole-dancing bars are directed at men and are seldom (if ever) intended for women; and
- Prostitutes offer men sex the world over but women very rarely pay for sex.

Many women CLAIM to orgasm during sex just because it makes them look good. The facts of female sexuality have been available since the 1950s:

(1) women have more difficulty with sexual arousal and orgasm during sex than men do and

(2) women need clitoral stimulation for orgasm so masturbation is a much easier source of female orgasms than intercourse.

It would be more useful to ask older women, who have less to prove, what they think of sex. I have tried talking to women of all ages about sex and the vast majority prefers to make no comment at all.

In fact, very few women are shouting from the rooftops about the joys of sexual pleasure. Unfortunately the majority is intimidated by the sexual ego of a tiny minority.

There is little support for providing younger women with information about enjoying their own sexual pleasure. My efforts meet with defensiveness, silence or fierce opposition.

Many people insist that women can 'enjoy' sex as much as men do but it is not clear that they are talking about orgasm. Women themselves are rarely able to explain how they orgasm during sex.

## Why is sexual pleasure still taboo?

If sex is so equal then why would anyone need to pay for sex? Prostitution exists because men's drive to enjoy sexual pleasure cannot always be satisfied through relationships.

Most women interpret their sexual experiences in emotional terms as 'making love'. Consequently, wives and girlfriends are often reluctant to offer more sexually explicit sexual pleasuring.

Given the strong associations with male gratification through the sex industry, sexual pleasure has overtones of immoral behaviour for women.

Since many women never experience sexual pleasure, they are simply appalled by the exploitative nature of the sex industry. It is men's enjoyment of a young woman's body regardless of any relationship that causes offence.

In the film '50 first dates' (2004) Adam Sandler's Hawaiian friend explains that his wife's mature figure no longer arouses him.

Some men only ever see sex as sex, but many others prefer sex with a woman they love. When men find that special woman, they may not get all slushy about love but they still choose to marry. Even the unisex term 'lover' indicates a link between love and sex.

As the film 'Cruel Intentions' (1999) points out, women can also exploit men through sex.

One day while I was waiting at the supermarket checkout I listened to two young women, each with babe-in-arms, comparing the money they got from their ex-partners.

Women often assume that a man will finance their dream of home and family without a thought for what a man might hope for in return.

### Women are not the only ones exploited through sex

So women today can get alimony from a man they are no longer having sex with. Young men should campaign for a male pill but men (unlike women) are worried about how hormones might affect their sex drive.

Certainly a man should put off having a family until he can be sure that a woman is willing to invest in a long-term sexual relationship with him.

If governments are concerned about teenage pregnancies then they should provide information about the obligations of family life. A woman will enjoy having a family much more with a partner than by facing the challenges of raising children alone.

Advice based on the reproductive aspects of sex (family and relationships) should include:

- Single parenthood is tough – raising children with a caring partner is much easier;
- A woman needs to find a man who cares about her enough to be willing to support a family; and
- A man needs to find a partner who cares enough about him to invest in their sexual relationship.

The problem with sex advice today is that girls are not given the facts about female sexuality to help them enjoy sexual pleasure.

A man's sex drive provides a woman with a means of keeping her man motivated to support the family. If a couple can open up to each other and explore eroticism together then they may discover more ways of pleasuring than young people ever try.

Advice based on enjoying sexual pleasure (sexual arousal and orgasm) should include:

- Men gain much more from the immediate rewards of a sexual relationship;
- Women need information about their sexuality if they are to enjoy eroticism and orgasm; and
- Men need to accept that if they want a longer-term sex life then they need to invest in finding ways to pleasure their woman.

If a woman cares about her man, she will appreciate how important sex is to him. If you can survive the ups and downs, it is definitely worthwhile exploring how to make sex more intimate and more adventurous (that means men as well as women!).

# Very few women talk about orgasm

After finding no answers from talking to experts, I decided to do my own research by talking to women I came across in everyday life.

I wrote about some of my experiences and conclusions and then asked women whether they would be willing to read what I had written. I made it clear that there was no obligation for reviewers to comment.

The first point to note is just how difficult it is to approach anyone on such a sensitive and personal subject. I quickly realised that very few women appeared amenable enough for me to dare even to ask them.

We can be fairly sure that a man is unlikely to object to or be insulted by a random reference to sex. It is much less certain that a woman will not be offended. Even as a woman, talking openly about sex and orgasm can easily come across as odd and even a little perverted.

I only approached women who I thought might have a sense of humour in the hope that even if they were embarrassed they wouldn't take irreversible offence. Even so, few were willing to comment.

*"Many women find it very difficult to talk about sex with their male partners.*

*More than a quarter of the women with whom I have discussed the subject say that they never talk to their partners about things they might do to improve lovemaking."* (Sheila Kitzinger; *Woman's Experience of Sex*; 1983)

### Even fewer women can explain how they orgasm during sex

Silence is difficult to interpret. Were they shocked, angry or embarrassed? I'll never know.

Of those who did comment they probably fell into five groups:

(1) Those who were 'shocked' by explicitly sexual behaviour. They assumed that a woman's sexual experiences more properly revolve around a loving relationship.

See 'A sexual relationship' – p30 and 'Female masturbation is relatively uncommon' – p52.

(2) Those who were confident that orgasm during sex just 'happens' the first time and every time. They drew comfort from popular

beliefs about female sexuality: 'Bluffers, fakers and sex surveys' – p234 and 'Some women never tune into eroticism' – p82.

(3) Those who were sexually 'jaded'. One woman in her late thirties, career and no children, said that all her friends agreed that women don't get anything out of sex

Women accept sex because they want a relationship (for companionship or family).

(4) Those who had the same experience as me and could only orgasm from masturbation alone.

See 'Women's sex drive to orgasm during sex' – p54 and 'Sex advice for women is often misleading' – p272.

(5) Those who were confident about orgasm and were able to explain their experiences. These women were relatively relaxed about talking about orgasm.

A couple of these explained orgasm with a partner either (A) by masturbation or (B) by using a position. They recognised the need for clitoral stimulation and also admitted to using fantasies during sex for arousal.

(A) Women who masturbate during intercourse: The women I spoke to (See 'Transferring masturbation techniques to sex' – p142 and 'Reaching orgasm' – p134) learnt to combine masturbation and sex early on so perhaps they developed fantasies in line with reality.

(B) Women who find a position for intercourse: One woman described this approach to me (See 'Positions and techniques for sexual intercourse' – p144) but the political correctness of this solution makes me doubt. I also question whether women used to direct clitoral stimulation during masturbation would be able to benefit from this approach, which provides little clitoral stimulation.

# Sexual pleasure

Self-evidently there are 'responsible' aspects of sex as well as the 'pleasurable' but sexual ignorance is of no use to anyone.

Young women today are more likely to end up pregnant as a result of pressure from men or from idealised images of motherhood than from any hope of enjoying sexual pleasure.

Providing girls with information about their sexuality is an important part of giving women the confidence to stand up for what they want in life.

It may be that a woman's sex drive is more likely to involve a desire to enjoy family rather than orgasm. But female sexuality can encompass more than this reproductive capacity.

Girls need information about how their sexual arousal works if they are to discover how to get the most out of a long-term sexual relationship.

Why would anyone want to discourage women from enjoying sexual pleasure? Unfortunately, many people fear that women always stand to be exploited through sex because men's arousal and orgasm are so much more easily achieved.

Thus sexual pleasure is more usually associated with women facilitating male gratification than with them enjoying their own orgasm.

Lack of understanding about female sexuality means that women are often reluctant to promote the clitoris, either through female masturbation or oral sex, to younger generations.

This may explain the custom in some primitive African communities of the surgical removal of a young woman's clitoris (grossly misnamed 'female circumcision') by older women in the tribe.

Although some women do explore sexual pleasure through genital stimulation, there is very little practical sex advice passed on by more experienced women to enable younger women to learn how to go about transferring orgasm techniques to sex.

## Sexual pleasure versus reproductive sex

Women can have a low expectation of sex because they lack knowledge about female sexuality.

Conversely, if women have the facts about the physical and psychological aspects of their sexuality then at least they are in a position to make personal choices. Sadly young women are not told about the orgasm techniques that women use to orgasm.

When I was in my twenties, I visited my doctor regularly for medication to relieve the discomfort that accompanied vaginal intercourse.

I accepted pain as part of my experience of sex because it was implicit that it was unfair to deprive my boyfriend of a sexual outlet. I also assumed that it was my personal failing that I could not naturally enjoy sex as my partner did.

A woman can accept a man's love-making, regardless of her menstrual cycle. This provides women with more flexibility in attracting and keeping a mate.

However, just because we are able to offer intercourse does not mean that we have to. Unfortunately, it may be that men achieve the best sexual satisfaction from thrusting simply because of the biology.

Oral sex or mutual masturbation are both obvious solutions if they work for you. Otherwise, on the basis of a loving relationship, you can offer your partner non-penetrative (outercourse) sex based on his orgasm.

This could include allowing him to masturbate himself (depending on your generosity, you could offer to suck him off or masturbate him) while you display yourself provocatively or allowing him to masturbate by riding between your breasts (if large enough!) or your buttocks.

*"With my boyfriend of four years, we pretty much stopped fucking, because it just wasn't working for me, and he doesn't want me to do it if I don't like it. He still comes, and I do too, and I don't have to worry about pregnancy." (Shere Hite; The Hite Reports; 1993)*

# Women who want to enjoy sexual pleasure

When I was growing up there was never any embarrassment over nudity at home. As divorcees, my parents naturally enjoyed sexual relationships with various partners from time to time.

So I have never seen any reason why I should not enjoy the same easy sexual arousal and orgasm apparently promised by erotic fiction. Especially since I have been lucky enough to have:

- enthusiasm for erotic literature, sexual fantasy and masturbation;
- a sexually attractive body (pretty with a good figure);
- a close relationship with my partner and an adventurous sex life.

I was naturally curious about eroticism because I recognised that sex was a natural part of adult relationships. I saw sex as an adventure to some extent and read avidly about the exploits of prostitutes and call-girls in an attempt to understand how to be a 'good lover'.

Being a 'good lover' appeared to involve being relaxed about nudity, physical sex play and sexually explicit activities.

I understood that an 'uninhibited' woman would naturally be able to respond to being pleasured in a similar way by a man.

Even though from the very first time, I realised that sex was for the enjoyment of the men in my life, I have been willing to invest in pleasuring them because I cared about them.

Their obvious sexual frustration meant that unless I had a good reason, I accepted going along with their desire for sex.

I came to realise that the eroticism and sex play that many men hope for is often based on situations where women are being paid for offering sex. The fact is that prostitutes are, after all, not engaging in sex for their own sexual pleasure. In other words, it's all an act.

Nevertheless, I have always been determined to make the most of my sexual experiences with a partner. I find it too humiliating (and insulting to my partner) to 'put up with' sex, 'lie back and think of England' or fake orgasm.

Over time this enthusiasm inevitably has had its ups and downs but even so I have been willing to invest effort over decades in exploring ways in which my partner might be able to return the favour.

## Sex for love or for money?

No one likes to admit it but men often pay for sex (whether by supporting family or paying for dates). Nevertheless, we can differentiate between:

(1) sex for pleasure where men pay directly for sex and

(2) sex within a loving relationship.

The proposal of the sexual revolution was that the line between these two would become blurred. The suggestion was that in a more liberated world, men and women could hope to share sexual pleasure when they enter into intimate sexual relationships.

*"Certain it is that many males reach orgasm before their wives do in their marital coitus, and many females experience orgasm in only a portion of their coitus. ... Masturbation thus appears to be a better test than coitus of the female's actual capacities; and there seems to be something in the coital technique which is responsible for her slower response there.*

*... The record indicates that the average (median) female ordinarily takes a bit less than four minutes to reach orgasm in masturbation, although she may need ten to twenty minutes or more to reach that point in coitus." (Alfred Kinsey; Sexual behavior in the human female; 1953)*

No one explains how women can hope to orgasm during sex when they need 20 minutes plus yet younger men orgasm within a few minutes. Are there really so many generous male lovers out there?

Sometimes a woman knows that something is missing from sex. Other times the man suspects that his partner is faking or hopes that she would be more enthusiastic about sex if she could enjoy orgasm during sex as he does.

In some cases, the man is much more driven by sex than the woman. In other cases the couple is keen to find new ways of making sex even better over the longer-term.

We would like to share some of these ideas with other couples, who have explored a variety of sex play together in a spirit of exploration and adventure and who are open to new ideas.

## Sharing physical intimacy with a partner

I always enjoyed sharing physical intimacy with a lover but this is very different to achieving my own sexual arousal. I always knew that true sexual arousal was missing because I was familiar with orgasm from the very first time that I had sex. Very few women discover female masturbation so early in their life.

From the very early days, I appreciated the sensual aspects of sex:

- Marvelling at the responsiveness of my lover's penis and his erection;
- Enjoying the different feel of hairy skin;
- The intimacy of full-on kissing;
- The sensuality of nudity; and
- The concept of penetration.

My partners enjoyed being affectionate through touching and kissing. Naturally, they have appreciated me returning a similar level of physical fondling of their body. Thereafter the follow through to intercourse and male orgasm was from their perspective an inevitable conclusion to close physical intimacy with someone they loved.

I accepted this and did not withdraw my affection even though I did not personally want sex on each occasion. I have put effort into responding sensually and lovingly because I knew that it would pleasure my partner.

My partners have always been quick to become noticeably aroused so learning how to pleasure a man was an easy way to demonstrate my love for him.

Men approach sex already mentally aroused and so they tend to take this aspect of sex for granted. Physical stimulation only works if you are already aroused in your mind (a man needs an erection before he can orgasm).

Women might talk about feeling horny but this is more likely to indicate that they are amenable to sex than that they are just about to orgasm.

Men experience spontaneous sexual arousal as a result of testosterone (the hormone responsible for sex drive) and by seeing a woman's body. Women have neither of these benefits. Women's sexual arousal has to be consciously generated.

Researchers have known for decades that clitoral stimulation helps with female orgasm but if a lack of clitoral stimulation during intercourse were the only issue involved then why do so many men and women ask about female orgasm?

Surely couples would simply try other means of providing clitoral stimulation e.g. by hand or mouth and the problem would be solved?

The popular suggestion that women are too timid to ask for, and men too clueless to provide, the necessary clitoral stimulation during sex is patronising to the modern sexually adventurous couple. My partner and I have been very happy to try almost anything over the years.

Right from day one I tried oral sex, masturbation with a partner, positions for intercourse etc. Nothing worked and, in particular, I have never found clitoral stimulation with a partner (either manual or through oral sex) arousing enough for orgasm.

Many years later I have realised that clitoral stimulation only works during masturbation because I use sexual fantasies first to achieve the necessary arousal required for genital stimulation to lead to orgasm.

*"Many women wonder if their lack of orgasms is due to some underlying emotional or psychological problem. However, this is usually not the case at all.*

*Frequently, not having an orgasm is simply due to unfavourable circumstances, or lack of understanding about how to achieve personal sexual pleasure." (Michael Carrera; Dictionary of Sexual Terms; 1992)*

But what if female orgasm happens most naturally during masturbation alone? Frustratingly, it would seem that women are described as 'dysfunctional' (or inhibited) simply because they do not respond sexually as men do.

Porn movies are good for getting turned on to sex with a partner but do not help me achieve orgasm during female masturbation.

I have found (post 35 when my clit has become less sensitive) that my partner can stimulate me much more effectively with his fingers. Penetration is nice, conceptually, but the vagina has few nerve endings – it is, after all, the birth canal.

## Some women do explore sexual pleasure

Slowly attitudes to sexual pleasure are changing and more couples are approaching their sex life with a willingness to try activities other than vaginal intercourse.

Basically, if you are struggling with lack of arousal during sex and genuinely want to share your own arousal with a partner then you will need to be prepared to explore activities other than intercourse.

Make a special effort once in a while to spice up your sex life.

This brings welcome variety for men as well as the opportunity for a couple to explore whether more explicit clitoral stimulation might increase the woman's arousal and even lead to orgasm.

For example, many women who explore sexual pleasure with a partner find that oral sex is how they enjoy their best orgasms.

*"There is no reason why physical intimacy with men should always consist of 'foreplay' followed by intercourse and male orgasm*

*and there is no reason why intercourse must be part of heterosexual sex." (Shere Hite; The Hite Reports; 1993)*

The pre-orgasmic woman (who can orgasm only during masturbation alone) faces a unique dilemma because of the difficulty she may have in trying to reconcile a sexual relationship without orgasm.

Presumably, with oral sex becoming more accepted, couples are content when the woman can climax in this way.

But perhaps even for these women there is a similar problem if a couple still feels that ideally orgasms should result from intercourse.

One advantage of vaginal intercourse, when combined with a face-to-face position, is that it allows for the loving aspects of sexual relationships.

Equally, for many people, penetration is the greatest turn-on because it symbolises the ultimate act of intimacy with another person.

Another form of sex play, that is highly taboo especially for women, is anal sex. If a woman is open-minded and has a sensitive lover then anal stimulation/penetration combined with clitoral stimulation is likely to lead to orgasm.

As with vaginal fisting, a professional lubricant from a sex shop and plenty of time to TAKE THINGS SLOWLY are critical.

Try the book by the young American women: Em & Lo called 'The Big Bang' (2004) on both of these.

*"Anal intercourse: This is something which nearly every couple tries once.*

*A few stay with it, usually because the woman finds that it gives her more intense feelings than the normal route and it is pleasantly tight for the man." (Alex Comfort; Joy of Sex; 1972)*

Alex Comfort (author of 'Joy of Sex') was perhaps a little optimistic about the sexual adventurousness of the average couple. I would be amazed if it were proven that 'nearly every couple' tries anal sex.

If it doesn't appeal then it's not likely to be very arousing. Given the inertness of the vagina, anal sex is simply one suggestion that may provide more sensation for the woman.

Heterosexuals, confident of the moral weight of society behind them, often condemn anal sex. Personally I am not tempted by 'filching' but so what?

It is inappropriate to be judgmental about activities that consenting adults may find pleasurable.

Women's rejection of suggestions for how they might enjoy sexual pleasure is yet more evidence that women have to make a more conscious choice to learn about how their sexual arousal works.

Many women are unfamiliar with their own sexual arousal and so they have no motivation to even try activities (including masturbation and oral sex) that may lead to orgasm.

One of the unfortunate consequences of the sexual revolution was to imply that all of a sudden women were transformed from what they were before (presumably just ordinary women – wives, housewives and mothers) into fully motivated sexual beings.

# How to pleasure a man

Tracy Cox (author of 'Hot Sex' 1998) tells the story of a woman who welcomes her partner home wearing a sexy nightdress, with champagne by the bed and a pornographic movie ready to play.

If she does this regularly over the longer term then I take my hat off to her! Her partner is a very lucky man.

More realistically such pampering to a man's sexual fantasies is likely to be an occasional treat.

Nevertheless, such episodes that live out men's sexual fantasies can fuel male sexual arousal and enjoyment of more 'bread-and-butter' style sex for a while.

Fantasy style sex is likely to be occasional. If inventive sex happened every day of the week, it too would become the norm.

Nevertheless, men still hope for this ideal of everyday fantasy sex.

While at college I had a dentist with a sense of humour. Once just before starting work he asked me cheerfully, with his drill raised, whether I had any last requests.

"Not really, just be as quick as you can!" I replied. "That's exactly what my wife always says to me!" he joked.

Men don't want sex to be a chore that is 'gotten over with' as quickly as possible.

Particularly, over the course of time a man hopes for his partner to be more engaged in enjoying their intimate time together than in the early years when he could carry the day with his own arousal.

### The best female lovers learn to share eroticism

In the film 'Ruthless People' (1986) an older man hires a prostitute to have sex with him in the back of his car.

He asks her to make as much noise as possible because his wife always lies there 'like a gunny-sack'.

The prostitute duly screams and moans so much that an onlooker (who admittedly is very stupid) mistakes the couple to be a murderer and his victim.

For men to enjoy sex they need to feed their sexual fantasies, which are most effective when based on their real sex life. Hence, men want to develop the variety, spontaneity and imagination of their relationship with a sexual partner.

Men hope a lover will enhance their sexual arousal by engaging on their enjoyment of eroticism and by responding appreciatively.

*"It isn't the same for the two sexes because male turn-ons are concrete, while many female turn-ons are situational and atmospheric. ...*

*You can't of course control your turn-ons any more than he can, but it helps if a woman has some male-type object reactions, like being excited by the sight of a penis, or hairy skin, or by the man stripping, or by physical kinds of play (just as it helps if the man has some sense of atmosphere).*

*It's the active woman who understands his reaction while keeping her own who is the ideal lover." (Alex Comfort; Joy of Sex; 1972)*

Women make better lovers than men because they can put aside their own sexual arousal and focus wholeheartedly on pleasuring a man.

Younger men especially are likely to have difficulty focusing on their partner's arousal rather than their own.

Porn movies may show women pleasuring men but it's important to recognise that they are being paid.

If a man starts out more enthusiastic about sex then, over the longer-term, he needs to be willing to invest effort in pleasuring his woman.

I don't like the taste of semen so I offer my partner fellatio just as a warm-up. A shared bath is a good venue for fellatio (starting with lathering his penis) when it can be combined with a gently probing finger in his anus.

A man enjoys being licked over the tight skin holding his foreskin in place (uncircumcised). I also simulate intercourse by massaging his penis firmly with my lips (teeth well out of the way).

Sometimes I take my partner's penis as far back into my mouth as I can but this increases jaw-ache.

# Spice up your sex life

A young woman, who had promised her father that she would remain a virgin until a certain age, complied with his request by having anal sex with her partners (Note: STD protection and contraceptives still required).

Unsurprisingly, she was very popular with men who tend not to be so hung-up about breaking sexual taboos.

To be fair though – we expect more of women.

There is no such thing as a male slut, no matter how 'wantonly' a man behaves. Some women do explore sexual pleasure but there are many unflattering terms for women who are sexually adventurous.

A strong argument against anal sex is that it is not 'natural'.

Unfortunately 'natural sex' is usually defined in terms of reproduction rather than sexual pleasure.

Looked at another way, the very fact that the anal area is an erogenous zone means that Nature designed it that way.

It is society that tells us to place moral restrictions on how we enjoy sexual pleasure even with a consenting partner.

Seriously though, can you imagine a sex life based on vaginal intercourse alone over a life-time?

No wonder couples stop having sex – boredom alone would kill anyone's sexual desire.

*"Since intercourse has been defined as the basic form of sexuality, and the only natural, healthy and moral form of physical contact, it has automatically been assumed that this is when women should orgasm." (Shere Hite; The Hite Reports; 1993)*

Many women experience a lack of arousal during sex because sex is not designed to facilitate female orgasm, either physically or psychologically.

## Sexual pleasure at any price

Men's drive to enjoy their sexuality is stronger than women's and so they are able to push aside any qualms about what is 'proper' more easily than we can.

Men might have difficulty understanding this limitation but then they are not usually the ones compromised by sex.

They are also more prone to opt for sexual pleasure at any price.

A woman told me that a gay friend had to wear a tampon in his rectum because the sphincter muscle around his anus had become loose from over indulgence.

As with all good things, moderation is key!

Em & Lo suggest in 'The Big Bang' (2004) that anal sex can even lead to a healthier awareness of the anal area.

Nina Hartley, who runs sex clinics in the US, also deals sensitively with this topic in erotic movies.

*"... with enough relaxation, communication, lubrication and TLC, anal sex can actually strengthen your sphincter muscles." (Em & Lo; The Big Bang; 2004)*

Our enjoyment of sexual pleasure will always depend to some degree on our willingness to indulge our sexual fantasies as well as to explore our own sexuality and our sexual relationship with a lover.

Ultimately we each need to find our own personal balance between reconciling our moral beliefs and enjoying our sexual experiences.

Heterosexual women need to come out of the closet over sex. Sex by its very nature cannot be pure.

The most taboo concepts are likely to be the most arousing.

Sexual fantasies are all very well but liberated women (if they are also sexually motivated) need to start admitting which sexual activities they find most effective for enjoying sexual arousal with a partner.

# Stories: Misconceptions

# Interpreting experiences of female orgasm

When a man is stimulated sexually by a partner he finds it difficult to avoid becoming aroused. Similarly, if a woman's response to penile thrusting (or any other physical stimulation technique) was automatic then women would presumably be unable to avoid becoming aroused whatever their conscious desires.

So in the movie 'Swordfish' (2001) Hugh Jackman hacks into the US Department of Defence, while threatened at gun point and seriously distracted by a hooker sucking him off. This scene simply would not work if the roles were reversed - quite apart from the fact that few top hackers are women!

*"I only ever orgasm with a partner through oral sex and only if he's really good at it. Lots of my girlfriends claim they come during intercourse but to be honest, I don't believe them. I'm sexually educated and have a high, healthy libido and if I don't have vaginal orgasms, I can't see why they would." (Tracey Cox; Hot Sex; 1998)*

If only we could all apply such good common sense! We have very few channels for sharing our sexual experiences. Sometimes we assume that others must experience real life quite differently to ourselves even though there is no logical reason why they should.

Just remember that bluffers, fakers and sex surveys do not provide reliable sex information.

*"Read all the sex surveys you want but you still won't really know what other people do in bed because what people say and what people do are two totally different things." (Tracey Cox; Hot Sex; 1998)*

## The sexual fantasy view of female sexuality

When I have tried to talk to others about sex (not as a teenager but as a mature woman), I have been shocked by how defensive people can be.

I am very happy for women who say they have orgasmic sex from day one. But this is not the case for all women.

Don't get me wrong – I would love to believe that couples can enjoy the mutual and easy sexual pleasure portrayed in porn movies and erotic novels.

It's just that, for me, reality never matched up and I think it is more useful to work with reality rather than hanker after some impossible-to-achieve fantasy.

Sexual ego is harmful if it prevents us from keeping an open mind and being willing to learn from our real life sexual experiences. As soon as I experienced a lack of arousal during sex with a partner, I suspected that descriptions of women's ability to orgasm easily during sex must be fictitious. So why have women not stood up and said:

"But that's ridiculous. My body and brain just do not react like that!"

One obvious reason is personal embarrassment. Another is that, although as heterosexual women our physical responses must be similar, our interpretation of those experiences can be quite different depending on our attitude and expectations.

Finally we are, often subconsciously, guilty of becoming defensive of our sexual fantasies and sexual egos. We cannot accept the facts even when they are laid out before us. The concept of 'that's just the way it is – take it or leave it' does not appeal.

*"Many males are disappointed after marriage to find that their wives are not responding regularly and are not as interested in having as frequent sexual contact as they, the males, would like to have;*

*and a great many of the married females may be disappointed and seriously disturbed when they find that they are not responding in their coitus, and not enjoying sexual relations as they had anticipated they would.*

*...in view of the diverse pre-marital backgrounds of the spouses in the average marriage, it is not surprising that they sometimes find it difficult to adjust sexually. It is MORE surprising that so many married couples are EVER able to work out a satisfactory sexual arrangement."*

(Alfred Kinsey; Sexual behavior in the human female; 1953)

Unfortunately, sex advice for women is often misleading because, for the most part, sex experts deal with sexual dysfunction and young people's ignorance of the basic sexual facts.

In fact, there is no intentional campaign to disseminate misinformation but simply a lack of understanding in an intensely personal area of our lives.

# Talking to women about female orgasm

Since the experts I talked to had no rational explanations, I decided to do my own research by talking to women I met in everyday life. I quickly learned just how highly embarrassing it is to approach women on such an intimate topic.

Very few women are willing to talk about sex at all and even fewer have anything to say about female orgasm.

The vast majority is silent so who knows what they think? We might imagine that at least some are quietly getting on with it; too busy doing to be talking about it.

But when I mention sex (only to those women I hope will not drop dead from shock at the mention of the word!) most women simply ignore me or change the subject.

They don't even risk a commonplace comment like 'How interesting!' or 'How brave!'. I can only assume that women's sexual experiences are not as sensational as we'd like to hope.

*"Because there is such wide variation in the sexual responsiveness and frequencies of overt activity among females, many females are incapable of understanding other females. There are fewer males who are incapable of understanding other males.*

*... Sensing something of this variation in capacities and experience, many females – although not all – hesitate to discuss their sexual histories with other females, ..." (Alfred Kinsey; Sexual behavior in the human female; 1953)*

Men may exaggerate their sexual abilities but they do not grossly misrepresent their sexuality the way that women do.

Naturally there is distrust between women who suspect that those, who claim to be sensationally orgasmic, are simply reacting to men's desire for a responsive sexual partner.

I have talked to women of varying ages. No doubt, people will tell me that I have encountered an unrepresentative group of women.

One woman suggested that I must 'live in a broom cupboard' because of the reactions I have reported. They have no idea.

## Most women show little interest in orgasm

Anyone who doubts that these attitudes exist should get out of their own broom cupboard.

I challenge anyone who thinks that everyone is happy to talk about their sex life to try approaching women they know: relatives, friends, neighbours, etc.

Many people claim to be relaxed about sex but they run a mile if you ask for details.

Likewise women may joke together as a group and compare notes over their lovers' sexual performance but never their own.

The women who were brave enough to talk to me admitted that they had never divulged the same details to anyone else not even to their closest friends.

A young woman in her mid-twenties told me that she was too embarrassed to talk to anyone about her inability to orgasm during sex. She had assumed that it was her boyfriend's fault and that perhaps she didn't love him enough.

Only once I told her some of the facts that might explain her experience was she brave enough to mention the issue to her mother.

Her mother, a medical doctor, replied (with slight bravado given her previous silence): "Of course you don't orgasm during sex!"

Some women accept such conclusions without questioning. Others want to understand why popular beliefs are so misleading.

I certainly did. Unfortunately, it isn't done to question because people feel uncomfortable when they have no answers.

One woman told me that she would never allow her adult children to have sex in her house. I do not understand this attitude towards sex but it was clearly impolite to ask for an explanation.

Even discussing the taboo nature of sex is a sensitive subject.

## Women who appear to want sexual pleasure

When I was 21, I met an Italian boy of the same age during a stay in Rome. Alfredo cared about how he dressed and would often check his appearance in the mirror. I teased him because I had always been taught that personal vanity was undesirable.

Alfredo wore designer sunglasses in the day but one evening as we were going out, I saw that he was wearing eye make-up. First I thought it odd but quickly realised how straight I was being.

After all, film stars wear make-up. I decided that it was a compliment and a turn-on that the man I was going out with had gone to the effort of making himself attractive. It's a shame that more men don't spend time and money on making more of their looks.

Most men would benefit from a complete make-over of their wardrobe by a woman friend. Start with some sexy underwear and nightwear.

Buy some figure hugging tee shirts for wearing under shirts: worn open at the neck. Make sure you have a smart jacket and designer jeans as a minimum for dates.

Heterosexual men often assume that it is only women who need to attract a lover. Dressing attractively is strongly associated with women and gays (who both dress to attract men), so many straight men see their disregard for their looks as a sign of their masculinity.

Heterosexual men don't dress up because women's sexual arousal does not arise from the provocative display of a lover's body as men's does. However by dressing sexily a man can acknowledge the effort that his woman makes for him. Naturally a man needs to work on getting rid of any beer gut first!

I have never felt it necessary to dress in a sexually provocatively way. I am lucky to be naturally attractive so I have never had a problem being able to attract the men I want.

Men don't always appreciate women's use of make-up and my male lovers have been pleased that I don't wear it. I didn't see the point in encouraging yet more passing compliments and advances from men.

Consequently I am always amazed when women claim to be unaware of the effect that the sight of their body can have on a man. Perhaps they have difficulty understanding because women do not become sexually aroused (get an erection) at the sight of a naked male body.

In fact, most women probably prefer to see a man dressed in a style that indicates his social status, for example: James Bond in black tie evening suit and Richard Gere in naval uniform in 'An Officer and a Gentleman' (1982).

As an attractive woman you get a great deal of attention when you look good. It's not just men that notice. So when a woman dresses provocatively it is more about competing with other women according to feminine values of attractiveness than about appealing sexually to men. For example, men would not necessarily define their ideal woman in line with the fashion industry.

Some women do dress in order to attract male attention but they still expect to be able to select the man they want. Men often assume that women are indicating a general enthusiasm for sexual pleasure.

This tendency for men to misinterpret women's motivations explains why, in more conservative societies, women cover up their bodies more than we do in the West.

Men often assume that women respond as men do but male sexuality is very different to female sexuality. Women are not fascinated by genitals, either their own or those of the opposite sex.

After puberty, men's sexual reaction to nudity is so strong that they have new associations with genitals. For women, the connection with going to the bathroom remains into adulthood.

Most people are still shocked by the idea that women might enjoy orgasm. When I asked a female doctor for information about female sexuality, she did not appear to understand the term.

Eroticism is strongly associated with women providing men with sexual pleasure, typically in an immoral context. Otherwise women's interest in sex is assumed to revolve around family and relationships.

An older male doctor referred me to the family planning library in London. I was truly depressed to find that the information related to the reproductive aspects of women's sexuality: contraception, pregnancy and childbirth. Most sex information today, even for men, comes from the sex industry rather than from more official sources.

# Bluffers, fakers and sex surveys

Pam, an attractive woman in her late forties, told me that she had never had a problem with sexual arousal and orgasm.

She started masturbating at the age of eight and after thirty years with the same man, she was still enjoying orgasmic sex as she had done from day one.

Women's sexual arousal and orgasm are not automatic for reasons of anatomy if nothing else – the clitoris is not directly stimulated during intercourse.

So it is difficult to know how to respond to someone who suggests that fantasy sex is a reality for them. The implication is that the rest of us have gone badly wrong somewhere!

In an attempt to identify some specifics of her sexual experiences, I asked Pam when she experienced orgasm.

She replied that the timing of her orgasm was 'a moving feast' and that she could orgasm before, during or after intercourse.

*"Even Sharon Stone admits that she did women a disservice in 'Basic Instinct' by suggesting that they could reach orgasm in about 30 seconds flat.*

*This is just not how the female body works, and anyone who suggests otherwise is either a good actress, deluded or blessed by the gods." (Marina Muratore; The Bluffer's Guide to Women; 1998)*

Are these women bluffing or are they just incredibly lucky? If this approach works for you then definitely stick with it!

## Fantasy sex where orgasms just happen

I was interested to find out some more details in order to find parallels with other women's experiences.

However, Pam replied that sex was not a subject that could be analysed. She suggested that orgasms just happened naturally, flowing from the passion of the sexual act.

People get away with claiming complete nonsense about sex just because no one challenges the common sense of their assertions.

As many women never experience real female orgasms they can bluff and be bluffed surprisingly easily. For example, eight-year-old girls may touch their genitals innocently but this is very different to the kind of adult sexual activity that leads to orgasm.

Most women never compare masturbation with sex because they never learn to masturbate to orgasm in the first place. They assume that sexual arousal and orgasm must come from the emotional aspects of a loving relationship.

I asked Pam whether she had continued to masturbate. She replied that masturbation was 'but a sneeze' compared with the orgasms she enjoyed with her partner.

Men continue to masturbate throughout their lives but women often imply that the emotional rewards of a sexual relationship replace any need to masturbate.

We all draw different conclusions from our sexual experiences. After thirty years in a relationship, Pam told me that she could not recall even one serious argument.

She and her partner bickered endlessly about trivial matters but had never fallen out over anything serious (even though they had raised children together).

This experience is so different from my own, or that of other couples I have observed, that it is easy to react cynically. Perhaps Pam's idea of bickering was my idea of a full-scale war.

However, let's be generous and allow that anything is possible, even the 'perfect' match. One explanation for this anomaly could be that the couple place few demands on each other.

Presumably, for a fortunate few, the erotic stories describing the overwhelming sexual arousal that fictional women have from vaginal penetration are a reality.

For the rest of us these stories remain in the realm of fiction – frankly unachievable.

## Is sexual arousal with a partner really so easy?

I approached my adult life in anticipation of a mutually enjoyable sex life. This optimism was fuelled by my love of erotic literature, which I read avidly as a teenager. I enjoyed exploring my sexual fantasies and by the age of seventeen I discovered orgasm through female masturbation.

When I had sex for the first time at the age of eighteen with a man I found attractive and admired (notice that only women are supposed to need these factors in order to enjoy sex), I was disappointed because the experience left me cold – not even the hint of any sexual arousal.

Apparently I was not the first woman to have this experience.

In fact, after consulting a sex clinic and reading all the available information I could find over many years, it seemed that my experience was – QUITE NORMAL.

So why were other women not as outraged as I was?

Don't other women want to tell younger generations that the suggestion that women's sexual arousal during sex is easy – is MISLEADING at the very least?

Few women challenge the media portrayals of the spontaneously orgasmic women because by doing so, they risk exposing their own sexual inadequacy. But this assumes women are just as sexual as men.

So it is assumed that most women must experience at least some sexual pleasure with a partner. I doubted this simply because I found so few women who were prepared to be open about sex.

Sure there was bravado but very little explicit detail about how women can enjoy sex.

Women who did claim to orgasm with a partner avoided questions by implying that anyone who doubted the mutual pleasure of sex must be sexually inadequate.

In fact, this is a form of intimidation or bullying. It is a defensive behaviour. We all know that there are women who are less than enthusiastic about sex but their point of view is discounted as irrelevant.

After taking fairly extreme steps, I was able to confirm that my partner and I were a perfectly normal couple. So when you press the point, experts do admit that a woman is likely to find orgasm considerably more elusive than a man does.

And yet, it is still difficult to find this fact publicised anywhere or anyone willing to agree that a man might stand to gain more (in a direct sense) from a sexual relationship.

The fact is that people who earn their living from the sex industry, only make money by providing the public with what we want to hear – fantasy more often than reality.

To me it was so evident when I met my first boyfriend that I couldn't understand why every woman didn't have the same reaction. Perhaps they were not as open with their men. How can you admire a man's easy erection and his orgasm without appreciating that women just don't have it as easy?

Even when we do orgasm it is just a pleasure – very nice and very enjoyable. But it does not provide the central meaning to life. Men just die with pleasure as soon as they get into your knickers. Come on! It's just not the same for women. I wish it were…

Of those women who have talked about their sexual experiences (the few that I can believe because they talk about their experiences in a way that tallies with the facts that I know about female sexuality from my own body's reactions) most have had much the same experience as me.

These women are in a minority because, after ten years of attempting to talk to women about sex, the vast majority of women say nothing and I suspect have no particular ambition to understand their sexuality.

I would like my daughters to have the experience of orgasm but I do not want them to be duped by all the claims of easy orgasm during sex with a partner. My daughters' generation should have more facts about how women can get the most out of sex.

Of course there will be people who object to what I am saying. I understand that. It is not possible to question the status quo without causing discomfort.

Sex is both highly political and highly emotional – not a good mix.

# Sexual fact versus sexual fantasy

Imagine the scenario: a woman, wearing a skirt and no panties, climbs a ladder. A man below enjoys a clear view of her genitals.

Imagine now that the genders are reversed: my point is that a woman is unlikely to appreciate the view in the same way that a man does.

Of course, someone will always disagree. A man said: "It depends from woman to woman, because if they want a quickie they like to take a look at your nakedness."

"Drop your pants" was an order I got from a girlfriend once in Brisbane who was a Buddhist, when she saw the size of me she stripped and said 'try to satisfy me – you are very big' and I did.

Second time I got that order was before I married in Tagbilaran. My now wife laid down and said: "Let's see how big you are – the bigger the better", that was before we got married and she went mad for me."

Men must think that women were born yesterday. Of course a sexually experienced woman appreciates the turn-on for a man if she emulates male sexual reactions.

It is also a fact that many women fake orgasm.

*"It is difficult for most males to comprehend that females are not aroused by seeing male genitalia. Some males never come to comprehend this." (Alfred Kinsey; Sexual behavior in the human female; 1953)*

Women can enjoy many aspects of physical intimacy with a lover but we are not automatically aroused, the way men are, because our bodies are not full of the sex hormone, testosterone.

Equally, we don't get a hard-on (clitoral erection) by looking at male nudity: even the body and genitals of our partner. Otherwise women would pay for sex and the sight of the male body more than they do.

No doubt there are women who pay for a male lap- or pole-dancer but, I think we all know, most would not.

If we are to accept the facts of female sexuality, we need to leave the sexual fantasy and look around the real world.

Men may be able to imagine that sexually attractive young women are always on the brink of orgasm. But what about other women?

Do we think that a stunning man enjoys sex more or is more sexually driven than an ugly man? No.

Even if a man is middle-aged, ugly, pigeon-chested or has a pot-belly, we know that he is just as likely to masturbate or pay for sex as the next guy. Similarly we know that, regardless of her looks, very few heterosexual women masturbate and almost none pay for sex.

Logic tells us that heterosexual women's sexuality is the same whatever the age or attractiveness of the woman. The rest is just part of the sexual game that men fall for. After all, men and women play for different stakes – who pays the bill, for example?

Some people believe the sexual fantasy regardless of the evidence: "I must shake my head in wonder as to what women you have spent time with (or possibly they are VERY, very, young women who have not yet discovered their own sexuality).

An older woman, say 30 to 55, is easily aroused. A well built man on a beach can absolutely stimulate a woman without her knowing him. Women are quite willing to 'act like a whore' in the bedroom and enjoy it, and as well they should, to the fullest."

Women who take a pro-active sexual role are described as acting 'like a whore' precisely because not every woman behaves in this way. Few heterosexual men are paid for sex because men tend to be enthusiastic about sex whatever the circumstances.

Women are more concerned about commitment and trust than about orgasm. Presumably this is why is it so often suggested that women's sexual arousal depends on her relationship with a lover or on the love-making skills of a particular lover.

Men have a much stronger sex drive than women so they want sex regardless of whether they are in a relationship. Men can enjoy sex with any attractive woman, even a prostitute.

Also for many men, the only way they can enjoy the delights of oral sex, for example, is by paying because most wives and girlfriends are not willing to engage on such explicitly sexual activities.

## Why it can be difficult to discuss our sexual experiences

One of the reasons that adults find it difficult to discuss sex openly is because of the personal nature of sex. It's important to consider how other people might feel as a result of what we say.

So men can be offended if it is implied that because they are enthusiastic about sex this necessarily means that they are less discriminating.

Not every man has been with a prostitute, for example.

Naturally there are women who are promiscuous but this is more down to personality and personal values than to sex drive. They have something to prove but it's not about enjoying orgasm during sex.

There is no value in judging people's sexual decisions but only in differentiating between men and women's motivations in a sexual relationship. These are likely to differ because it is much more difficult for a woman to orgasm during sex.

The evidence supporting women's greater difficulties with sexual arousal compared with men are well documented.

Nevertheless, it takes great courage to be truly open and honest about our personal sexual experiences.

Anyone who does so makes an easy target for others who may not be so ready to put their own experiences under the spotlight!

It's great that some women experience easy sexual arousal with a partner. But this is certainly not true for all women.

It's important, when offering advice, not to insinuate that any woman who does not orgasm during sex is sexually inadequate.

In over 10 years of talking to women about sex I have found very few who are willing to be explicit.

The vast majority of women are offended by any sexual phenomena as explicit as clitoral stimulation or sexual fantasies.

They approach sex through their relationship and assume that sex revolves around emotional and sensual (rather than explicitly sexual or erotic) pleasures.

*"For most males, discussions of sex often provide some sort of erotic stimulation.*

*They do not provide anything like the same sort of stimulation for the average female, and in consequence she does not have the same inspiration for engaging in such conversations." (Alfred Kinsey; Sexual behavior in the human female; 1953)*

Women who are confident that orgasm with a partner is easy may want to consider whether we are talking about the same experience.

A woman who masturbates appreciates how to take a mental state of sexual arousal to orgasm through genital stimulation.

If we are to encourage women to be more open about sex it is important to respect each other's experiences.

I am specifically offering reassurance to women who are familiar with orgasm from female masturbation and who would like to experience something similar with a partner.

A woman who masturbates (as an adult activity with the aim of enjoying sexual arousal and orgasm) is likely to be hoping for true sexual arousal from sex because she is familiar with orgasm.

It's a real positive that men slow down a bit as they grow older (post 35) – older men stand to make better lovers!

It is much more difficult for a younger man to focus on his partner's arousal because his own orgasm is his top priority.

Equally the clitoris becomes slightly less sensitive and so a lover may be able to stimulate a woman's clitoris more directly – still gently and over the hood though.

Over time, the man needs to learn how to pleasure a woman using erotic and sensual massage. Even if orgasm is missing, a woman will appreciate a sex life that is more two-way.

# Why do so few women comment on sexual pleasure?

I am not so crazy as to approach just any random woman on the subject of sex. I know that most women will be irreversibly offended even at the mention of sex. So I choose women who appear to be fairly liberated and then I approach the subject tangentially.

Of the women I have been brave enough to approach, the vast majority have shunned me. It is this almost fearful reaction that so many women have to any mention of sex that causes me to question the assertion that women are just as enthusiastic about sex as men are.

To date, not one woman has said "Wow, aren't you brave! I would love to compare notes. Please feel free to ask me any questions you want to." Let's face it, openness about sex is much more difficult for women because of misunderstanding about female sexuality.

Of the few women who have been willing to discuss their sexual experiences, only a couple have talked about easy orgasm. See 'Some women never tune into eroticism' – p82 and 'Bluffers, fakers and sex surveys' – p234.

Both women talked about sex in terms of their relationship. One was openly disgusted by any form of eroticism and the other was dismissive of female masturbation even though these are both fundamental to men's sexuality.

The modern liberated view is that women reach orgasm during sex almost as easily as men do. The more conservative view is that a woman only finds sex rewarding as part of a loving relationship.

Ironically both of these approaches imply that women enjoy sexual arousal 'naturally' during sex and make it difficult for women to compare notes on how to orgasm with a partner.

The popular belief is that women need do nothing other than be on the receiving end of male thrusting to enjoy sex fully.

So although the average woman is shocked by the idea of sexual fantasies and never masturbates, we still assume that she experiences sexual arousal and orgasm during sex.

How on earth can this logically be?

Although everyone assumes that women enjoy sex as much as men, the fact is that relatively few women ever comment on sex.

I am challenging women who say that orgasm with a partner is easy, not only because their experience does not tally with the known facts but also because they are contributing towards the continuing misunderstanding of female sexuality.

The fact is that women do not experience spontaneous sexual arousal as men do. This explains why most women do not masturbate and why women often interpret their sexual experiences in terms of their relationship.

The sensations arising from a woman's loving emotions may be very pleasant but it is not likely that they equate to the phenomenon that men call orgasm.

The idea that female orgasm is achieved through emotional feelings is misleading because:

- When these women claim to orgasm easily during sex, women who are asking about lack of orgasm with a partner assume that we are all talking about the same experience; and

- Unfortunately emotional passion tends to wane over the longer-term and men, hoping for an active sex life, have difficulty understanding why women are no longer interested in sex.

There seems to be a surprising amount of resistance to asking women to account for their sexual experiences. I simply want to get a more open discussion of the facts so that we can be sure that we are all talking about the same kind of experiences.

I am taking all the risk and yet other people are so easily defensive. Surely it is in all our interests to improve our understanding of the facts?

I have legitimate questions and I am looking for answers in a society that claims to support rational explanations.

# Taking the ego out of sex advice

Why do adults so often assume that they know everything about sex when most people have never even read a sex manual?

Everyone is entitled to their own opinion but why do they have to flaunt their own sexual ego? Whatever our own personal views there is absolutely no need to express them in a way that belittles other people.

Despite their inexperience, women can be supremely confident in offering advice: "I love sex and I am sure I love it just as much as men do. If you are not enjoying sex you need a new partner. You should be enjoying sex! ... I have had many lovers which I completely and thoroughly enjoyed wild, hot, passionate sex just for sex sake! "

If women were truly willing to be helpful, they would express their views with more humility. They make highly inflammatory comments when, in truth, they know very little about sex. It is this arrogant and intimidating approach that holds other people back from talking about sex.

Are such women even aware that orgasm exists? They talk about 'enjoying' sex but rarely about true female sexual arousal and orgasm. They are happy with their sexual experiences because sex totally fulfils their expectations. They never appreciate that some women approach sex with an expectation for orgasm.

I am discussing sex on a different and more questioning level. For example, when I had sex for the first time I already knew how to masturbate myself to orgasm. Most women never learn how to masturbate, never mind how to orgasm during sex. Other women only learn about orgasm through masturbation much later. So they have nothing to compare sex with.

As recently as the 1950s (sex has been around for eons), society was shocked to the core when Alfred Kinsey proposed that women might even be capable of orgasm. So if orgasm is just as easy for women as it is for men, then it must be the best kept secret ever.

Equally (if women orgasm easily) why is there so much advice on how a man can give his woman an orgasm?

Even today, with all the information we have, our liberated views and easy access to sexual partners my point is that it cannot be that every women in the world (or even just in western society) now experiences orgasm during sex. Most people still don't even appreciate that the clitoris is the female sex organ and the source of a woman's orgasm however she claims to achieve it.

This is because clitoral stimulation only works once a woman is aroused enough in her mind for genital stimulation to be effective. Even if a woman realises that her sexual arousal works through focusing on complex erotic scenarios during female masturbation alone, it is much less intuitive for her to even consider using similar orgasm techniques during sex with a partner.

Women who are claiming that it is all so easy need to start offering more factual substance to back their claims of orgasm. Any woman who knows anything about her own sexual arousal knows that women have to work up to sex. A woman who admits that arousal takes longer, for example, or that she has to work at achieving her own arousal is more credible.

It is a FACT that since very few women masturbate, by definition, most women approach sex without any knowledge of what orgasm feels like or how to achieve it. So they ASSUME that female orgasm occurs as easily as male orgasm does. The pleasures they enjoy during sex, whether sensual pleasure or sharing physical intimacy, they attribute to arousal and orgasm.

Dating is easy because of the romance that often accompanies sex. Try being married for ten to twenty years and many couples find that a good sex life requires a little investment. Again if it all continues blissfully for you, great, but there's no need to patronise others. You may think that you have all the answers but if you are to help others you will need to provide specifics.

*"Our data suggest that there may be as many as two-thirds of the marriages which, at least on occasion in the course of the years, run into serious disagreement over sexual relationships. In a considerable number, there is constant disagreement over sexual relationships.*

*In perhaps three-quarters of the divorces recorded in our case histories, sexual factors were among those which had led to the divorce." (Alfred Kinsey; Sexual behavior in the human female; 1953)*

# The sexual revolution set false hopes for female sexuality

Up until the 1950s society believed that women only had sex either for the purposes of procreation or to satisfy their partner.

Alfred Kinsey's revelation in 1953 that women also experience orgasm caused a sensation.

His report was attacked for being 'anti-family' in claiming high incidences of male infidelity (40%) and homosexuality (37%) as well as female masturbation (62%), which others thought to be unrepresentative.

Nevertheless the media jumped on the idea that women could match men's experience of orgasm, especially during sex.

Kinsey's findings indicating women's much lower levels of sexual responsiveness (based on incidences of orgasm) compared to men were simply ignored.

Women who did not achieve sexual arousal and orgasm during sex as easily as men, who had previously been labelled 'frigid' were now considered to be sexually dysfunctional.

The fact that this 'dysfunction' was so prevalent among women, and yet unheard of in men, was never questioned.

This new definition of female sexuality implied that, once relieved of the old-fashioned female inhibitions, truly modern and liberated women's minds and bodies would respond just the same as men's had always done.

Women were pressured into exaggerating both their sexual desire and their sexual arousal as well as into faking orgasm to keep men happy.

Others understood that women's sexual role is to satisfy men's sexual desire and that some women are more manipulative than others. What have women to gain by admitting to any sexual inadequacy?

So women fake orgasm rather than visit a sex clinic. They assume that sex is one of those areas of human life that will never be truthful (and as I found they are right).

## The power of female sexuality is to arouse men

When girls become women they learn that men's response to their body provides them with a tremendous advantage both in earning easy admiration and in their relationships with the opposite sex.

In the film 'Dangerous Liaisons' (1988) Glenn Close asserts that sex involves women using their sexuality to manipulate men. Women's advantage comes from the fact that men need sex so intensely whereas women do not need sex at all.

This power causes resentment between women because those who pander to men's sexual fantasies are seen to be capitalising on this male vulnerability and thereby often threatening the stability of marriage and family.

As a teenager, I was naive (or optimistic) enough to believe in the promises of the sexual revolution. Later, after meeting with so little sympathy and so much defensiveness, I decided to highlight the difficulties for women who hope to orgasm during sex.

*"Since the frequencies of masturbation depend primarily on the physiologic state and the volition of the female, they may provide a significant measure of the level of her interest in sexual activity.*

*Heterosexual activities ... are more often initiated by the male partner and, in consequence, they do not provide as good a measure of the female's innate capacities and sexual interests."*

(Alfred Kinsey; Sexual behavior in the human female; 1953)

So despite the claims of orgasm during sex, women rarely initiate sex. Kinsey acknowledged that female masturbation was used as the basis for observing women's sexual responses including orgasm.

My familiarity with orgasm from masturbation made it more difficult for me to accept a lack of arousal during sex. That said, although orgasm is a very pleasant feeling it is still not something that I would think life was not worth living without.

Female orgasm is important not only to some women today but also to many men who want their partner to be aroused through sex. A woman can ignore the problem to a degree because she doesn't have the same need that men have to orgasm with a partner. So the modern pressure on sexual relationships is often driven by men's insistence that women should orgasm.

# Stories: Understanding men

# Men are fascinated by sex

When I was seeing Bruce, a sexual psychologist, Peter also went along for one session by himself. It was a rare opportunity for two men to compare notes on techniques for female sexual arousal.

Peter told Bruce how he had masturbated a woman on a transatlantic flight. He had told her about some sexual fantasy scenarios while stimulating her clitoris.

Apparently, Bruce was very impressed with this story.

His interest in the story (given he was a sex professional) highlighted to me how little adventure the average person has. Real life sexual adventures appear to be particularly important to men.

A female magazine editor was amazed at the response to an article about women's underwear. Their offices were inundated with correspondence from men interested in women's panties.

Men's sexual arousal relies on fairly basic concepts whereas women look for a more sophisticated sexual context.

Lonnie Barbach was disappointed when she approached several writers of erotic fiction.

*"'Do you really want real experiences?' One woman wrote. 'Mine are awfully depressing, by and large. However, I have some fictional scenes that are quite exciting.'*

*Another said 'Alas, I am sorry to say that I cannot recall any turn-on real life experiences. I live a very bland existence. The only fun I have is with my book characters.'"* (Lonnie Barbach; pxiv Pleasures; 1984)

## Men are more easily tempted by sexual pleasure

On a business trip to Germany, Peter's foreign colleagues met him at the airport. As they drove into the city, they invited him to join them for the evening as they visited the brothels of the city.

Men seem to think it quite natural that, whether he is married or not, a man is free to consider opportunities for sexual pleasure while he is away from home.

*"To most males the desire for variety in sexual activity seems as reasonable as the desire for variety in the books that one reads, the*

*music that one hears, the recreations in which one engages, and the friends with whom one associates socially.*

*On the other hand, many females find it difficult to understand why any male who is happily married should want to have coitus with any female other than his wife." (Alfred Kinsey; Sexual behavior in the human female; 1953)*

On another business trip to the USA, my partner was shown to his room by one of the hotel maids.

As he was putting his bags down, the maid pulled up her skirt to reveal that she was wearing no underwear. She asked if he needed any other services.

Firstly it is worth noting that if the genders were the other way around, it is likely that a female guest (unless she was extremely liberated or had a good sense of humour) would complain to the hotel about the sexually offensive behaviour of its staff.

Secondly, in offering sex without any provocation the maid must have been fairly confident that at least some men would be interested in having sex with a stranger.

It would seem that men take up sexual opportunities as they arise much more readily than a woman would in the same situation.

Naturally there are always exceptions. A young woman in her late twenties told me about a girlfriend of hers.

The friend regularly walks up to strange men, perhaps as many as a handful in one evening, and without even introducing herself starts kissing the man on the mouth. I asked whether any of the men ever objected.

The woman looked at me quizzically and laughed, "What a man object to being kissed by an attractive stranger? Of course not!"

It is inconceivable that a man would reject the advances of a woman and yet few women would welcome the same advances from a man even after an introduction.

# Men's sexual fantasies

In pursuit of knowledge and understanding of sexual arousal, I went to a large newsagent in London's Oxford Street to review the covers of fifty or more pornographic magazines lined up on the top shelf.

Over 90% were directed towards heterosexual men. Most of the remainder was male homosexual pornography. The few pornographic magazines for women were for lesbians.

Although pornography is labelled 'adult' as if this is a unisex indulgence, the truth is that the vast majority of women never engage on the subject.

Censorship protects not only minors but also the many adult women who are disgusted and offended by men's enjoyment of the physical.

Officially, human sexuality is always presented in terms of a relationship. This allows male and female sexuality to be viewed purely through social liaisons and reproduction.

Little importance is placed on the massive sex industry because of the taboo over men paying women for sex.

The British magazine 'Men's Health' (March 2000) refers to men's 'secret porn stash'.

Men's sexual arousal is usually easy and men buy pornography because (in the absence of the real thing) they need assistance with releasing their sexual frustration caused by their daily arousal.

*"After thinking about sex every six seconds for six days, men are beginning to need to do something about it." (Anthony Mason; The Bluffer's Guide to Men; 1998)*

Younger men can make do with masturbation (sometimes as much as two or three times a day) for days at a time but eventually (usually by the weekend!) they want to engage in some real action.

If men were happy to masturbate indefinitely as a substitute for sex then there really would be a chance that the human race could die out!

Men may find thrusting during penetrative sex to be the most satisfying way of releasing their sexual emotions simply because nature intended it that way.

## Men's sexual fantasies map onto reality more easily than women's

Perhaps it is worth stating the obvious that men do not reach orgasm simply through looking at images of the female form.

In their minds, they also need to contemplate what they would like to be doing with a sexual partner.

Men have a much easier time, than women typically do, of transferring orgasm techniques to sex.

On the physical side, the vagina may not grip the penis as firmly as a hand but the penis is still directly stimulated.

Equally men's sexual fantasies map fairly easily onto a real life sexual encounter.

Instead of looking at pictures of naked women, a man now has the real thing in front of him.

*"Reality and fantasy are further apart for women than for men ..." (Rachel Swift; Satisfaction Guaranteed; 1996)*

Initially, the turn-on of a new sexual partner is enough for a man to reach orgasm without any further assistance. However, over time men also use sexual fantasies to help them through more routine sex by visualising more adventurous sexual episodes.

*" ... people who report most guilt about having fantasies during intercourse have higher levels of sexual dissatisfaction and dysfunction than those who are relatively guilt-free." (Masters & Johnson; Human Sexuality; 1995)*

Since a woman is not biologically driven to reach orgasm, she approaches sex appreciating how her body causes a man to become sexually aroused.

A woman enjoys her own sexual arousal by focusing on fantasies that revolve around imagining a man's desire to enjoy her body sexually and to penetrate her (take her).

Women's sexual psychology is naturally tuned into being on the receiving (as opposed to initiating) end of sex. So women get turned on by the idea of things being done to them.

# The marvel of male sexuality

The film 'The Way We Were' (1973) stars Barbra Streisand and Robert Redford (the Brad Pitt of my mother's generation).

She's the young woman from a humble background driven by political ideals; he's the young man from a privileged family who has no ideals.

Of course she's a virgin and she ends up one night with him in the bed naked. He's so drunk that he's just thrown up in her bathroom.

Nevertheless she hopes that he will notice a naked woman lying next to him: she undresses and gets in beside him. Well we're watching movies so, of course, he revives enough to climb on top of her.

It's not clear what happens but enough for her to ask afterwards: "You realise it's me, Katie?" Her main concern is not orgasm but that she should matter to him; that he should care about her as a person.

Instinctively we do not expect a woman to enjoy an equal sexual pleasure from sex. Neither do we expect her to approach sex insisting on her own orgasm before his. Nature has designed women to be more co-operative and accommodating than men.

When a woman has sex with a man she marvels at his ability to perform sexually. We have no similar experience. A man's sexual passion for a woman can be intoxicating. The marvel of sex, for a woman, is not her own arousal but that of her man.

Male sexuality and male sexual desire (fuelled by an appreciation of the female form) is the true glory of heterosexual sex.

*"But, by and large, coitus in marriage occurs with a regularity which is not equalled by any other type of sexual activity in the female, ...*

*This suggests that it is the male rather than the female partner who is chiefly responsible for the regularity of marital coitus." (Alfred Kinsey; Sexual behavior in the human female; 1953)*

The woman's sexual arousal is a different and less romantic story. Why do bridal magazines rarely discuss a woman's aspirations for her sexual relationship?

Of course women think that to keep a man happy they must simply be attractive. So they diet, they eliminate body hair and they put on make-up. The fact is that most men want a woman to be more adventurous in bed.

Men feel guilty if it is suggested that women get less out of sex than they do. They shouldn't. Women enjoy their children; men enjoy sex.

The travesty of the sexual revolution was that it set false hopes for women with sexual aspirations. Women cannot be men any more than men can be women. Neither can women hope to experience sex the exact same way a man experiences it.

Sex is a gift that a woman offers to a man she loves. She offers her body for his pleasure without necessarily hoping for anything in return except his devotion to her. In the end, all any of us want is to be loved and appreciated – just in different ways.

Boys grow up trying to impress their fathers. Perhaps they don't realise that girls are never able to impress men in the same way.

When a woman offers a man sex, she can enjoy being the object of his sexual desire, the key to his sexual arousal and orgasm.

The woman hopes for his adoration of her beauty and his appreciation of her ability to arouse him sexually.

That sexual adulation is important because a woman worries that if it's not there then he may be devoted to someone else. Sex is the barometer of the relationship but more importantly the sign of the man's commitment to the woman and her goals for family.

Sadly this novelty wears off and male sexual arousal is not so automatic after years with the same partner.

The couple's sexual relationship comes under pressure because men look to sex for their emotional sense of well-being. I have certainly questioned why I have needed to make effort when I have less to gain directly from sex.

It's important for men to realise that over the longer-term they need to overcome their inhibitions and communicate over sex and relationship issues.

# Men's sexual arousal is usually easy

Young men wake up each morning with an erection and have spontaneous erections throughout the day as sex-related thoughts occur to them or simply as a result of seeing someone they find attractive.

A boy has no choice but to learn about his sexual arousal and orgasm but, for women, learning how to orgasm is a much more conscious process.

*"What's pink and hard first thing in the morning? Answer: The Financial Times!" (The FT is a high-brow UK newspaper printed on pink paper).*

Her man's erection is a novelty in a woman's first sexual relationship since her own anatomy provides her with no comparable experience.

If a woman has an erection (of the clitoris) at all, it is only once she has the experience to know how to become highly aroused.

A man's sexual arousal can be very flattering and in the early days, a man's devotion is reward enough.

I remember that I was fascinated by the way my partner's penis appeared to have a separate identity of its own in our sex life!

Whole books have been written about the personality of the penis, the cocky blighter, with or without his hat on.

But the clitoris? The clitoris is like a demure flower that hides in the face of an audience like a blushing virgin.

*"There are two types of penis. One expands and lengthens when becoming erect (The Grower). The other appears big most of the time but doesn't get much bigger (The Shower). A Men's Health survey shows 79% of men have growers 21% have showers." (Men's Health Magazine June 2007)*

## Male sexuality involves a high sex drive

Most boys discover masturbation fairly automatically in early teens. The penis is naturally the focus for physical stimulation and visual pornography provides men's psychological sexual arousal.

Men's sexual fantasies tend to relate well to sex with a partner and so transferring orgasm techniques to sex is usually straightforward.

*"It has been said that 90 per cent of men admit to masturbation and the other ten per cent are liars. ... Masturbation is almost certainly less common among females than among males." (Andrew Stanway; Loving Touch; 1993)*

In her book 'Hot Relationships' (1999) Tracey Cox tells how one lover was so engrossed in his book that, despite sucking him off, she failed to gain his attention. This scenario is so far removed from my experience of physical intimacy with men that I have to wonder whether she was in bed with a shop dummy.

Male sex drive represents a big part of how we define masculinity yet, due to embarrassment over sex, differences in sex drives are rarely admitted. Apparently there are even couples who never notice a difference. Not every man has a strong sex drive but equally not every woman is willing to acknowledge her partner's sexual needs.

*"Women aren't automatically excited the way men are." (Kramer & Dunaway; Why Men don't get enough Sex and Women don't get enough Love; 1994)*

Men approach sex eagerly anticipating the easy pleasures of physical intimacy. They often fail to appreciate that for a woman to want to demonstrate her love for a partner through sex she must feel that she has been a receiver elsewhere in the relationship.

Affectionate companionship (emotional intimacy) is just as important to women as sex (physical intimacy) is to men.

*"Men want more sex than they usually get. ... It's no wonder, then, that couples argue most often about sexual frequency..." (Kramer & Dunaway; Why Men don't get enough Sex and Women don't get enough Love; 1994)*

Alcohol may slow men down a little but they still usually manage to come, especially in their younger years. My experience is that there is no chance of female orgasm after even one drink, whether through masturbation or during sex.

So if the aim of a sex session is for the woman to enjoy orgasm, make sure you do all your wining and dining after sex not before.

# Male sexuality involves a high sex drive

Faking illustrates how women are more concerned about keeping their partners happy or not appearing inadequate than they are about reaching orgasm. Otherwise, they would admit their problem and try to find a solution.

Likewise, the debate over which body part needs to be stimulated for female orgasm arises because many women don't know how to orgasm.

It is unthinkable that a man would not know that his penis is the source of his orgasm because men tend to know how to achieve their own orgasm.

Men deal with sexual frustration on a daily basis so their ability to orgasm is vital to them. In relatively new relationships, the novelty of the experience is arousing enough for a man to reach orgasm regardless of his partner's response. His own sexual arousal is his top priority and he does not need the reassurance of his partner's.

*"In the beginning of a relationship, sexual arousal is much more automatic and quick for a man." (John Gray; Mars & Venus in the Bedroom; 1995)*

Later on, sexual arousal is no longer as automatic so a man needs to build some variety and sexual fantasies around what can become a repetitive act within long-term sexual relationships.

The man now looks for a more involved sexual partner who knows how to pleasure a man by engaging on his sexual fantasies and sexual arousal.

*"The bottom line of what makes sex fulfilling and memorable for a man is a woman's fulfilment. When a man is successful in fulfilling her, he feels most fulfilled." (John Gray; Mars & Venus in the Bedroom; 1995)*

### Men want to hold onto their sexual fantasies

Men tend to be so absorbed in their own sexual arousal and need for orgasm that they are usually quite oblivious to how women feel.

Men have difficulty empathising with the female perspective for a variety of reasons:

- They want to hold on to their sexual fantasies;

- They fear losing out on opportunities to have sex;

- We often hold men responsible for women's sexual arousal and men are pressured by feeling inadequate; and

- They are led to expect that a woman should keep a man happy in bed.

*"Men's illusions about women are long on fantasy and short on reality and are often based on male-oriented published material ...*

*These media stereotypes become the stuff of male fantasy, even, though as any woman knows, they bear little resemblance to the vast majority of real women either emotionally or sexually. ...*

*Of course, the more experience a man has with women in the real world, the more clearly he realises how inaccurate the media and locker-room stereotypes are.*

*He continues to hold on to his illusions, however, because he lacks anything more reliable with which to replace them." (Kramer & Dunaway; Why Men don't get enough Sex and Women don't get enough Love; 1994)*

Men may be more sexual than women but there is one aspect of sex where men can learn from women. Since women do not approach sex already aroused, they enjoy a greater variety of sensual sex play.

Men are affectionate when they want sex but once they have had their orgasm they lose interest in touching or kissing. A good lover devotes time to pleasuring his partner.

Men are either

(1) highly aroused and focused on reaching orgasm as soon as possible or

(2) having come, disinterested in any sexual contact.

Men need to acknowledge that their sex drive works like an on-off switch. An ideal male lover should re-think his approach to sex and be prepared to build in some sensual pleasuring around obtaining his own orgasm.

# Holding men responsible for women's sexual arousal

Men are often blamed, unfairly, for the difficulties that women have with orgasm during sex. For example, it is suggested that, by coming too soon, a man fails to provide enough stimulation.

In fact, intercourse is unlikely to provide women with enough clitoral stimulation regardless of how long the man keeps thrusting for.

*"Closely linked with the traditional pressure on men to maintain long erection and thrusting during intercourse is the idea that it is a man's role to 'give' the woman an orgasm during intercourse. ...*

*In addition to the pressure created by this role, this idea also often puts the man in a no-win situation since the information he has been given – that thrusting during intercourse should bring a woman to orgasm – is faulty*

*This places him in a vulnerable position, leaving him to doubt his masculinity whenever female orgasm does not occur and also possibly pressuring the woman to fake orgasms." (Shere Hite; The Hite Reports; 1993)*

Older generations of women never hoped for orgasm from their relationships, but equally a man never felt obliged to facilitate a woman's orgasm during sex. The sexual revolution has made men feel just as inadequate as women.

The difficulty for couples today is matching reality with the unrealistically high expectations (fuelled by the media) that we have for our sex lives.

### Sexual arousal depends on the mind more than the body

Sex advice today often plays on male insecurities by suggesting that a man can 'give his woman an orgasm' or even (for heaven's sake!) multiple orgasms. This is ludicrous.

The fact is that most women use fantasy to reach orgasm and no man can control what is going on inside a woman's head.

A woman can arouse a man simply by revealing her body. This is just the way nature intended things to work and not down to her individual talents (pole & lap dancing aside!).

A male lover does not have the same natural advantage because most women do not become aroused enough for orgasm simply by enjoying male nakedness. So there are few male lap dancers!

Many women do not know how their own sexual arousal works so small wonder that men struggle to find techniques to turn their woman on!

In 'The Hite Reports', a male respondent points out:

*"It seems that women have only recently discovered the nature and depth of their own sexuality... Yet women are angry at men for not understanding their sexuality already...*

*as if men should be experts at something about women that even women didn't know!" (Shere Hite; The Hite Reports; 1993)*

Touché! Perhaps, because men appear to enjoy sex so spontaneously, women assume they have some innate understanding of sex that we fundamentally lack.

So we leave the initiative to the man hoping against all odds that something will happen as if by magic. Unfortunately, women's sexual arousal and orgasm are not automatic and so pleasuring a woman is not easy.

My partner joked that he will most likely to die of old age before he gets around to trying all the different suggestions on the web for locating a woman's G-spot!

The G-spot may be amazing but if it is so obscure then just how useful is it to the average couple? This search for the Holy Grail is yet another indication of how many women struggle with orgasm during sex.

Personally, I have never found the so-called 'G-spot' nor have I experienced multiple orgasms. There are plenty of jokes about nymphomaniacs but I have never met a woman with this condition in real life.

Whether these aspects of female sexuality are myths or simply rare occurrences, they undermine any attempt to generalise about the average woman's experience of sex.

# How men appreciate sex and love

My mother never talked to me much about sex but she did tell me to respect a man's sexual ego. She believed that a man's sexual performance relies on a sensitive lover who understands how to play to a man's sexual fantasies.

A man hopes for a lover who is enthusiastic about sharing physical intimacy and their intimate time together as lovers. Essentially, sex is no fun if it is one-sided. More than this, a man wants to feel that his love-making is pleasing his woman.

But where does a woman reasonably draw the line?

I could not lie by pretending to reach orgasm from intercourse. However, I have put effort into being a responsive lover during sex. I kiss back. I move to his rhythm. I grasp his buttocks or stroke his balls. I run my fingers down his back.

I have approached sex with a willingness to pleasure a man that I now realise other women may not always offer. However, this generosity towards my lover has also meant that I have hoped for more in return. I have questioned why I should always be enthusiastic about sex when my own sexual arousal has been so elusive.

Men are lucky because their experiences of sex and love are closely aligned. When men are physically intimate with someone they find attractive, sexual arousal is usually automatic. This connection between sex and love is much less evident for women.

This is why 'Sex in the City' (2008) is more about women's passion for shopping than their passion for sex. This is not about attitude. It's just the way women are. Female sexuality is not geared towards women 'sowing their oats' as men often want to.

It makes senses that sex is more important to men. It would hardly be fair if women enjoyed sex as much as men do as well all the aspects of reproduction that men can never experience. We might just as well ask why men don't want to devote their lives to their children as many women do.

For the survival of our species it is vital that women are devoted to their children. The skills of pleasuring a man through sex are a luxury: nice to have (perhaps even very nice to have!) but not vital to our survival.

After all if men wanted to marry women who were 'good in bed' they would simply trawl the brothels for a woman who was well-versed in how to pleasure a man sexually.

Likewise, the old-fashioned custom of virgin brides indicates more a desire for a wife who cannot question her husband's prowess as a lover than one who is knowledgeable about sexual pleasure.

Nevertheless men seem to need to express their love for a woman through sex and women find this difficult to relate to because we don't have the same need. Sometimes a woman can feel that a man loves sex more than he loves her.

Men's easy sexual arousal makes the early days of a romance fairly effortless for a woman. Sadly, sex can become one-sided because a woman's arousal is so much more difficult to achieve.

Orgasm and sexual pleasure are so important to a man that, if a woman is a generous and sensitive lover, he is often willing to be generous in return by being devoted to her.

One woman was shocked when a female colleague brazenly admitted that she waits for her husband to be in that state of post-coital gratitude before she asks him to pay for the next household item.

Sex needn't be as manipulative as this. My partner's devotion to me encourages him to spend more time with the family and with me talking about our goals for our lives together.

Since sex and enjoyment of orgasm are much more important to men than they are for women, it tends to be women, not men, who are offended by eroticism.

There is a contradiction for men: although they may use plenty of gutsy words to describe a woman they find sexually attractive, they would not like to hear another man talking about a woman they care about in that way.

Emotionally, men need women more than women need men because men do not get the same emotional rewards from same sex friendships and from caring for their children.

So although men want sex intensely they also benefit from the emotional intimacy or affectionate companionship that women provide through family, friends and the wider relationship with their man.

# Long-term sexual relationships

Why in our liberated times do women still accept 'putting up with sex' just to avoid being single? I am not judging anyone else's experiences. If other women are content with sex as they find it – I'm very happy for them.

But are they really? Or are they simply more accepting?

A woman in her early thirties said that she didn't see the point of sex unless a couple was planning a family. Suddenly I realised how idealised my aspirations had been for a partner to be both my lover and my friend. I grew up assuming that adult life naturally included a mutually enjoyable sexual relationship.

Few women appear to care about orgasm and sexual pleasure. Even if she does care, a woman often has to accept that sex is more about appreciating her man's arousal and about making the most of physical intimacy, than about orgasm.

Sex is much, much more important (both emotionally and physiologically) to most men than it is to women. Conversely men are less motivated by relationships and family.

So sex is what keeps them bought into supporting women in their life-goals of providing a home and raising children. Men hope when they marry that they can look forward to sex for life.

*"As a general guideline, a woman needs to be emotionally fulfilled before she can long for sexual contact. A man, however, gets much of his emotional fulfilment during sex." (John Gray; Mars & Venus in the Bedroom; 1995)*

Women need information to make the most of their sexual experiences but equally men need to be encouraged to invest in pleasuring their partner rather than seeing sex purely as an opportunity to enjoy their own orgasm.

## Sex helps motivate men to engage on family

A man in his late sixties commented to me: "It's a good job that men are interested in sex because otherwise the human race would die out!" The fact is that even in committed sexual relationships, sex is rarely about producing children.

There are two views of sex. There is 'reproductive sex' based on intercourse, which since it leads to family is often the only view that many women have of sex.

Then there is 'sex for pleasure', which since it is associated with men paying for sex (either directly or indirectly) naturally revolves around male gratification.

The fact that prostitutes and mistresses exist is evidence that men enjoy sexual pleasure. Within a committed relationship, a woman has the choice of providing her man with sex or risking him going elsewhere.

Unfortunately, many women are not always well informed either about female sexuality or about enjoying sexual pleasure within a sexual relationship.

*"How do we explain the imbalance between the genders?" asks Bel Mooney. " ... the modern woman does not feel bound by what was once seen as marital duty – encapsulated in the phrase 'conjugal rights'.*

*If this was not so common why are there so many sad jests about 'headaches'?" Bel suggests that perhaps the answer lies in men's focus on sex alone whereas women talk more about affection and companionship*

*She observes that "Couples who keep on having fun together, who share activities, who go out for a meal to talk, ... " are more likely to survive long-term relationships. (Bel Mooney's column page 9 The Times UK newspaper Wednesday 28th September 2005 entitled: 'I love my wife, but she doesn't want sex. What can I do about it?')*

Men have a need for regular sex throughout their lives. Sexual frustration causes men to become bad tempered whereas good sex makes them more amenable. Not much of a choice really!

So a woman needs to learn how to keep arousing her man over a lifetime. If she can also learn how to get some sexual pleasure for herself then so much the better.

# Men hope a lover will enhance their sexual arousal

The sex industry (prostitution and pornography) is a clear indication that men's desire to enjoy their own sexual arousal and orgasm cannot be satisfied through their relationships with women alone.

It's easy for a woman to figure out that men want sex... but they also want to be loved and appreciated through their sexual relationship.

- Men's sexual arousal is usually easy and immediate. Despite the evidence to the contrary they like to hope that a woman feels the same way about sex that they do.
- A man can feel that sex represents the most important way of demonstrating that he loves his partner.
- At the same time, he perceives a woman's enthusiasm for sex with him as confirmation of her love for him.
- If a man wanted a loving, sexless relationship with a woman he would never have left his mother.

Men need sex, both physiologically and emotionally, more than women. Men's relationships with others are not as emotionally intimate as women's tend to be.

So a man looks to the woman in his life for the emotional support he needs and sex is the mechanism that men use to express their loving emotions.

*"The failure of an unresponsive sexual partner to provide these physical or emotional stimuli may, on the other hand, do considerable damage to the effectiveness of the relationship. ...*

*Such failure leads not only to disappointment, frustration, and a sense of defeat, but sometimes to contrary emotional responses which become anger and rage." (Alfred Kinsey; Sexual behavior in the human female; 1953)*

Despite acknowledging this not inconsiderable pressure on a woman to 'respond' to a man's love-making, the male authors of Kinsey's report never appear to consider the possibility that women might need to exaggerate their sexual responsiveness to meet male expectations.

## How to pleasure a man

From early on, the sensitive female lover learns how to pleasure a man, co-operating quite instinctively during intercourse by moving with the man's rhythm. She also learns how to play along with men's sexual fantasies and acts out the part of the appreciative and responsive lover in order to help him reach orgasm.

Sometimes a woman may caress her lover's body or make encouraging noises to enhance the man's arousal. Some women even exaggerate their sexual arousal to the point of faking orgasm.

This explains why in the film 'The Duchess' (2008), Kiera Knightley playing the virgin bride, lies inert as her husband thrusts into her on their wedding night.

Women only learn over time that responding as a lover encourages the male orgasm that nearly always ends sexual activity between a man and a woman. A woman appreciates that if she continues to be unmoved by her partner's love-making, her man will feel that he is failing to please her or that she does not love him.

By contrast, the mistress in the film has learnt to make the appreciative noises that sexually experienced women often use as a male turn-on during sex.

*"The fact is, we usually co-operate quite extensively during intercourse in order for the man to be able to orgasm. We move along with his rhythm, keep our legs apart and our bodies in positions that make penetration and thrusting possible, and almost never stop intercourse in midstream unless the man has had his orgasm." (Shere Hite; The Hite Reports; 1993)*

Unless a woman learns how to orgasm during sex with a partner, the role of the female lover can become burdensome in long-term sexual relationships. Even if a man never explicitly acknowledges the assistance of a female lover, a woman has the reward of knowing that she has helped her partner find the sexual release that is so vital to his happiness.

From a woman's perspective, making effort to be more involved in 'love-making' reduces the sense of uselessness that arises from participating in a sexual act in which (without the woman's sexual arousal and orgasm) the woman is effectively merely a bystander.

# Sex for life

One great aspect of men growing older is that they become slightly less obsessed with their own sexual arousal and need for sexual release.

Now that his own need for orgasm is less pressing, my partner is able to focus on my arousal and can bring me to orgasm through using a combination of anal and clitoral stimulation.

As a young woman I was never conscious of my own physical arousal and my body appeared to be almost inert to any stimulation from my partner. Sometime around my mid-thirties, I found that my body went through a remarkable change – it was as if I blossomed sexually.

Even intercourse became more sensual due to increased natural lubrication (still no arousal though). From time to time, my mind gets turned on now and I am conscious of the pelvic area behind the external clitoris being swollen and physically aroused (gross but true).

For the first time, I experienced orgasm from my partner arousing me via manual stimulation of the clitoris.

These physical orgasms are different to those I get from masturbation when I use sexual fantasies.

They are often intensely pleasurable but the increase in heart rate and breathing as well as the sense of releasing sexual emotions with the subsequent relaxation are all missing.

*"Orgasms vary, both between women and for the same woman at different times.*

*We experience different qualities of orgasm depending upon the degree and kind of stimulation we receive and also on what is going on in our minds." (Sheila Kitzinger; Woman's Experience of Sex; 1983)*

## Men's need for sexual reassurance

Experts try to reassure women by suggesting that orgasm is unimportant. Unfortunately, a woman who is familiar with orgasm from masturbation, assumes that the whole point of sex is the sexual pleasure of orgasm (just as a man does).

However, ultimately a woman can live with non-orgasmic sex because women do not experience the same sex drive and consequent sexual frustration that men do. Men's desire for sex is driven as much by emotional factors as by physical.

A man in his sixties, suffering from prostate cancer, was worried that he might not be able to continue to have sex.

He was so depressed about losing his ability to become sexually aroused that he felt, without sex, life would not be worth living.

Male sexuality, including sexual arousal and orgasm, represents not only a man's masculinity but also his emotional foothold on the world. A long-term sexual relationship fuels his ability to succeed in the otherwise emotion-less world of men.

Men hope a lover will enhance their sexual arousal over the longer term. So some women do explore sexual pleasure because, like myself, they consider faking to be humiliating and they are willing to invest in keeping a marriage (and family) together.

Perhaps other women, who have made do with intercourse over decades, are more adept at using sexual fantasies.

Perhaps other men accept a 'lie back and think of England' partner and use affairs to assist with their sexual arousal.

I told Bruce, the sexual psychologist I went to see, that in over twenty years of investing in my sexual relationship, the only orgasms I have experienced are from anal stimulation.

Bruce, quite evidently thinking that I was being overly particular, asked unsympathetically: "So what's your problem?"

*"Anal intercourse is no longer considered to be abnormal and is enjoyed by many homosexual and heterosexual couples.*

*As long as the decision is mutual and without coercion or guilt, most professionals believe that anal intercourse is simply another way for a couple to find pleasure with each other."*

*(Michael Carrera; Dictionary of Sexual Terms; 1992)*

# Stories: Sex advice today

# Sex advice for women is often misleading

Natalie, a woman in her late twenties, had a close relationship with her mother who was a doctor. I approached Natalie hoping that a mother with a medical background might be more likely than others to have discussed her sexual experiences with a daughter.

When young women have difficulty reaching orgasm during sex, it can be difficult for them to find answers.

Natalie was relieved and grateful on realising that she was not alone in experiencing a lack of arousal during sex.

She was too embarrassed to talk to me but wrote: "On reading your book, I spoke to my mum who said (I quote!):

'OF COURSE YOU DON'T ORGASM DURING SEX!' Like this was a well known fact!!!!"

*"The married female reaches orgasm in only a portion of her coitus, and some 10 per cent of all the females in the available sample had never reached orgasm at any time, in any of their marital coitus." (Alfred Kinsey; Sexual behavior in the human female; 1953)*

For me, Natalie epitomised the modern professional young woman: successful, attractive and confident. Tall and slim, she wore her blond hair cut short, which gave her a sweet elfish look.

I envied the easy-going friendships she maintained with her male work colleagues both within and outside the workplace. Despite her predicament, it was evident that Natalie had never been either brave or curious enough to research explanations for women's sexual arousal through reading or talking to someone.

"Everything you talk about in your book, particularly with reference to your problems with having an orgasm during sexual intercourse, I had been having the same problem. For many years, I had thought there was something wrong with me but was just too embarrassed to talk to anyone about it."

"In fact, I once heard on a radio talk show someone called in and said they couldn't orgasm during sex. The response to the person having the problem was to blame this on the man!" Holding men responsible for women's sexual arousal makes men feel inadequate and puts pressure on women to fake orgasm.

We think we live in an information age and at a time when people have relatively relaxed attitudes towards sex, yet this educated young woman was unable to find explanations for her sexual experiences or even to talk to her friends or to her mother.

Young women often don't know how to orgasm and unfortunately there are very few sources of information to help them learn.

Natalie told me: "As a result (of reading your book) my relationship with my partner has stepped up a level. I had been reluctant to have sex with him for about a year as I had it in my head that HIS inability to make me orgasm during intercourse must mean I didn't love him or don't want to be with him...!"

*"Waiting for the Right Man to make us orgasm is like waiting for the prince to come." (Shere Hite; The Hite Report; 1976)*

Why is it so difficult to find answers? Female orgasm is not required either for men's enjoyment of sex or for successful reproduction.

To keep her man happy and to have a family, a woman is more likely to be concerned with the basics of whether vaginal intercourse is possible than with orgasm (the cherry on the cake!). Most women are too embarrassed to ask for more.

So typically sex experts deal with sexual dysfunction (primarily problems with male sexual performance). Any problem with female sexual performance, even though considered to be a sexual dysfunction, is not as well understood.

Since relatively few women are seeking answers there is little funding to improve our understanding of female sexual arousal and orgasm.

*"Shocking though the statistics are, many women have found it secretly comforting to discover they are not the only ones who experience this enormous discrepancy between masturbation and intercourse.*

*For years I was unable to have an orgasm except by masturbation, and assumed I was a freak. I remember the relief when I discovered Hite..." (Rachel Swift; Satisfaction Guaranteed; 1996)*

# Explanations for women's sexual arousal

Some people assert confidently that women orgasm easily during sex. Yet, when I ask for details, the responses are frustratingly vague and defensive.

Many people assume that all women 'naturally' orgasm during sex. I have been advised to read a sex manual as if only extreme ignorance can explain a lack of orgasm.

Alternatively, with a sympathetic expression I am asked about my feelings for my partner: "Do you find him attractive? Do you love him?" The implication is that female orgasm arises from true love.

*"Orgasms are natural, but intercourse is not, for many of us, the easiest way to have them." (Sheila Kitzinger; Woman's Experience of Sex; 1983)*

More informed sources commonly explain women's lack of arousal during sex and their failure to orgasm during sex by:

- some deficiency on the part of the woman (i.e. that she is either physically or psychologically abnormal in some way);

- or ignorance (i.e. that we are not doing it right) including the suggestion that the man might be an incompetent lover.

A popular suggestion is that women have emotional hang-ups about sex and yet it is not logical that women should be more inhibited in their intimate relationships than men are.

Given women's much closer emotional intimacy with friends and their children, it seems more likely that if anyone is going to be emotionally inhibited it would be men not women.

While men's sexual arousal clearly depends on eroticism, women's sexual arousal is assumed to depend on romance. So women are told that they need a loving relationship to enjoy sex.

Of course, the ultimate fall-back is the suggestion that female orgasm is unimportant, which is only true from a reproductive point-of-view and when a woman is unfamiliar with orgasm.

## Women need clitoral stimulation for orgasm

Most boys work out how to enjoy orgasm through masturbation by the age of 12 or 13. Some women discover orgasm in their late teens, or in their twenties or thirties.

Many others never discover orgasm throughout the whole of their lives. Facts such as these are diagnosed as women's sexual dysfunction but there has to be a more reasonable explanation.

*"Men, imagine having sex without having your penis stimulated. It would certainly not be very much fun." (John Gray; Mars & Venus in the Bedroom; 1995)*

All those magazine articles proposing a million ways to give a woman a mind-blowing orgasm sound very promising but why are they needed in the first place?

You rarely see an article explaining how to give a man even one orgasm, mind-blowing or otherwise. These articles prove that there are many women who struggle with orgasm of any description during sex.

It's about time that sex experts stopped patronising the average couple out there. There are whole books written about female sexual arousal and orgasm so how can it be so straightforward that every woman achieves it as we'd like to think?

Even the terms 'arousal and orgasm' refer to women's experiences because men's sexual arousal is usually easy. Yet so often we are told that the solution is as simple and obvious as pressing a button – the clitoris. Evidently, clitoral stimulation is not everything.

Increasing numbers of women ask about orgasm during sex but there are few answers. Sex experts can rarely focus on this one issue as I have. From my extensive research, I can vouch for the fact that female arousal is not easy.

Anyone who implies otherwise is misguided: they have either misinterpreted their own experiences or they are simply quoting popular beliefs.

*"... since female orgasm is not necessary during intercourse for reproduction to occur, why should nature provide stimulation for female orgasm during intercourse?" (Shere Hite; The Hite Reports; 1993)*

# The truth about female sexuality

Sex is a difficult subject to analyse because it relies on our emotions rather than our powers of logical reasoning.

How many women have been as interested in sex as I have been?

Having masturbated since the age of seventeen, I knew that orgasm was missing from sex. I consulted sex experts and had it confirmed that my partner and I are completely normal.

I have read extensively and have my own personal library of erotica and sex manuals. I have explored sex with a partner on a regular basis over many years. I have spent over ten years writing about sex and talking to others about sex.

Despite this experience, all it takes is one sixteen-year-old to claim that sexual arousal and orgasm were easy for her the first time and every time or one twenty-something-year-old to talk about multiple orgasms.

Suddenly, anyone's interest in a more realistic discussion deflates like a balloon – we all prefer the more sensational report. And yet these claims do not tally with anyone's real life experiences of sex.

I may be doubting women's claims of easy orgasm during sex but I am certainly not anti-sex – quite the reverse.

I am asking: why do so many women dislike the eroticism that lies at the heart of our sexuality and our enjoyment of our sexual arousal?

I want to put an end to the intimidating and humiliating advice that is typically given to young women today. The fact is that any woman who asks about lack of sexual arousal during sex is very unlikely to be:

- Ignorant of the basic sexual facts;

- Sexually inhibited, have emotional hang-ups about sex or psychologically traumatised in some way; or

- Lacking the appropriate loving feelings for her partner.

Yet, I have been patronised and humiliated with all of these opinions by amateurs and professionals alike, even as an experienced woman (over the age of thirty five).

It is a crime that this 'sex advice' is given to young women on the web every day.

Modern day sex advice is discriminating against women by suggesting that orgasm is unimportant or that women can hope to orgasm without any of the techniques that men employ (eroticism for arousal and genital stimulation for orgasm).

The FACTS of female sexuality are lost:

(1) that women need clitoral stimulation for orgasm and

(2) that women are likely to have much more difficulty using their sexual fantasies effectively during sex compared with masturbation alone.

No man is thought to be odd because he masturbates. This is because every man masturbates. Masturbation is much less common for women so it is assumed to be an optional extra or even to prevent a woman experiencing orgasm with a partner.

Adult masturbation involves knowing what turns you on, how to achieve sexual arousal and orgasm. Many women never learn how to orgasm through genital stimulation (and I personally question whether there is another way to orgasm).

If my experiences were truly abnormal in some way, then others would be more sympathetic. They would be able to explain how they are able to overcome the known facts about female sexuality instead of claiming that it all happens 'naturally'.

I have no agenda. I am not trying to make money out of anyone. I am simply trying to establish some facts and provide other couples with more logical and realistic information about female sexuality.

# Sex experts deal with sexual dysfunction

In the film 'Doc Hollywood' (1991) Bridget Fonda asks Michael J Fox whether doctors know more about sex than normal people.

This is a natural mistake to make because of the misconception that sex is a mechanical or biological aspect of our bodies. In fact, doctors are unlikely to know any more about sex than the rest of us.

Sex is primarily about our psychology and our emotions. There are recommended positions and techniques for sexual intercourse but ultimately sexual arousal depends on what happens in the brain.

Most of us accept sexual pleasure for what it is and only seek help if there is a major problem. This is why the vast majority of people who consult sex experts are men with sexual performance problems.

People who go to sex experts are unusual because most people are not prepared to discuss possible sexual dysfunction with complete strangers, especially when they have to pay by the hour to do so!

By the time I was twenty I had read loads about sexual pleasure and imaginative sex play so my difficulty was not ignorance of technique.

Instead I wanted to know why (although everything worked by the book for the man) my body and mind did not respond as I assumed they were supposed to.

As a well-informed couple, we had tried all the foreplay techniques in the book.

### Sexual pleasure remains very personal

When I consulted therapists in the UK, I was asking: "How do women become sufficiently aroused during sex to enable them to orgasm?"

After meeting with defensiveness and incomprehension over my concerns about orgasm, I came to realise that therapists don't know the answer to this highly personal question any more than anyone else.

Why should they?

People who qualify as sex experts learn about human sexuality through textbooks full of theories, laboratory research and detailed analysis of phenomena such as orgasm.

There is no particular reason why female sex experts would have explored their own sexuality, either through masturbation or through sex with a partner, any more than the average woman.

We can all be fairly sure that a man knows how to orgasm both alone and with a partner.

But many women have sex without ever knowing how to become aroused enough to orgasm.

So there is no guarantee that a woman, even if she is advising others, knows how to masturbate herself to orgasm; let alone how to succeed with similar techniques during sex.

Some people claim to be unembarrassed about sex but only because they discuss other people's sex lives.

Very few women (even sex experts) are willing to talk about their own experiences of sexual arousal and orgasm during sex.

So therapists' understanding of the average woman's experience of orgasm is based on the findings of surveys.

Unfortunately these can be highly misleading:

(1) given the belief that orgasm is the normal experience many women assume they orgasm when they don't; and

(2) women often interpret their sexual experiences in the light of emotional rather than sexual criteria.

Lack of understanding means that women's sexual arousal is still highly taboo.

Even experts are confused when faced with couples who have unrealistic expectations.

Evidently female orgasm is not an issue for the vast majority of couples today.

## How do women reach orgasm with a partner?

Everyone says "but it all works fine for other women". My question is "How?"

Men have more testosterone. Men get turned on by anything that moves in a skirt with legs. All men naturally masturbate throughout their sexually active lives. They heckle, they ask women to dance, they proposition, etc. etc.

And women? They wait to be asked. Is this a sign of sex drive or sexual arousal?

When you look around the web it is relatively rare for a woman to describe exactly how she reaches orgasm with a partner. There's lots of talk about female orgasm and what it feels like but women know this from female masturbation.

I can quite see why women might be embarrassed to admit to their fantasies since suggested themes include: lesbianism, sadism, domination and rape. But I'm not asking women to divulge these most personal secrets.

A man would just say: "I like women with big tits, I enjoy porn and when I'm with a partner I GET TURNED ON before she has even taken her clothes off. I can easily orgasm BY STIMULATING MY PENIS via oral sex, intercourse or masturbation."

This explanation has logic and reason because it includes how men get turned on (in their minds) and how they use genital stimulation to reach orgasm. I am simply asking women the same question.

Expert advice about lack of orgasm often focuses on the suggestion that women might be suffering from some vague psychological trauma or have relationship difficulties. Others question whether orgasm is even that important. All these comments indicate that we are talking about women because men would not relate to this advice.

Some experts suggest that women need to employ relaxation and muscle tensing exercises in order to orgasm with a partner. Imagine suggesting this to a man! Exactly how does it help with arousal if you clench your pelvic muscles? Everyone still seems to be convinced that intercourse works for women. No one ever comments on the mental aspects of arousal.

Other experts use intimidation tactics. Some suggest that if a woman knows how to orgasm from female masturbation then all she has to do is the exact same thing during sex. Others suggest that women need to be more assertive in telling their partner what physical stimulation they need during sex. The effect is to trivialise the difficulties that women have with orgasm.

By patronising women and implying that female orgasm with a partner is easy, experts silence women. In fact, they use these techniques to have their suggestions accepted, however ineffective they might be. Some women may be able to orgasm with a partner with additional (manual or oral) clitoral stimulation but this does not mean that all women will be able to.

Experts never disclose how they (or their partners, in the case of male experts) achieve the psychological sexual arousal necessary for orgasm. The implicit assumption is that women experience the same kind of spontaneous arousal from a lover's body that men do and that physical stimulation techniques are all that is required for women to orgasm during sex.

If men have such significant stimuli (Kinsey acknowledges that women are not aroused by the body and genitals of a sexual partner as men are) to induce or aid their natural sexual arousal (Kinsey acknowledges that men are aroused by the thought of sexual activity but women are not), then how do women achieve the exact same result (orgasm) that men do?

Despite the fact that women use fantasy during female masturbation, there is no discussion of how women might also use sexual fantasies during sex. If they do not use fantasy then what do they substitute during sex in place of fantasy? We know that women do not get turned on by a lover's body in the same way that men do.

I don't mind being proven wrong. If other women want to come forward and tell me how their sexuality works to enable them to reach orgasm pretty much as spontaneously as men, then I'd really like to hear from them.

In fact, I would like to hear from any woman on the planet who is willing to stand by her sexual instincts. I don't mind if she's never had a sexual urge or orgasm in her life. That at least is believable. What is not believable is anyone who suggests that women respond sexually much as men do.

# Defending the modern image of female sexuality

As a young woman I never understood why I did not experience sexual arousal as a natural part of my sexual relationship.

Much later I decided to talk to experts, assuming that they would have some answers, but I was met only with evasion and silence.

The issue of women's sexual arousal and orgasm with a partner is surrounded by mis-information, contrary opinions and, above all, defensiveness. More often than not, our 'knowledge' today revolves around debating OPINIONS rather than the FACTS.

A male doctor claims: "Many, if not most, women by the time they are 30 regularly achieve orgasm during penetrative sex or immediately afterwards with mutual masturbation".

In the SAME article (The Times, 4th October 2008), a female therapist contradicts: "There is no avoiding the fact that orgasm is problematic for a significant percentage of women".

On the basis of a survey (notoriously unreliable), a UK medical site states: "the average British female first learns to reach orgasm at age 19". Even if this statement refers to orgasm from masturbation, it is ludicrously optimistic about women's orgasmic ability.

It is often implied that women can generate sexual arousal from purely loving emotions. This indicates a misunderstanding about how sexual arousal is achieved. Even men need to use eroticism (erotic images or the body of a sexual partner) for sexual arousal.

Women are still told they will orgasm 'naturally' when they love a man. Romance may cause a woman to be amenable to sex but anyone who is familiar with orgasm will know that reaching orgasm involves a release of SEXUAL emotions not LOVING emotions.

## Female sexual arousal is a political issue

Having been brave enough to ask personal questions about sex, I have been shocked by just how superior and openly hostile people have been. There were no answers and little sympathy.

Small wonder more women don't ask questions.

Some women claim orgasms during sex 'just happen' but they are rarely able to explain how their arousal works. When faced with women who do not share their experience of easy sexual arousal and orgasm they can be easily offended and quickly become defensive.

This has made it very unpleasant to try to understand female sexuality by comparing notes with others.

*"There are some who advocate the perpetuation of our ignorance because they fear that science will undermine the mystical concepts that they have substituted for reality." (Alfred Kinsey; Sexual behavior in the human female; 1953)*

The FACT that many women never learn how to orgasm during sex threatens people's emotional beliefs. Even experts prefer to assume that female orgasm 'just happens' rather than have to explain how a woman can learn to orgasm with a partner.

One woman was 'highly offended' by anyone questioning whether women orgasm as easily as men. I'm sorry to burst anyone's bubble but the evidence is there for anyone to see even if they claim that their own experience makes such a thing impossible.

She continued "Many reports note that in heterosexual sex relationships, the woman's inability to orgasm is in part due to her partner's inability to give her an orgasm, among other reasons." That's very nice isn't it? Let's blame it all on men.

So men are told that thrusting or the G-spot will 'make her scream pure bliss and beg you not to stop all night long'.

If female orgasm is so easy why is this advice necessary and why does no one ask about male orgasm? Are men really so selfish?

I also question not only WHY but also HOW exactly is a man supposed to give a woman an orgasm? Isn't this patronising towards women?

Shere Hite concluded in the 1970s that the women who succeeded with orgasm (not all by any means) did it for themselves.

Women LEARN how to orgasm by applying their orgasm techniques (learned from masturbation) to sex.

# The problem with sex advice today

The suggestion is that female sexuality is identical to male sexuality. Yet women don't approach sex with the same genital erection (of the clitoris) that men tend to have so how can women hope to orgasm during sex as easily as men do?

Many women have difficulty with orgasm during sex but this is rarely acknowledged by anyone, least of all the feminists, who are blinded by the need to prove women's sexual 'equality'. Yet the sex industry only exists to satisfy men's much greater interest in sex.

Anyone who earns their living from presenting women sexually through pornography or sex advice must appeal to the male consumer. Since couples' sense of inadequacy over a lack of female orgasm during sex generates massive revenues why burst the bubble?

However the suggestion that women need a good relationship and a considerate lover to enjoy sex implies a difference.

Also the suggestion that orgasm is unimportant implies a difference in sexual expectations because this advice is NEVER given to men.

Many women dislike the eroticism that leads to enjoying sexual arousal and so they do not understand why anyone would want to stimulate their genitals.

Consequently experts continue to advise that woman's psychological sexual arousal with a partner depends more on her emotions and her relationship rather than on any appreciation of eroticism even though this is contrary to the male experience of arousal and orgasm.

Since female sexuality (for heterosexuals) is not associated with genital stimulation (of the clitoris), experts recommend panting exercises or flexing pelvic or buttock muscles. The fact that women need clitoral stimulation for orgasm is often missing completely.

Women are sometimes advised to eliminate distracting or negative thoughts (imagine needing to tell men to do this!) when approaching sex with a partner. There is no appreciation of how women can use sexual fantasies to achieve sexual arousal.

Some experts imply that women are being timid or bashful for not explaining to their partner how to provide them with the correct circumstances for orgasm.

Any woman who knew how to orgasm would understand that, unlike men, women are not able to orgasm in multiple ways and almost on demand as men can. On the contrary, women are lucky if they find ONE way to orgasm.

I am sorry to be critical but it really does seem to be a case of the blind leading the blind. It's almost as laughable as the scenes from 'The Chicken Run' where they are trying to teach the chickens to fly...!

Explanations for how women reach orgasm often miss the point completely. Sex involves our enjoyment of:

- **SEXUAL AROUSAL** through an appreciation of eroticism (men use images women use scenarios); and

- **ORGASM** through genital stimulation (direct stimulation of the penis/clitoris).

Women who ask about orgasm are told that they are dysfunctional but no one mentions the FACTS about female sexuality that GUARANTEE that women will have difficulties with orgasm during sex.

How can every woman orgasm with a partner when most women limit their sexual experiences to vaginal intercourse, which provides insufficient clitoral stimulation for orgasm?

Images of naked men do not cause women to become aroused enough for orgasm. Instead they use sexual fantasies during masturbation.

In fact clitoral stimulation is only effective during female masturbation when combined with sexual fantasies.

Many women do not identify with the explicit eroticism involved in achieving true sexual arousal. So although it is known that women use sexual fantasies for sexual arousal during sex this fact is rarely acknowledged.

Unfortunately, some women find that they cannot use their fantasies during sex because of the mental focus required to reach orgasm through fantasy alone.

## What sex experts have told me

When my partner and I decided to get married, his work-mates took him out for a beer to convince him that marriage would mean the end of his sex life.

Naturally no woman ever gave me similar advice. I accepted early on that a woman needs to invest in sex for her man's sake. Even so, I was prepared to believe that there was something wrong with me.

So when I first talked to therapists, I simply wanted to understand how other women were able to reach orgasm during sex. What surprised me was that my questions were met with so much defensiveness.

They insisted not only that women have an equal sex drive but that they 'naturally' reach orgasm during sex. Later I realised that my own starting point of orgasm through masturbation was part of the problem. Many women, even sex experts, have been unenthusiastic about female masturbation.

Sex experts are never required to acknowledge the limits of their own sexual experiences. So women (and even men) can advise on female orgasm without any direct knowledge of how a woman reaches orgasm even through female masturbation. This explains why sex experts cannot agree on whether clitoral stimulation is needed for female orgasm.

The male editor of an on-line sexuality journal told me: "We don't have enough data to say that clit stim is "required" as is fantasy. The fact that some women find that works well for them does not prove it is required.

Some women report orgasm by fantasy alone, some by massage of the skin alone, some by BDSM. Kinsey pointed out the huge range of human sexual behavior."

I agree that BDSM (Bondage, Domination, Sadism & Masochism) may cause sexual arousal. But once a person is aroused why wouldn't they want to stimulate their genitals (clitoris/penis) in order to experience orgasm? Men certainly do.

## Very few women are familiar with orgasm

Women insist that they orgasm from intercourse but they never describe HOW they reach orgasm. If women use clitoral stimulation and sexual fantasies to orgasm during female masturbation, how do they achieve a similar result during sex? Women would be more convincing if they were less defensive and more willing to provide explicit explanations for orgasm.

A female director of a UK sex clinic wrote: "I also believe that you are still over focused on the clitoris and the view that clitoral stimulation is 'the real thing' and that women generally are not satisfied through intercourse; again because of your own experience.

I agree with you that in many cases this is the fact, but there are also many women who can have satisfying orgasms through sexual intercourse."

Other experts tell me that laboratory experiments indicate that the clitoris has as many nerve endings as the penis and, that as an organ, the clitoris extends back into the body and so it is comparable in size with the penis. Is this a competition or what?

I do not doubt these facts but ... SO WHAT? I question what they have to do with women's real life experiences of sex.

I know that a woman can become sexually aroused but how often do women experience this level of arousal in practice? And what do experts suggest is likely to cause physical sexual arousal (including a clitoral erection) in the average woman?

Another female expert was enraged by the idea that women might struggle with orgasm: "You mention nothing of the G-spot or the fact that the clitoris extends deep into the body cavity and therefore can be stimulated through thrusting. It's still true that fewer women enjoy orgasm through penetration..."

So why is the fact that some women never orgasm through vaginal intercourse not published as part of the whole picture of female sexuality?

Why does no one mention that many women never orgasm at all?

Equally no one admits that women who enjoy masturbation alone, often never learn how to share the same experience with a partner (and not through lack of trying!).

# Advice on female orgasm

Given the practical nature of sex (book-learning only gets you so far!) we tend to assume that sex experts have personal experience to support their 'expertise'.

Such is our embarrassment over sex that even when a person is advising others about sex we think it improper to ask them to account for their sexual experiences. Yet these experiences contribute towards their authority and support their qualifications.

Most women, sex experts or not, never learn how their own sexual arousal works and that genital stimulation is required for orgasm as much for women as it is for men.

We even accept men advising on female orgasm because of the misconception that women respond to physical sex play much as men do. But women do not approach sex aroused enough (in their minds) for physical stimulation to be effective (lead to orgasm).

Given that so many women either mistake orgasm or fake it, it seems unlikely that many men have ever been with a woman who knows how to achieve her own orgasm.

In any event, while a woman simply lies there waiting for a man to give her an orgasm, she will never take responsibility for achieving her own sexual arousal.

The fact is that men learn about how their mental arousal works through masturbation. But heterosexual women can claim to reach orgasm during sex without any need to acknowledge how they achieve sufficient psychological arousal for orgasm.

## Being explicit about how female orgasm is achieved

Some people object when intimate details are provided to describe sexual activity between two people. They assume that the author is either trying to impress or to shock. I have provided personal details of my sex life for two main reasons.

When I first started out, I was tempted to talk about sex generally because it was embarrassing to be explicit. Over time I learned that it was easy to end up talking at cross purposes unless you are specific.

One person's 'you know what I mean' is not necessarily the same as another's. In fact, shockingly they can be quite the opposite.

Unsurprisingly, since the vagina has few nerve endings, I experience no arousal whatsoever from intercourse.

My best orgasms come from masturbation alone but I also enjoy highly pleasurable sexual arousal (and a physical orgasm) from anal sex.

Naturally all of this is very shocking. But if heterosexual women want to enjoy orgasm then they need to admit to some erotic or 'naughty' thoughts and deeds.

How else does a person become aroused enough for orgasm?

Women who insist that vaginal intercourse works for them despite all the known facts cause unnecessary confusion over how female orgasm is achieved.

The other reason that I want to be explicit about the details of my sexual experiences is so that I can reassure people that I know as much about sex and orgasm as any woman is likely to.

All too often when a woman admits to a lack of orgasm during sex, other people assume she must be sexually inhibited, sexually ignorant or with a partner who is sexually incompetent.

So I need to tick all the boxes. OK – I have not had sex with hundreds of different men. But women who are promiscuous can be criticised for setting a 'bad example' to younger women.

So I am heterosexual. I am college educated. I have lived with my partner for over twenty years and we have made the most of exploring sex together.

Over the years, like many other couples, we have found that achieving female orgasm during sex is not easy.

Others will claim otherwise but they never provide enough factual detail to make it clear that it is not just sexual bravado.

# Bringing more realism to sex advice

It is natural that female sexuality is misrepresented by the media. We all watch films and read books in part to be entertained. We don't necessarily want to see real life because we know what that's like. We want to be uplifted by a fantasy view of the world.

Unfortunately this huge gap between sexual fantasy and reality means that men and women today are often disappointed when real life does not match up. Until we change our sexual expectations, sex will always be taboo because we end up feeling inadequate.

One sex expert admitted that sex advice is appallingly bad today but, as he put it, he is not prime minister and so cannot change what people think. I suppose it's like global warming. The problem is so huge that no one person feels able to do anything about it.

I have to disagree. Public health organisations should provide advice that reflects women's real life experiences. Although, erotic literature, as a form of fiction, can reflect our sexual fantasies, educational books should publish the facts about female sexuality.

Very few sources today offer sex advice or information to couples on the basis of the facts that Shere Hite highlighted in the 1970s.

So today young people are still not told that vaginal intercourse is rarely orgasmic for women or that a woman is likely to struggle with orgasm during sex by any means.

The fact that female masturbation is relatively uncommon is glossed over when talking about women's knowledge of how to achieve their own sexual arousal.

Even when experts acknowledge that women do not orgasm during sex, they seem oblivious to the relationship issue. Women may accept that sex doesn't provide female orgasm but many men expect a partner to be equally enthusiastic about sex.

Self-evidently, women's sexual performance is not a show-stopper and so most people assume that women do not have sexual problems. Relatively few women ever consult sex clinics.

How many are concerned enough about lack of orgasm to pay out over $100 an hour to find a solution? Even in my own case, I went to a clinic more for my partner's sake than for my own.

No one seems to think it wrong that the current definition categorises huge numbers of women as sexually dysfunctional. Yet this is purely because women are assumed to respond sexually as men do. Since female orgasm is not required for reproduction I don't see how it makes a woman dysfunctional if she doesn't orgasm with a partner.

Kinsey commented in 1953 on the astounding variety of experiences that women report: from never having an orgasm throughout their lives to others who claim to orgasm easily and even multiple times often with minimal stimulation of any kind (physical or psychological).

It's surprising (to me at least) that no one EVER questions how a woman can be MORE sexually responsive than a man is.

Is it that we (men in particular) are fascinated by such fantastical stories, no matter how unrepresentative they may be of women in general?

Let's be honest… We are mesmerised by stories of women who orgasm multiple times a session not just because this would be unheard of for a man.

The truth is that a similar story about a man would hold little interest because there is nothing newsworthy about male orgasm.

But just how helpful is it to suggest that every woman responds sexually as men do? And how fair is it to imply that women are dysfunctional if they cannot match these experiences?

We never admit that there are many reasons why people say things. They want to impress. They say what they think other people want to hear. They need to make money and have to print what people will read or what sells.

Why do men apologise to women for sexual innuendo? Why do women rarely make sexual remarks? Why do men buy women flowers? Why does experience improve men as lovers and yet younger women are thought sexier than experienced women?

I wanted to know the answers to questions like these and I am surprised that no one else wonders. No one seems to demand that one and one must add to two. Emotional taboo and sexual politics mean that all rational argument is suspended.

# Appendix

# About the author

Standing in the street outside a sex clinic on London's Harley Street, I paused a moment to consider: "What on earth am I doing here?"

Well, quite simply I wanted to know why, despite being able to enjoy orgasm through masturbation since adolescence, I had never felt anything like the same sexual arousal during sex.

Many women approach sex purely through their relationship.

Sex fulfils all their expectations for a sexual and emotional act with a man they love. They never notice that something is missing from their lives. Not all women have this experience.

I, for one, was bitterly disappointed when sex did not deliver the easy arousal portrayed in erotic fiction.

I also could not believe that I was the only woman on the planet to have noticed that sex was so much more rewarding for men.

Of course at first I thought there must be something wrong with me.

Much later I came to realise that the explanations that would have helped me are not generally promoted due to lack of understanding about women's use of orgasm techniques.

*"The woman-in-the-street (most of us) still has the impression that it is 'normal' to orgasm from male thrusting." (Shere Hite; The Hite Reports; 1993)*

I had questions from the very first time I had sex but there was no one to ask. Years later when I tried to find answers I met with embarrassment, defensiveness and silence even from the experts.

This is wrong. Given so few women question non-orgasmic sex, experts assume that other women don't have the same problem.

So women who can masturbate to orgasm are offered therapy but few specifics to explain how women achieve orgasm during sex.

## Sharing sexual experiences

By talking to women in everyday life I learned that my 'problem' was that my expectations were set too high.

Like Oliver Twist, I was dumb enough to ask for more than my due. My naïveté was to assume that anyone else knew any better.

At best, other women accept that sex involves only emotional and sensual pleasures. Most never experience orgasm by any means.

Overall men are much more interested in discussing female sexual arousal and orgasm than most women ever are.

Some women claimed easy orgasm during sex and yet they were shocked by the eroticism that leads to sexual arousal.

Very few women showed any interest in enjoying orgasm and even fewer wanted to compare notes on orgasm techniques.

At the start I was just an educated woman with an interest in erotic novels and sex manuals. After over 10 years researching the content for **Ways Women Orgasm**, living with my partner for more than twenty years and raising three daughters together, I continue to be passionate about improving understanding of female sexuality.

For more about Jane go to www.nosper.com.

Sex remains a highly personal and embarrassing topic for most people. I hope that my efforts will save other couples some of the difficulties we have had in learning how to make the most of our sexual relationship.

If you think your sexual experiences can help others, either by reassuring or informing, please e-mail me jane @ wayswomenorgasm.org. There are some tips for doing this on the 'Contact' page.

My eternal gratitude goes to Alfred Kinsey and to Shere Hite for their work on female sexuality; also to Sheila Kitzinger for pointing out that many women are not particularly bothered about female orgasm and to Tracey Cox for her enthusiasm for female masturbation and sexual fantasies.

For modern wisdom on relationships I have relied heavily on the bible 'Why Men don't get enough Sex and Women don't get enough Love' by Jonathan Kramer and Diane Dunway as well as the legendary John Gray.

# My story

During adolescence, I read books that gave me both sexual knowledge and an insight into eroticism. So that even before I had sex for the first time, I had the impression that sex would be sensationally pleasurable. Erotic fiction showed women enjoying the same sexual arousal and easy orgasm during sex as men.

I learnt about female masturbation from books. I never felt any compulsion to masturbate so it was simply curiosity that motivated me.

When I was seventeen, I found that I could become aroused by imagining a sexy scenario (whilst lying in bed contemplating sleep) and then I discovered orgasm by pushing my fingers against my vulva and down towards my clitoris in a gentle massaging rhythm.

I met my first boyfriend in the South of France. David was a chef from Liverpool and at twenty-two, four years older than me, he had plenty of sexual experience. Sadly, losing my virginity was severely disappointing because absolutely nothing happened.

When I remarked that I had felt very little (in fact a complete lack of arousal during sex) David replied that other virgins had said the same thing.

Pleasing my partner was easy and since none of it moved me in the least, I resigned myself to the fact that our sex life focused on his sexual arousal and orgasm. Back in the UK we lived together for two years.

Unfortunately, we never talked about sex so whenever David pressed and I found it difficult to say "no" I offered the minimum: basically missionary style intercourse-to-male-orgasm every time.

## Accepting a lack of orgasm during sex (only because I had to)

Six months after we split up, I met an Italian boy called Alfredo. At twenty-one, although I was resigned to a lack of orgasm during sex, I found the prospect of a sexual relationship exciting.

Alfredo was good with his hands and he succeeded in arousing me through clitoral stimulation. This fuelled the hope that I might one day learn how to orgasm during sex.

Later the same year, I met Peter and we fell in love. Despite my reluctance to become involved in a sexual relationship, I accepted that sex accompanies any intimate relationship with a man.

There was an almost inevitable cycle that once started would naturally end in sex. Simply being affectionate with a man was enough to lead him on (stimulate his need for orgasm).

As with my earlier sexual relationships, I was open about the fact that sex failed to arouse me. Peter was keen to try but my body seemed to be inert to any stimulation.

I continued to be severely disappointed but there was nothing I could do about it. I read sex manuals galore but all the indications were that adults of both sexes naturally find sex mutually rewarding.

Rather than carry on in ignorance, we went along to relationship therapists early on. They used the book 'Treat yourself to Sex' by Paul Brown & Margot Faulderby, which suggested sensual massage and foreplay but this did not improve my levels of sexual arousal.

We ended the sessions none the wiser and I put on hold any ambition of finding an answer to my 'problem'.

Fifteen years later, our relationship hit rock bottom. At 35 I was masterminding a household of three young children, a daily nanny and a live-in au-pair while my partner and I both worked in full-time careers often travelling abroad. In addition my partner felt I should be orgasmic during sex.

No wonder we are called the 'have it all' generation! I resolved to visit a sex clinic.

After five hours of talking to their consultant psychologist, he concluded that there was nothing wrong with either of us. His therapy focused on physical stimulation techniques but, frankly, after being sexually active for over fifteen years, I could not see how any sexual position, however unusual, was going to increase my sexual arousal sufficiently to enable me to orgasm.

# Contact

Many people describe their sex life, including evidence of female arousal, as if it came straight out of erotic fiction.

I have come to question these stories because, despite their initial bravado, no one is ever willing to provide any detail.

Naturally most women are too embarrassed to comment. They conclude that their experiences of sexual arousal must be abnormal.

They assume that other more 'experienced' or more 'sexy' women must have a more 'normal' experience.

Women, who do comment, tell me that they become aroused just as men do by appreciating their partner's body but I know that women's minds and bodies do not respond sexually as men's do.

In fact most women are hugely offended by any 'adult' material: including language, imagery or erotica relating to the genitals of either sex.

So women are too embarrassed to speak up but why are men unwilling to say how their partners get the clitoral stimulation needed for female orgasm?

Why do so many men still believe that women are aroused through vaginal intercourse?

There is no shame in a woman never discovering her own sexual arousal especially with a lover.

Female sexual arousal is MUCH more obscure than male and in this sense understanding female sexuality, for what it truly is, IS like rocket science!

It is a misconception that we live in a modern and sexually sophisticated world. From an emotional standpoint, humanity might just as well be in the Stone Age.

## True female sexual arousal and orgasm

Women can be utterly convinced (and convincing!) in describing their sexual experiences as orgasmic.

Such stories are worthless unless women can explain their orgasm techniques in enough detail to allow others to learn from them.

Unless she knows what orgasm is from masturbation, a woman can easily mistake orgasm during sex. Unfortunately the confusion over female orgasm undermines women's confidence in their less sensational but more realistic experiences.

*"The trouble with the world is that the stupid are cocksure and the intelligent full of doubt." (Bertrand Russell 1872-1970)*

There's always an element of personal interpretation but a genuine story will ring true if it strikes a chord with other women.

Forget the bluffers! What matters is making the most of our own experiences whether we describe them as orgasmic or not.

Once we accept that female orgasm from intercourse is difficult, the more interesting question is how women orgasm during sex BY ANY MEANS (oral sex or manual stimulation of the clitoris).

How can a woman who is familiar with orgasm from masturbation alone learn how to experience something similar during sex?

Please e-mail me, jane @ wayswomenorgasm.org with your story.

**Some ideas for context that might help others:**

- Please provide some basic personal background: age, sexual experience, relationship history etc.
- Can you masturbate yourself to orgasm (if so, how exactly, how often, since when)?
- If you can orgasm with a partner: what technique do you use, how long did it take for you to learn to orgasm during sex in this way and how do these orgasms compare with those from masturbation (if relevant)?
- What role do sexual fantasies play in both masturbation and sex with a partner?
- What impact does the relationship have on your ability to orgasm? Can you orgasm during sex with different partners?
- How often do you initiate sex with your partner and/or masturbate alone on average?

# Member Forum

Welcome to the Members' Forum! This page is dedicated to members only for sharing ideas on how women can get more out of their sexual relationships with men. Please show your support by leaving a positive comment.

Let's face it, very few couples are lucky enough to have a sexual relationship where they can talk openly about female sexual arousal and orgasm. **Ways Women Orgasm** is for couples who are looking for ways to improve on what they already have.

If you are in a long-term sexual relationship of any kind then you are probably unusual. If you have moved beyond missionary style intercourse and can discuss more general pleasuring as a couple then you are almost certainly exceptional.

I don't expect everyone to agree with me. **Ways Women Orgasm** PROVOKES debate by offering a DIFFERENT view to other sources. Tell me if you disagree but please provide a reasoned explanation that tallies with the facts of women's sexuality, together with supporting evidence either from women's real life experiences or from the published conclusions of the experts.

If you have not found any answers elsewhere you may find my more logical presentation helpful. If not, then no harm done. Women should feel free to share their experiences whatever they are. At the end of the day much of what is said about sex is purely opinion. If we are to find a common basis for discussion, we have to first find other people who share our own opinions.

Ultimately the aim is for **Ways Women Orgasm** to facilitate an open and constructive dialogue, covering questions or experiences from women and their partners, who are interested in understanding more about female sexuality.

Please feel free to ask or share as you like...

### Ways Women Orgasm – the sexuality forum where female orgasm matters

There is a scene in the film 'The Chicken Run' (2000) where Ginger, our hero, returns from solitary confinement after her umpteenth escape failure. Another chicken tentatively suggests that, since the chances of them breaking out of the chicken farm are evidently 'a million to one against', perhaps Ginger should consider giving up on her dream.

A demoralised Ginger pauses to reflect for a moment and then quietly but resolutely, replies: 'Then there's still a chance!' What a girl! At times, my experience of trying to bring more realism to modern day sex information has felt a little like the prospect of escaping from a concentration camp: so impossible that it has seemed futile even to try.

If you are a woman who is keen to learn how to masturbate then take a look at my stories 'How a woman can learn to masturbate' – p64 and 'How to enjoy your sexual fantasies' – p136.

If you are a woman who can masturbate to orgasm but struggles with orgasm during sex, you may be reassured to read: 'Men hope a lover will enhance their sexual arousal' – p266, 'Women who fake orgasm' – p36 and 'How we enjoy our best orgasms' – p70.

If you are interested in the conclusions of the experts about how women reach orgasm with a partner then read my stories: 'How to orgasm' – p108, 'Techniques women use to reach orgasm' – p62 and 'Positions and techniques for sexual intercourse' – p144.

If you have tried every PHYSICAL stimulation technique in the book then read my stories about women's PSYCHOLOGICAL sexual arousal: 'Clitoral stimulation is not everything' – p118 and 'Women's sexual arousal relies on sexual fantasies' – p126.

It takes trust and practice to explore some of the naughtier ideas for making the most of a sexual relationship, including anal sex and vaginal fisting. Take a look at 'Some women do explore sexual pleasure' – p220 and 'How a woman can enjoy sex play' – p180.

**Ways Women Orgasm** is not offering specialist advice about sexual problems. Lack of female orgasm during sex is rarely a dysfunction. It is simply a normal state of affairs for any woman who realises that something is missing from sex.

Unless diagnosed with a specific medical condition, every woman can assume that she and her sexual experiences are quite normal.

# Bibliography
## Reference
Sexual behavior in the human female – Alfred Kinsey, Wardell Pomeroy, Clyde Martin & Paul Gebhard (1953)

The Hite Report (on Female Sexuality) – Shere Hite (1976)

The Hite Report on Male Sexuality – Shere Hite (1981)

Dictionary of Sexual Terms – Michael Carrera (1992)

Human Sexuality (fifth edition) – William Masters, Virginia Johnson and Robert Kolodny (1995)

Sex toys a playfully 101 uninhibited guide – Rachel Venning & Claire Cavanah (2003)

## Sex information
Everything you wanted to ask about sex but were afraid to ask – David Reuben (1969)

EveryWoman – Derek Llewellyn-Jones (1971)

Joy of Sex – Alex Comfort (1972)

The Loving Touch – Andrew Stanway (1993)

EveryMan – Derek Llewellyn-Jones (1980)

Healthy Sex – Miriam Stoppard (1998)

The Big Bang: Nerve's Guide to the Sexual Universe - Emma Taylor & Lorelei Sharkey (2004)

## Women's experiences
My Secret Garden – Nancy Friday (1973)

Woman's Experience of Sex – Sheila Kitzinger (1983)

The Hite Reports – Shere Hite (1993)

Women's Pleasure – Rachel Swift (1993)
Satisfaction Guaranteed – Rachel Swift (1996)
Hot Sex – Tracy Cox (1998)

## Relationships

Treat yourself to sex – Paul Brown & Margot Faulder (1977)
Men are from Mars Women are from Venus – John Gray (1992)
Why Men don't get enough Sex and Women don't get enough Love – Jonathan Kramer & Diane Dunaway (1994)
Mars & Venus in the Bedroom – John Gray (1995)
Go Ask Alice – Columbia University's Health Education Program (1998)
Hot Relationships – Tracy Cox (1999)

## Light-hearted

Man's Best Friend – Gray Jolliffe & Peter Mayle (1984)
The Bluffer's Guide to Women – Marina Muratore (1998)
The Bluffer's Guide to Men – Anthony Mason (1998)
Why women can't read maps… – Allan & Barbara Pease (1999)
Why men don't listen… – Allan & Barbara Pease (1999)

## Sex stories

Emmanuelle – Emmanuelle Arsan
The Happy Hooker – Xavier de Hollander
The Story of O – Pauline Reage
Mixed Doubles - Zoe le Verdier
Erotic Stories (DVD) - James Avalon (archel in the UK)

www.ingramcontent.com/pod-product-compliance
Lightning Source LLC
Chambersburg PA
CBHW070547050426
42450CB00011B/2745